MAKING SCHOOL AND COMMUNITY RECREATION FUN FOR EVERYONE

MAKING SCHOOL AND COMMUNITY RECREATION FUN FOR EVERYONE

PLACES AND WAYS TO INTEGRATE

edited by

M. Sherril Moon, Ed.D.
Associate Professor
Department of Special Education
University of Maryland
College Park

·P·A·U·L·H·
BROOKES
PUBLISHING C°

Baltimore • London • Toronto • Sydney

Paul H. Brookes Publishing Co.
P.O. Box 10624
Baltimore, Maryland 21285-0624

Typeset by Brushwood Graphics, Inc., Baltimore, Maryland.
Manufactured in the United States of America by
The Maple Press Company, York, Pennsylvania.

Library of Congress Cataloging-in-Publication Data
Making school and community recreation fun for everyone : places
   and ways to integrate / edited by M. Sherril Moon.
      p.   cm.
   Includes bibliographical references and index.
   ISBN 1-55766-155-3
   1. Handicapped—United States—Recreation.   2. Recreation areas
and the handicapped—United States.   3. Physical education for
handicapped persons—United States.   I. Moon, M. Sherril, 1952–
GV183.5.M35 1994
790.1'96'0973—dc20   94-28438
                                                                  CIP

British Library Cataloguing-in-Publication data are available from the
   British Library.

CONTENTS

LISTING OF TABLES AND FIGURES

CONTRIBUTORS

Paula J. Beckman, Ph.D.
Professor
Department of Special Education
1308 Benjamin Building
University of Maryland
College Park, Maryland 20742

Martin E. Block, Ph.D.
Assistant Professor
Department of Human Services
405 Emmet Street, Ruffner Hall
University of Virginia
Charlottesville, Virginia 22903-2493

Patricia Johnson Brown, Ph.D.
Director, Continuing Education and
  Community Programs
827 West Franklin Street, P.O. Box 2508
Virginia Commonwealth University
Richmond, Virginia 23284

Rikki S. Epstein, M.Ed., CTRS
Program Manager
National Recreation and Park Association
2775 South Quincy Street, Suite 300
Arlington, Virginia 22206

Robin Friedlander, M.Ed.
Community Recreation Liaison
Project REC
Children's Hospital
Institute for Community Inclusion
  University Affiliated Program
Boston, Massachusetts 02115

Debra Hart, M.Ed.
Special Projects Coordinator
Children's Hospital
Institute for Community Inclusion
  University Affiliated Program
Boston, Massachusetts 02115

William Kiernan, Ph.D.
Director
Institute for Community Inclusion
  University Affiliated Program
Children's Hospital
Boston, Massachusetts 02115

Frances L. Kohl, Ph.D.
Associate Professor
Department of Special Education
1308 Benjamin Building
University of Maryland
College Park, Maryland 20742

Cheska Komissar, B.S.
Community Recreation Liaison
Project REC
Children's Hospital
Institute for Community Inclusion
  University Affiliated Program
Boston, Massachusetts 02115

Melanie Sloniker Larson, B.A.
Project Manager
Natural Supports Transition for Students
  with Moderate to Severe Disabilities
TransCen, Inc.
451 Hungerford Drive, Suite 700
Rockville, Maryland 20850

John N. McGovern, J.D., CTRS
Executive Director
Northern Suburban Special Recreation
  Association
P.O. Box 8437
Northfield, Illinois 60093-8437

M. Sherril Moon, Ed.D.
Associate Professor
Department of Special Education
1308 Benjamin Building
University of Maryland
College Park, Maryland 20742

Paula Rogerson, B.S.
Integration Specialist
483 Southampton Street
South Boston, Massachusetts 02127

Paula Sotnik, B.S.
Project Director
The Technology Training Project
P.O. Box 341
Lincoln Center, Massachusetts 01773

Cheri L. Stierer, Ph.D.
Regional Team Manager
Virginia Department of Mental Health,
    Mental Retardation, and Substance Abuse
Office of Mental Retardation Services
P.O. Box 1797
Richmond, Virginia 23214

George P. Tilson, Jr., Ed.D.
Senior Vice President
TransCen, Inc.
451 Hungerford Drive, Suite 700
Rockville, Maryland 20850

Gina Wagner, CTRS
Coordinator of Therapeutic Recreation
    Programs and Community Integration
    Services
Howard County Department of Recreation
    and Parks
Executive Center, Suite 170
3300 North Ridge Road
Ellicott City, Maryland 21043

Pam Walker, M.A.
Research Associate
Research and Training Center on
    Community Integration
Center on Human Policy
200 Huntington Hall
Syracuse University
Syracuse, New York 13244-2340

Laura Wetherald, CTRS
Supervisor of County Wide Programs
Howard County Department of Recreation
    and Parks
Executive Center, Suite 170
3300 North Ridge Road
Ellicott City, Maryland 21043

Billie Wilson, CTRS
Coordinator of Therapeutic Section
Montgomery County Department of
    Recreation and Parks
12210 Bushey Drive
Silver Spring, Maryland 20902

Laura L. Zygmunt, M.S.
Teacher
Montgomery County Public Schools
14201 Wolf Creek Place
Silver Spring, Maryland 20906

PREFACE

To some of us, it seems that things have moved slowly in the domain of leisure and recreation services for people with disabilities. However, the early 1990s have brought a multitude of philosophical and programmatic initiatives. With the enactment of the Americans with Disabilities Act (ADA) in 1990, we moved from a time when therapeutic recreation usually involved separate or different activities for those with disabilities to one in which inclusive public and private recreation programs are mandated by federal law. Over time we discovered that instructing people with disabilities in specific leisure skills is not nearly as critical as creating supportive leisure environments in which anyone can have fun. Fostering awareness and sensitivity in participants without disabilities and providing a variety of supports for participants with disabilities are of central importance to inclusive programs, overshadowing the need to improve learner readiness or competence, which were the focus of most therapeutic recreation or adaptive physical education programs up to the mid-1980s.

This text offers case studies, models, and specific techniques to those individuals or groups who are interested in assisting children, teenagers, and adults with disabilities to participate more fully in local school and neighborhood social and leisure activities. These ideas revolve around a variety of concepts that have changed our perceptions about the capacity and desire of people with even the most severe disabilities to participate in community life. Volunteerism, school inclusion, new technology, natural supports, emphasis on cooperation rather than competition, quality-of-life emphasis, and advocacy for choice making among people who have disabilities have made inclusive social and leisure activities more accessible. New legal mandates for inclusion, including the Individuals with Disabilities Education Act (IDEA) and the ADA, challenge us to experiment with new ways to include people of all skill levels in school and community recreation programs.

Whether you are an advocate or family member working to include a person with a disability in existing school or community activities, an educator who desires to have all students learn and play together regardless of their ability levels, a therapeutic recreation service provider who has been mandated to make your program inclusive, or an innovator who wishes to create diverse leisure options for all citizens, this volume can assist you in accomplishing your goal. As you read on, you will find that the authors of these chapters avoid technical jargon and outline tried-and-true strategies for including persons with disabilities in leisure activities. Our hope is that anyone who becomes familiar with these strategies can have a direct hand in replicating them.

Each of the chapters in this volume focuses primarily on one or more of the state-of-the-art elements necessary for successful inclusive recreation programs. However, there are three basic themes running throughout the book that tie the chapters together. One is that of using a community leisure facilitator (CLF), either a professional or volunteer, to support people with disabilities in community programs. As the authors point out, recruiting committed people to assist in a variety of capacities is the key to successful efforts at inclusion. Another general theme is the importance of discovering local groups and activities such as sports, arts-and-crafts classes, and cultural events for people of all ages. A final recurring theme is that of helping people with disabilities to try new activities, to choose, cope, and experience either joy or dislike. The most important aspect of participation is not success or failure, but choice itself, the opportunity to discover and express preferences. This process adds new dimensions to the role of the facilitator: encouraging connections between people, searching for appropriate activities, and educating the public become just as important as teaching individual skills.

This volume is organized into four topical sections. After an introductory chapter that describes the philosophy behind our efforts, the first section, comprising Chapters 2, 3, and 4, emphasizes the logistics of "how-tos" of establishing inclusive leisure options. The role of the CLF is outlined and specific methods typically used by the CLF are delineated. Finally, several case studies and examples of inclusive school and community activities are presented.

The second section, which includes Chapters 5 and 6, highlights two of the newest tools at our disposal in facilitating inclusion. Chapter 5 describes federal laws that mandate inclusive recreation and other services in schools or the community. Special emphasis is put on the ADA, since this new law has the greatest implications for most recreation programs. Chapter 6 describes new accessibility standards and explains how programs can be made more accessible through a variety of adaptations.

The third section, Chapters 7 through 9, provides specific examples of inclusive activities that are appropriate for persons of all ages, from preschool through adulthood. Commercially available toys, adapted physical education programs, and various groups and activities for adults are highlighted.

The final section of this volume, Chapters 10 through 12, illustrates how various organizations—municipal recreation and parks programs, extracurricular organizations at high schools, and a network of city summer camps—have been adapted to accommodate all interested citizens, regardless of ability levels.

Because inclusive community recreation and leisure participation for people with severe disabilities is a relatively new concept, we have much less research or recommended-practice data to draw on in this area than in other life-skill areas such as those in the academic or vocational domains. In other words, we are at the point where it makes sense to try anything and everything so long as participants seem to enjoy the effort. It is alright to make mistakes during this process as long as we are willing to try again and again. We have to be ready to discuss with the public people's "differences" on a continuous basis while at the same time making quick judgments about changing some participants' involvement when behavioral differences or the attitudes of others become a barrier. We have to keep looking for appropriate activities, suitable facilitators, and accepting program directors, and while doing this we have to support families and encourage them to take chances.

It is a difficult job, but none could be more rewarding or fun, as we discover when we see someone making a friend, playing a new sport, or learning a new hobby. Anything is possible, and everything is worth a try. That's the challenge that we face and the beauty of working and playing together in this area.

Acknowledgments

I would like to thank Dr. Bill Kiernan and the rest of my colleagues at Boston Children's Hospital Institute for Community Inclusion University Affiliated Program for supporting Project REC's efforts. Project REC, which was funded through the Office of Special Education and Rehabilitative Services (OSERS) from 1989 through 1993, would not have been so successful without the guidance and support of our project officer, Dr. Anne Smith. This project, which was responsible for the development of many of the activities and techniques described in this book, also succeeded because of the participation of so many great people in the metropolitan Boston area. It was a pleasure to work with the recreation activity participants, recreation departments, schools, YMCAs, Arcs, Scouting groups, and families in Newton, Wellesley, Waltham, and other towns.

I would also like to acknowledge the work done in this area by Stuart Schleien, Tip Ray, Paul Wehman, Paul Bates, Adelle Renzaglia, John Dattilo, Luanna Meyer, Susan Hamre-Nietupski, John Nietupski, Lou Brown, and their colleagues. Much in this book further validates the earlier and ongoing work of these prolific researchers, practitioners, and writers.

My co-workers at the University of Maryland have also been incredibly supportive of my finishing this book. Phil Burke, my department chair, has been great, as have the faculty members I work so closely with, especially Francey Kohl and Debra Neubert. Barb Gruber has really been helpful as we experiment together with inclusion techniques in the work we do in schools and community organizations. My deepest appreciation must go to Carolynn Rice, who typed and retyped a major portion of this manuscript; I absolutely could not have finished this project without her.

Finally, I want to thank all the people at Brookes Publishing Company for their encouragement. The extra support, content suggestions, and thoughtful editing of Theresa Donnelly have made this volume a reality.

*To Adelle Renzaglia and Paul Wehman, my teachers,
mentors, and good friends, with whom learning and
working has always been fun! Thank you for teaching me
so much about so many things, but especially about
the importance of recreation for everyone.*

MAKING SCHOOL AND COMMUNITY RECREATION FUN FOR EVERYONE

~one~

The Case for Inclusive School and Community Recreation

M. Sherril Moon

One of the front-page stories in *The Washington Post* of June 12, 1993 (Buckley) was about Cecelia Pauley, a 15-year-old freshman with Down syndrome who attended only inclusive classes at Churchill High School in Montgomery County, Maryland. This article on successful school inclusion described the involvement of Cecelia's peer "buddies" at school, who helped her adjust in class and who eventually became her friends. This group of volunteer students received training from TransCen, Inc. (see chap. 12, this volume). Another recent article in *The Washington Post* (Greene, 1993, May 17) related the story of Christine Hoehl, an 18-year-old Girl Scout with mental retardation from Clinton, Maryland, who had just received the Girl Scout Gold Award, the organization's highest honor. This article espoused the benefits of inclusion as exemplified by the efforts lately undertaken by the Girl Scouts of America. Chapter 4 of this text provides many other examples of organizations that are beginning to open their doors to people of differing abilities. Likewise, a front-page article in the *New York Times* of May 16, 1993 (Henneberger) reported that the emphasis in physical education in this country is shifting from competition to cooperation, allowing children with disabilities to more easily participate alongside their peers. Inclusion, wellness, diversity, and fitness have become more important goals than discipline and the pursuit of excellence, according to new standards set by the National Association for Sports and Physical Education (see chap. 8, this volume for methods for adapting physical education classes so that all kids can participate).

Reports in the popular media on inclusion in school and recreational programs illustrate how dramatically things are changing; people with disabilities and their families are more frequently choosing to participate in community activities rather than entering separate programs, and their decisions are now supported by laws such as the Americans with Disabilities Act (ADA) and the Individuals with Disabilities Education Act (IDEA), as well as by advances in technology, the self-advocacy movement, and the more-accepting attitudes engendered by the growing ethnic and racial diversity of our nation's population. Thus, those of us whose professions revolve around supporting people with disabilities and their families must learn how to help these citizens gain access to school and community recreation and leisure activities. This volume offers a variety of ways to achieve this goal.

DEFINING LEISURE AND RECREATION

Webster's dictionary (1977) defines *leisure* as the freedom provided by the cessation of activities, or time free from work or duties. This same source defines *recreation* as the refreshment of strength and spirits after work. The two terms are often used synonymously, and this text will use *leisure* and *recreation* to refer to any activities or programs that people participate in for fun, relaxation, diversion, or amusement. Leisure and recreation activities have been classified in a variety of ways, usually according to the behaviors associated with them or the environments in which they occur. Most typical leisure activities can be categorized along several dimensions: 1) physical, cultural, or social; 2) outdoor or indoor; 3) spectator or participant; 4) formal or informal; 5) independent, cooperative, or competitive; and 6) sports, games, hobbies, or toy play (Moon & Bunker, 1987).

Regardless of the type of activity, it cannot really be classified as recreation unless the person participating is having fun, is enjoying herself or himself. In fact, this is probably the one element that differentiates leisure or recreation from any other type of activity. A leisure activity must also include some element of choice on the part of the participants (Wehman & Moon, 1985). Dattilo (1991b) defines leisure as an individual's perception of his or her freedom to choose to participate in certain experiences. He goes on to say that the goal of providing leisure services for people with disabilities is to give them skills and experiences that will enable them to feel free to participate in particular chosen activities.

Therapeutic Recreation

Therapeutic recreation services are designed to assist people with physical, mental, emotional, or social limitations to develop an appropriate *leisure lifestyle*, a term that refers to the day-to-day expression of leisure attitudes, awareness, and activities. Therapeutic recreation specialists provide programs or services that assist the individual in eliminating barriers to experiencing leisure, developing leisure skills, and optimizing leisure involvement (National Therapeutic Recreation Society, 1982; Schleien, Green, & Heyne, 1993). These services typically include therapy aimed at improving specific functional behaviors, providing leisure education (instruction in skills and attitudes related to leisure), or encouraging voluntary participation in recreation (Reynolds, 1993).

Therapeutic recreation specialists (TRSs) typically complete undergraduate or graduate university training programs and can become certified through the National Therapeutic Recreation Society (NTRS). TRSs are hired by residential facilities, rehabilitation hospitals, park and recreation departments, child care centers, private rehabilitation and education agencies, and disability advocacy and service organizations such as the National Association for Retarded Citizens (NARC) and the United Cerebral Palsy Association (UCP).

Although in the past therapeutic services have usually been offered only in segregated settings, attitudes have changed dramatically in the past two decades. Experts in this field now assert that therapeutic recreation services should be provided, whenever possible, in inclusive settings in which age-appropriate skills can be learned alongside peers (Lord, 1983; Schleien & Ray, 1988). Reynolds (1993) points out the changes in the role of the therapeutic recreation specialist brought about by the passage of the ADA in 1990. He emphasizes the need to help all citizens, both those with and those without disabilities, to enjoy leisure pursuits focused on cooperative rather than competitive involvement. Others (Ray, 1991) have emphasized the need to facilitate the inclusion of people with different abilities in community settings and for therapeutic recreation to be focused on encouraging the development of friendships and social skills (Schleien et al., 1993). Therapeutic recreation specialists are also working more frequently with schools in developing plans to allow students to participate in recreation programs in the community as they move from school to adulthood (Wehman, 1992).

Community and School Recreation

The phrases *community leisure* or *recreation programs/activities* and *school leisure* or *recreation programs/activities* will appear throughout this volume to refer to activities that members of a community or students in a school participate in for fun, enjoyment, or enrichment. Hobbies, sports, fitness and wellness activities, arts and crafts, music, social opportunities, dance, art, drama, outdoor excursions or nature appreciation, and learning another language or studying cultural or ethnic practices would all be included in this category. Typically, community recreation opportunities are provided by park and recreation departments, community colleges, churches, or private organizations such as country clubs, YMCAs, YWCAs, or Boys' and Girls' Clubs. Establishments such as bowling alleys, movie theaters, and arcades also provide many community recreation options (some typical school and community recreation activities that children and young adults enjoy are described and categorized in Chapter 3). Including people with disabilities in community or school recreation programs that they choose to participate in is now a primary objective of most therapeutic recreation secialists, special educators, and advocates working in this area (Reynolds, 1993).

The majority of leisure and recreation activities that young people enjoy usually fall under the broad category of "sports" (see chap. 3, this volume). While young people are in school, they learn to participate in and enjoy most sports and fitness programs during physical education classes. Therefore, both general physical education instructors and adapted physical education specialists can be considered important members of the team that delivers recreation services. As Sherrill (1993) points out, adapted physical educators serve much the same function as therapeutic recreation specialists in that they facilitate the inclusion of students with disabilities in general physical education and provide them with leisure education related to sports and fitness. Chapter 8 of this volume provides specifics on the roles of both adapted and general physical educators and on ways to include students of differing ability levels in physical education.

Inclusive Recreation

Organized recreation programs for people with disabilities were first initiated in residential institutions in the early 1900s, and they flourished throughout the 1930s (Gray, 1977; Reynolds, 1993). It was not until after World War II that community-sponsored and school-based recreation programs for people with disabilities were first instituted. Even then, most activities were still provided by advocacy and service organizations, such as NARC or UCP. In the 1960s and 1970s, more specialized programs were developed for people with disabilities as private organizations, municipalities, states, and the federal government began to recognize the benefits of recreation for everyone. Still, even through the early 1970s, nearly all recreation options for citizens with disabilities were segregated. The development of the Special Olympics—designed specifically for people with mental retardation—during the 1960s and 1970s is one of the best examples of the growth of a special recreation program with an emphasis on sports participation (Block & Moon, 1992).

The mid-1970s saw a number of developments that gradually brought people with disabilities into some community recreation activities. The reasons for this can be traced to the deinstitutionalization movement and the passage of several landmark pieces of nondiscriminatory federal legislation, including the Rehabilitation Act of 1973 and the Education for All Handicapped Children Act of 1975 (Reynolds, 1993; Schleien & Ray, 1988). Chapter 5 of this volume describes how these and other more recent federal laws affect the provision of inclusive leisure programs in schools and communities.

The 1980s and 1990s have brought increased inclusion as the school mainstreaming and inclusion movements and the increasing self-determination of persons with disabilities (St. Peter, Field, & Hoffman, 1992) have had an impact on all facets of human services provision. The growing belief that people with disabilities have a civil right, guaranteed by the Fourteenth Amendment to the Constitution, to participation in all elements of American life, including friendship and social activities, has resulted in a call for a policy of inclusion in all school and community programs (Sailor, Gee, & Karasoff, 1993). The civil rights movement for people with disabilities led to the 1990 passage of the ADA, which mandates that all public and private recreation programs be inclusive (see Chapter 5).

In summary, any leisure program can be considered inclusive so long as people with disabilities have the same opportunities to participate as everyone else. Ideally, placement in existing community recreation programs should be based only on personal preferences and age. This "integration of generic existing programs" as described by Schleien et al. (1993) has the advantage of allowing continuing contemporary, age-appropriate, high-interest activities within a community. This approach provides those with disabilities the opportunity to join extensive social networks, and it is also probably more cost effective, at least initially. Chapter 11 of this volume provides an extensive illustration of how children with disabilities in one town were included in existing summer camps. This generic approach was cost effective, popular with parents, and led to the development of extended social networks among campers.

Two other approaches to inclusion described by Schleien et al. (1993) are the creation of new programs in a school or community that can include anyone, regardless of ability, and reverse mainstreaming, in which people without disabilities join previously segregated activities for people with disabilities. Examples of creating new programs include the friendship clubs and activity periods described in Chapter 4 of this text and the social groups for adults detailed in Chapter 9. As well, the organizers of Special Olympics have successfully used reverse mainstreaming to make some new programs inclusive (Block & Moon, 1992).

In the long run, it doesn't really matter how the inclusion is implemented as long as everyone has a chance to participate in a meaningful way and fun and enjoyment are the outcomes for those involved.

ELEMENTS OF STATE-OF-THE-ART SCHOOL
AND COMMUNITY INCLUSIVE RECREATION PROGRAMS

A number of education and therapeutic recreation experts have described important characteristics or elements in the design and implementation of inclusive leisure programs (Dattilo, 1991b; Davis, 1987; Falvey, 1989; Moon & Bunker, 1987; Schleien et al., 1993; Wehman & Schleien, 1981). The elements most commonly described, and those to which the most attention is devoted in this text, include: 1) enjoyable use of free time; 2) expression of choice of age-appropriate leisure activities; 3) family involvement; 4) volunteer, peer, and professional roles; 5) partial participation and the adaptability of activities; 6) leisure education for participants with disabilities; 7) disability awareness for participants without disabilities; 8) friendship and peer relationship development; and 9) enhancement of physical fitness and motor skills. Each of these program characteristics is briefly described below, with references to chapters that provide more detail.

The Enjoyable Use of Free Time

People with disabilities often have significantly more free time than those without disabilities. Often, they are under- or unemployed, have not learned to use community facilities, have had to face inaccessible transportation systems, and may be overprotected by guardians and prevented from actively participating in the community (Wehman, 1992). In fact, if a person with a disability is reinstitutionalized, the reason is often his or her lack of the skills necessary to occupy time without supervision (Novak & Heal, 1980). Studies have also shown that instruction in leisure activities can reduce inappropriate behaviors such as self-abuse and property destruction that sometimes occur during free time (Favell, 1973; Moon & Bunker, 1987).

Because so much of our free time is spent at home, people should be given opportunities to enjoy leisure activities that can be pursued in home environments. For children this usually involves toy play; for teens and adults it can include a variety of options—from hobbies such as collecting and woodworking, to arts and crafts such as painting or needlework, to pursuits such as playing the piano or guitar, to fitness activities such as aerobics and weight training.

Both children and adults with disabilities also need to learn how to use the community facilities in which leisure programs are offered. This can entail transportation training, educating families about the options offered in different settings, teaching community providers about the needs and preferences of potential participants with disabilities, and facing the logistical challenges of offering multiple participation opportunities. It takes a tremendous amount of planning by families, teachers, caregivers, and recreation providers to actually begin this process.

Every chapter in this book will provide assistance in helping people to have fun, but you should keep in mind that there is no right or wrong way to achieve this goal. A chosen strategy may not work in certain situations or with particular people, but you can't lose anything by trying. The important thing about introducing someone to a recreational activity is that you are giving them another choice. The main objective is to give each person with a disability the chance to try a number of options and then choose the things that he or she finds most fun. When fun and enjoyment are the key objectives of leisure participation for a person with a disability, the following questions can help you determine whether you are proceeding in the correct way:

Have you observed what the participant likes to do with different people in various environments?

Does the participant get ample opportunities to take part in particular activities so that he or she can really decide how he or she feels about them?

Have you experimented with different adaptations to enhance participation and enjoyment?

Does the participant still chose a particular activity when presented with other choices?

Do other participants seem to enjoy, or at least accommodate, the presence of the participant with a disability?

Do the participants laugh and smile or indicate in some way that they are enjoying the activity?

Does the participant ask to do it again?

Choice

Self-determination, self-advocacy, self-esteem, and empowerment are beginning to have more meaning for people with disabilities (St. Peter et al., 1992). These constructs, which involve making choices, expressing preferences, taking risks, assuming responsibility, and feeling a sense of control over the results of one's own actions have always been important to most people without disabilities. However, only recently have professionals in the human services field recognized that they are valuable for all people and that some of our past practices have actually prohibited self-determination by promoting dependence and limiting choice and decision making by people with disabilities (Wehmeyer, 1992).

Research has shown that being able to express choice in leisure activities increases participation (Dattilo, 1988; Realon, Favell, & Lowerre, 1990). We also now have the technology to assess both preferences and choice-making ability (Guess, Benson, & Siegel-Causey, 1985) and to teach relevant skills even to people with the most significant disabilities (Dattilo, 1985; Dattilo, 1991a). The real challenge for leisure service providers is to develop a repertoire of preferred recreation options for an individual with a disability and then to support that person's efforts to self-initiate a chosen option at the appropriate time (Moon & Bunker, 1987).

Age Appropriateness

When helping a person with disabilities to develop a repertoire of leisure preferences, it is crucial to introduce activities that his or her same-age peers can participate in within local, home, school, and community settings. This concept of age appropriateness (Baumgart et al., 1982) dictates that toys, games, and activities that a 3- or 4-year-old child would enjoy are never appropriate for a 13- or 14-year-old, regardless of his or her mental or physical capacity. Some experts have asserted that only leisure skills that can be performed in the presence of or in interaction with same-age peers should be encouraged (Silberman, 1987). Research has shown that adults without disabilities perceive other adults with disabilities as more competent and more "normal" when they are participating in a typical age-appropriate leisure pursuit such as reading a magazine, doing aerobics, or playing cards, as opposed to participating in activities such as Special Olympics, coloring, or playing a children's board game (Calhoun & Calhoun, 1993; Storey, Stern, & Parker, 1991).

Family Involvement

Turnbull, Turnbull, Bronicki, Summers, and Roeder-Gordon (1989) state that one of the major issues that parents of a child with a disability have to consider in planning for their son's or daughter's future is what leisure or cultural activities he or she might want to pursue. Therefore, it is crucial that families become involved in the planning of school and community recreational pursuits at the earliest stages. Family preferences should be one of the major factors that determine what, when, and how leisure activities are implemented, since the family is likely to have the greatest long-term effect on a child's leisure participation (Falvey, 1989; Wehman & Schleien, 1981). Chapter 3 of this text is particularly pertinent to this issue, as it describes specifically how family preferences can be built into community leisure programs.

It is also crucial for professionals and advocates to work with families so that, together, this team can work through some of the barriers that often exclude people with disabilities from community participation. Such barriers typically include attitudes toward inclusion, accessibility issues such as lack of public transportation options, and training for recreation providers on the needs and desires of people with disabilities. In fact, Dattilo (1991b) lists the area of family perceptions about leisure needs and strategies for the removal of barriers to leisure involvement as one of the top priorities for future research efforts. Chapter 2 of this text provides a number of specific topics on which families usually need information and training, as well as information that should help families and advocates reshape the roles of the professionals who are most involved in leisure programs for their sons and daughters.

Professional Roles

One of the most important elements of successful community leisure program inclusion is the support and assistance of a competent individual or group of individuals who can work effectively with people with disabilities, families, program providers, and school and community agencies (Goodall, 1992; Ray, 1991; Schleien & Ray, 1988). As Reynolds (1993) asserted, the TRS, who traditionally provided separate activities for people with disabilities, must now assume completely different responsibilities in order to facilitate the inclusion of people with disabilities in general programs. The TRS must now act as a direct service provider, family and community educator, and coordinator of services between agencies and schools.

Other professional or volunteer service providers must also get involved in the process of implementing inclusive community leisure activities and programs. For example, special education teachers must be aware of what opportunities for leisure participation are available in the school and community and then build recreational activities into students' curricula. Teaching age-appropriate play skills, fostering friendships with peers without disabilities, working with families to investigate community recreation opportunities, including leisure activities in the formal individualized education program (IEP) and individualized transition plan (ITP), and including students in physical education and extracurricular activities are only part of what must be accomplished by teachers.

As a student gets older, community professionals such as rehabilitation counselors who work with state vocational rehabilitation agencies and service coordinators who work with state developmental disability agencies can help families and individuals by providing information on community options and by coordinating with community providers to allow entry into these programs. It is essential that TRSs, teachers, rehabilitation counselors, and service coordinators work together to educate each other about existing leisure options or those that should be created within a particular community.

Advocates and volunteers who work in programs that serve people with disabilities must also understand the value of inclusive leisure participation. People in advocacy or volunteer positions can educate people with disabilities about community options and even accompany them to these activities. Advocates, particularly, can work to change segregated programs and start new recreation activities. It has been the experience of this author that advocates and volunteers, with some basic education, can be as effective as professionals, an idea that lies at the heart of this volume.

Leisure Education

Quality of life has been defined as satisfaction with one's situation and contentment with one's experiences (Taylor & Bogden, 1990). This concept is now a primary influence in the design of services and support networks for people with disabilities as we move from systems into which consumers of services must somehow fit to systems in which individuals choose the types of assistance or support that enable them to have the life they want (Dennis, Williams, Giangreco, & Cloninger, 1993). Quality of life is now being employed as a conceptual framework for evaluating transition outcomes and the outcomes of schooling, and one of the major factors considered in this context is a student's leisure and recreation participation or his or her use of free time to pursue interests (Halpern, 1993).

Including leisure participation as a measure of the adequacy of transition services means that educating people with disabilities about recreation must become part of their formal education program and documented on either the IEP or ITP (Dattilo & St. Peter, 1991; Moon & Inge, 1993). Leisure education can include a variety of components or methods, including direct instruction in skills through behavioral technology, courses on leisure participation, the provision of help with program entry, and education and support of families. Dattilo and St. Peter (1991) describe a leisure education model that includes teaching people with mental retardation to appreciate leisure time, to make decisions about what they want to do, to gain knowledge about local leisure resources, and to interact socially with people without disabilities.

Successful leisure education requires that people with disabilities not only have access to school and community programs but also be taught how to appreciate and participate in these programs. This means that families, teachers, counselors, TRSs, and advocates must determine how to become involved in providing leisure education. Teachers, particularly, can provide skill instruction and practice in activities that students have chosen as leisure pursuits. Teachers are also in the best position to work on preference development and choice making. They can also teach students about the use of community facilities and programs as part of a community-based training program. Teaching social skills and providing opportunities for interactions with peers are prime components of leisure education ideally suited to educators.

Physical Fitness and Motor Skills

Recreational activities are usually the most ideal way to work on improving fitness, gross motor, and fine motor skills (Schleien et al., 1993), which can be taught and practiced across numerous activities and settings and are also requisite to other skill domains, particularly those relevant to successful employment (Moon, Inge, Wehman, Brooke, & Barcus, 1990).

Inclusive leisure activities and leisure education efforts emphasizing fitness and motor skill development have proved to be very successful in increasing motor and aerobic capacity and in reducing weight (Moon & Renzaglia, 1982). Some programs have even helped reduce the occurrence of behaviors such as self-stimulation and self-abuse (Schleien et al., 1993). Other fitness and motor-skills training programs that have included peers without disabilities have been highly successful, and in some cases, the presence of peers seems to be more motivating than any other factor (Moon, 1983). Anderson and Brady (1993) showed that interactions with peers improved basic motor responses such as the use of a walker and holding the head upright. Halle, Gabler-Halle, McKee, Bane, and Boyer (1991) showed how a peer-mediated conditioning program could enhance the aerobic fitness of young people with severe disabilities. These researchers wrote an implementation manual describing their efforts, which could be replicated in school and community programs.

Fitness and motor skills are typically learned during the school years as a part of a student's physical education program. Because this is the logical place for training in these areas, it must also be one of the places targeted for inclusion. Chapter 8 of this volume illustrates how all students can be included in general physical education. In the community, fitness and motor-skill development are enhanced by joining organizations such as the YMCA or YWCA, or aerobic, walking, or running clubs, and, for children, by attending summer camp. Chapters 4, 9, and 10 of this volume provide examples, case studies, and techniques revolving around inclusive participation in community fitness and motor-skills programs.

Partial Participation

Even though people with disabilities may not be able to function independently in every situation, they still should be encouraged to participate, with the necessary assistance, to whatever degree possible (Baumgart et al., 1982). The most important point of any activity is that each participant exert some degree of control over the environment and express some degree of choice and satisfaction or dissatisfaction with his or her involvement. The idea of partial participation is especially important in leisure participation by people with disabilities because this is the one life domain in which the main goal is having fun, not completing an activity or producing a product. A person's skill level or perceived degree of competence or independence should not preclude his or her enjoying most noncompetitive activities.

Partial participation in inclusive school and community leisure activities can be made possible in a number of ways, but particularly through the creation of natural support networks and the sensible adaptation of particular aspects of an activity. Natural supports include assistance, training, or "co-production" of some outcome that arises from informal or naturally occurring sources within a particular situation, rather than from paid human services or educational professionals (Smull & Bellamy, 1991). Natural supports would include co-workers or supervisors on a job, family members or neighbors in a home, and participants without disabilities in a leisure activity. Adaptations to an activity can include physical changes to a facility, equipment modifications or additions, and procedural or rule changes. Chapters 4, 6, 8, and 9 should be especially helpful in designing partial participation opportunities for people who may never be independent participants in certain recreational activities.

Peer Relationships

Recreational activities are the most natural places in which to promote and support positive social interactions and even friendships between people with and without disabilities. In fact, these friendships may be best facilitated within the context of structured recreational programs involving age-appropriate activities that both participants are sure to enjoy (Haring, 1991). Designing leisure alternatives that emphasize friendship, or at least social interaction, may be the most crucial element of all, since this is the one area where people with disabilities have had the least opportunities and human services professionals have had the least experience (Amado, 1993).

There are reports in the literature of a variety of strategies being successfully used to encourage or enhance friendships and other types of supportive relationships (Kohl, Moses, & Stettner-Eaton, 1984; Strully & Strully, 1985). Supported membership in organizations is one method in which members with and without disabilities are paired for participation in certain activities (Ferguson & Ferguson, 1993). After-school or in-school opportunities such as clubs, Scouts, 4-H, and sports organizations are all excellent places to help people become friends. Circles of friends (Forest, 1987) have also been created to help friendships grow and to increase participation in inclusive school and community activities. Structured situations involving the cooperative grouping of people of varying skill levels can also enhance positive relationships (Schleien et al., 1993). Regardless of what strategy is used to promote relationships, most of the elements mentioned earlier—choice, age-appropriateness, partial participation, and leisure education—must almost always be incorporated into the program.

Recently, a survey was conducted to see how special education teachers perceived their involvement in facilitating friendships between students with significant disabilities and their typically developing peers (Hamre-Nietupski, Hendrickson, Nietupski, & Sasso, 1993). These teachers felt that friendships were possible and beneficial for everyone and that they definitely could do things to enhance these types of friendships. In terms of preferred strategies, teachers rated collaboration with general education teachers, teaching social interaction skills, cooperative learning, ability awareness training, and peer tutors/partners as being most effective, while organizing circles of friends was rated as one of the lowest four preferred strategies. Schleien et al. (1993) report that ability awareness training can be very helpful in promoting friendships, especially when this training for peers without disabilities includes: 1) information that emphasizes similarities among all children, 2) specific information about the child's disability and exercises that provide experience on how it feels to have a particular disability, 3) discussions on how to include a specific student with a particular disability, and 4) a question-and-answer period. The author has found that using a combination of methods, especially awareness training for peers, supported membership, and cooperative grouping, is the most effective way to enhance relationships.

CONCLUDING COMMENTS

As described throughout this chapter, successful inclusive recreation programs involve a variety of elements—from family involvement and professional support, to participant choice of age-appropriate activities and the utilization of partial participation techniques. These activities can also revolve around different purposes—from the simple provision of opportunities for choice making, to leisure education or peer relationship development. The remaining chapters of this book provide descriptions and illustrations of how all these elements have been built into actual inclusive recreation and sports programs in a variety of school and community settings.

REFERENCES

Amado, A.N. (Ed.). (1993). *Friendships and community connections between people with and without developmental disabilities.* Baltimore: Paul H. Brookes Publishing Co.

Americans with Disabilities Act of 1990 (ADA), PL 101-336. (July 26, 1990). Title 42, U.S.C. 12101 et seq: *U.S. Statutes at Large, 104,* 327–378.

Anderson, N., & Brady, M. (1993). Improving motor responses in students with severe disabilities using adult instruction and peer social interactions. *Education and Training in Mental Retardation, 28*(1), 47–56.

Baumgart, D., Brown, L., Pumpian, I., Nisbet, J., Ford, A., Sweet, M., Messina, R., & Schroeder, J. (1982). The principle of partial participation and individualized adaptations in educational programs for severely handicapped students. *Journal of The Association for the Severely Handicapped, 7*(2), 17–27.

Block, M., & Moon, M.S. (1992). Orelove, Wehman, and Wood Revisited: An evaluative review of Special Olympics ten years later. *Education and Training in Mental Retardation, 27*(4), 379–396.

Brown, L., Branston-McClean, M.B., Baumgart, D., Vincent, L., Falvey, M., & Schroeder, J. (1979). Using the characteristics of current and subsequent least restrictive environments in the development of curricular content for severely handicapped students. *AAESPH Review, 4,* 407–424.

Buckley, S. (1993, June 12). Making room in the mainstream: Down Syndrome student turns trepidation to triumph in Potomac. *The Washington Post,* pp. 1, 10–11.

Calhoun, M., & Calhoun, L. (1993). Age-appropriate activities: Effects on the social perception of adults with mental retardation. *Education and Training in Mental Retardation, 28*(2), 143–148.

Dattilo, J. (1985). Incorporating choice into therapeutic recreation programming for individuals with severe handicaps. In G. Hitzhusen (Ed.), *Expanding horizons in therapeutic recreation* (Vol, XI, pp. 63–83). Columbia: Curators, University of Mississippi.

Dattilo, J. (1988). Assessing music preferences of persons with severe disabilities. *Therapeutic Recreation Journal, 2*(2), 12–23.

Dattilo, J. (1991a). Mental retardation. In D. Austin & M. Crawford (Eds.), *Therapeutic recreation: An introduction* (pp. 163–188). Englewood Cliffs, NJ: Prentice Hall.

Dattilo, J. (1991b). Recreation and leisure: A review of the literature and recommendations for future directions. In L.H. Meyer, C.A. Peck, & L. Brown (Eds.), *Critical issues in the lives of people with severe disabilities* (pp. 171–193). Baltimore: Paul H. Brookes Publishing Co.

Dattilo, J., & St. Peter, S. (1991). A model for including leisure education in transition services for young adults with mental retardation. *Education and Training in Mental Retardation, 26*(4), 420–432.

Davis, D.H. (1987). Issues in development of a recreational program for autistic individuals with severe cognitive and behavioral disorders. In D.J. Cohen & A.M. Donnellan (Eds.), *Handbook of autism and pervasive developmental disorders* (pp. 371–383). Silver Spring, MD: V.H. Winston & Sons.

Dennis, R., Williams, W., Giangreco, J., & Cloninger, C. (1993). Quality of life as context for planning and evaluation of services for people with disabilities. *Exceptional Children, 59*(6), 499–512.

Education for All Handicapped Children Act of 1975, PL 94-142. (August 23, 1977). Title 20, U.S.C. 1401 et seq: *U.S. Statutes at Large, 89,* 773–796.

Education of the Handicapped Act of 1970 (EHA), PL 91-230. (April 13, 1970). Title 20, U.S.C. 1400 et seq: *U.S. Statutes at Large, 84,* 121–195.

Falvey, M.A. (1989). *Community based curriculum: Instructional strategies for students with severe handicaps* (2nd ed.). Baltimore: Paul H. Brookes Publishing Co.

Favell, J. (1973). Reduction of stereotypes by reinforcement of toy plan. *Mental Retardation, 11,* 21–23.

Ferguson, P., & Ferguson, D. (1993). The promise of adulthood. In M.S. Snell (Ed.), *Instruction of students with severe disabilities* (pp. 588–608). New York: Merrill.

Forest, M. (1987). *More education/integration: A further collection of readings on the integration of children with mental handicaps into the regular school system.* Downsview, Ontario, Canada: The G. Allan Roeher Institute, York University.

G. & C. Merriam Co. (1977). *Webster's New Collegiate Dictionary.* Springfield, MA: Author.

Goodall, P. (1992). *Integrated leisure options for individuals with severe traumatic brain injury.* (Special Topical Report #1). Richmond: Virginia Commonwealth University, Medical College of Virginia.

Gray, D.E. (1977). The case for compensatory recreation. *Parks and Recreation, 12*(11), 23.

Greene, M. (1993, May 17). Surmounting disability, teen wins Girl Scouts' highest honor. *The Washington Post.* pp. D1, D7.

Guess, D., Benson, R., & Siegel-Causey, E. (1985). Behavioral control and education of severely handicapped students: Who's doing what to whom? and why? In. D. Bricker & J. Filler (Eds.), *Severe mental retardation: From theory to practice* (pp. 230–244). Washington, DC: Council for Exceptional Children.

Halle, J., Gabler-Halle, D., McKee, M., Bane, S., & Boyer, T. (1991). *Enhancing the aerobic fitness of individuals with moderate and severe disabilities: A peer mediated aerobic conditioning program.* Champaign, IL: Sagamore Publishing, Inc.

Halpern, A. (1993). Quality of life as a conceptual framework for evaluating transition outcomes. *Exceptional Children, 59*(6), 486–498.

Hamre-Nietupski, S., Hendrickson, J., Nietupski, J., & Sasso, G. (1993). Perceptions of teachers of students with moderate, severe, or profound disabilities on facilitating friendships with nondisabled peers. *Education and Training in Mental Retardation, 58*(2), 111–127.

Haring, T.G. (1991). Social relationships. In L.H. Meyer, C.A. Peck, & L. Brown (Eds.), *Critical issues in the lives of people with severe disabilities* (pp. 195–218). Baltimore: Paul H. Brookes Publishing Co.

Henneberger, M. (1993, May 16). New gym classes: No more choosing up sides. *The New York Times,* pp. 1, 37.

Individuals with Disabilities Education Act of 1990 (IDEA), PL 101-476. (October 30, 1990). Title 20, U.S.C. 1400 et seq: *U.S. Statutes at Large, 104,* 1103–1151.

Kohl, F.L. Moses, L.C., & Stettner-Eaton, B.A. (1984). A systematic training program for teaching nonhandicapped students to be instructional trainers of severely handicapped schoolmates. In N. Certo, N. Haring, & R. York (Eds.), *Public school integration of severely handicapped students: Rational issues and progressive alternatives* (pp. 185–195). Baltimore: Paul H. Brookes Publishing Co.

Lord, J. (1983). Reflections on a decade of integration. *Journal of Leisurability, 10*(4), 4–11.

Moon, M.S. (1983). *The effects of nonhandicapped peer participation and different reinforcement procedures on the maintenance of performance of fitness activities in severely handicapped adolescents.* Unpublished doctoral dissertation, University of Virginia, Charlottesville.

Moon, M.S., & Bunker, L. (1987). Recreation and motor skills programming. In M.E. Snell (Ed.), *Systematic instruction of persons with severe handicaps* (pp. 214–244). Columbus, OH: Charles E. Merrill.

Moon, M.S., & Inge, K. (1993). Vocational preparation and transition. In M. Snell (Ed.), *Instruction of students with severe disabilities* (pp. 556–587). New York: Merrill.

Moon, M.S., Inge, K.J., Wehman, P., Brooke, V., & Barcus, J.M. (1990). *Helping people with severe mental retardation get and keep employment: Supported employment issues and strategies.* Baltimore: Paul H. Brookes Publishing Co.

Moon, M.S., & Renzaglia, A. (1982). Physical fitness and the mentally retarded: A critical review of the literature. *The Journal of Special Education, 16*, 269–287.

National Therapeutic Recreation Society. (1982). *Philosophical position statement of the National Therapeutic Recreation Society.* Alexandria, VA: National Recreation and Park Association.

Novak, A.R., & Heal, L.W. (Eds.). (1980). *Integration of developmentally disabled individuals into the community.* Baltimore: Paul H. Brookes Publishing Co.

Ray, T. (1991). *SCOLA leisure activity guide.* Ramsey, Co., Minnesota, Association for Retarded Citizens.

Realon, R.E., Favell, J.E., & Lowerre, A. (1990). The effects of making choices on engagement levels with persons who are profoundly multiply handicapped. *Education and Training in Mental Retardation, 25*, 299–305.

Rehabilitation Act of 1973, PL 93-112. (September 26, 1973). Title 29, U.S.C. 701 et seq: *U.S. Statutes at Large, 87*, 355–394.

Reynolds, R. (1993). Recreation and leisure lifestyle changes. In P. Wehman (Ed.), *The ADA mandate for social change* (pp. 217–240). Baltimore: Paul H. Brookes Publishing Co.

Sailor, W., Gee, K., & Karasoff, P. (1993). Full inclusion and school restructuring. In M. Snell (Ed.), *Instruction of students with severe disabilities* (pp. 1–30). New York: Merrill.

Schleien, S., Green, F., & Heyne, L. (1993). Integrated community recreation. In M. Snell (Ed.), *Instruction of students with severe disabilities* (pp. 526–555). New York: Merrill.

Schleien, S., & Ray, T. (1988). *Community recreation and persons with disabilities: Strategies for integration.* Baltimore: Paul H. Brookes Publishing Co.

Sherrill, C. (1993). *Adapted physical activity, recreation and sport* (4th ed.). Madison, WI: WCB Brown & Benchmark.

Silberman, R. (1987). Report of the working group on recreation and leisure. In A.M. Covert & H.D. Fredericks (Eds.), *Transition for persons with deaf blindness and other profound handicaps: State of the art* (pp. 141–146). Monmouth, OR: Teaching Research Publications.

Smull, M.W., & Bellamy, G.T. (1991). Community services for adults with disabilities: Policy challenges in the emerging support paradigm. In L.H. Meyer, C.A. Peck, & L. Brown (Eds.), *Critical issues in the lives of people with severe disabilities* (pp. 527–536). Baltimore: Paul H. Brookes Publishing Co.

St. Peter, S., Field, S., & Hoffman, A. (1992). *Self-determination: A literature review and synthesis.* Wayne State University.

Storey, K., Stern, R., & Parker, R. (1991). A comparison of attitudes toward typical recreational activities versus the Special Olympics. *Education and Training in Mental Retardation, 25*, 94–99.

Strully, J., & Strully, C. (1985). Friendship and our children. *Journal of The Association for Persons with Severe Handicaps, 10*, 224–227.

Taylor, S., & Bogden, R. (1990). Quality of life and the individual's perspective. In R. Schalock & M.J. Bogale (Eds.), *Quality of life: Perspectives and issues* (pp. 27–40). Washington, DC: American Association of Mental Retardation.

Turnbull, H.R. III, Turnbull, A.P., Bronicki, G.J., Summers, J.A., & Roeder-Gordon, C. (1989). *Disability and the family: A guide to decisions for adulthood.* Baltimore: Paul H. Brookes Publishing Co.

Wehman, P. (1992). *Life beyond the classroom: Transition strategies for young people with disabilities.* Baltimore: Paul H. Brookes Publishing Co.

Wehman, P., & Moon, M.S. (1985). Designing and implementing leisure programs for individuals with severe handicaps. In M.P. Brady & P.L. Gunter (Eds.). *Integrating moderately and severely handicapped learners* (pp. 214–237). Springfield, IL: Charles C Thomas.

Wehman, P., & Schleien, S. (1981). *Leisure programs for handicapped persons: Adaptations, techniques, and curriculum.* Baltimore: University Park Press.

Wehmeyer, M. (1992). Self-determination and the education of students with mental retardation. *Education and Training in Mental Retardation, 27*(4), 302–314.

~SECTION ONE~

GETTING STARTED

As discussed in the preface and introductory chapter, including people with disabilities in general school and community leisure or recreation activities is a relatively new idea. Research in this area is just beginning, and model programs and replications of successful inclusion strategies are scarce. The three chapters in Section One summarize, or in some cases illustrate in detail, major concepts in inclusive recreation as described in the literature and, more importantly, as they are revealed in real applications across school and community settings. These chapters build on the philosophical foundation, presented in the first chapter, for including all citizens in organized leisure programs and activities.

Chapter Two is devoted to the concept of using a community leisure facilitator (CLF) to directly support people with disabilities as they begin to participate in school or community activities. Many experts assert that having a competent, dedicated person serve as a professional or volunteer CLF may be the most crucial element in the process of inclusion. Chapter Two describes the "who, what, where, and when" of this type of position. Organizations interested in converting a more traditional position to that of a CLF or in creating a new CLF position should find the longitudinal data from a program that hired two CRFs most helpful.

Chapter Three provides specific strategies that professionals, volunteers, and families can use to facilitate inclusive recreation activities. These nonintrusive techniques revolve around participant, family, and activity-provider preferences and satisfaction and should serve as the framework for recreation program evaluation. Easy-to-use forms that correspond to each of the strategies are also provided.

Chapter Four rounds out this section with examples of inclusive recreation activities that have been implemented in typical schools or communities. Actual case studies illustrate the role of the facilitator as described in Chapter Two and the use of the strategies outlined in Chapter Three. These examples and case studies should serve as guides for parents, advocates, and professionals who are trying to make inclusive recreation a reality.

~two~

The Community
Leisure Facilitator

M. Sherril Moon, Debra Hart,
Cheska Komissar, Robin Friedlander,
Cheri L. Stierer, and Patricia Johnson Brown

The involvement of a competent, respected person or group of people who will support persons with disabilities as they participate in school and community leisure or recreation activities is the most crucial element in successful inclusion (Dattilo & St. Peter, 1991; Goodall, 1992; Ray, 1991). The community leisure facilitator (CLF) can be either a paid professional or volunteer and can provide a wide variety of services, depending on the needs of the participants. In the past, this type of position has been given a number of names; CLFs have been referred to as leisure or recreation coaches, leisure support specialists, mainstreaming or integration coordinators, community bridgebuilders, community recreation or leisure planners, or community recreation facilitators. Each of these terms describes a person who assists or supports people with disabilities as they become involved in recreation, leisure, sports, or cultural or social activities organized by schools or community groups.

Many professionals, including therapeutic recreation specialists, special educators, residential counselors, service coordinators, rehabilitation counselors, adaptive physical educators, and special needs coordinators (see Moon, chap. 1, this volume for descriptions of several of these positions) spend a significant portion of their time facilitating the involvement of persons with disabilities in community recreation programs. In effect, a number of these professionals actually serve as CLFs in addition to fulfilling their other job duties. Increasingly, positions that entail part-time CLF duties are being converted to full-time CLF positions due to the growing recognition of the importance of integrated leisure participation (Lord, 1983).

Family members, friends, neighbors, and community and school volunteers often fill the role of leisure facilitator for specific activities or events. In addition,

Development of this chapter was supported through a grant from the Office of Special Education and Rehabilitative Services of the United States Department of Education (#H086U00030) to the Training and Research Institute for People with Disabilities at Children's Hospital, Boston, Massachusetts.

those who typically participate in recreation, as well as recreation instructors, team coaches, and teachers frequently take a keen interest in participants with disabilities. With the right information, training, and experience, any of these dedicated individuals can become a CLF. The purpose of this chapter is to outline the factors involved in serving as a full- or part-time professional or volunteer community leisure facilitator.

WHAT IS THE ROLE OF A CLF?

Helping citizens with disabilities to enjoy the same leisure pursuits as other community members can sometimes be a complicated and time-consuming process (Ray, 1991). Some surveys have shown that organizers of inclusive recreation services find them harder to provide than segregated activities (Rynders, Schleien, & Mustoven, 1990). Thus, the role of the CLF entails a wide range of activities that may include anything from making a simple telephone call to assisting in identifying adaptations in the physical and/or programmatic environment that will make it possible for an individual to participate in an activity. As Stierer (1988) and Dattilo and St. Peter (1991) have suggested, the person serving in this position acts in much the same way as a job coach or supported employment specialist (Moon, Inge, Wehman, Brooke, & Barcus, 1990), matching the preferences and skills of the participant with available community and school resources.

Providing Direct Service to People with Disabilities

The most important function of a CLF is to directly assist citizens with disabilities to gain access to and participate in recreation activities of their own choosing. The type and amount of direct assistance provided varies depending on the needs of the person and his or her family. Table 1 includes examples of typical situations in which CLFs might be expected to provide support. Some individuals may need one-to-one support every time they attend or participate in an event. This demands that the CLF plan to be at a particular site over an indefinite period of time. In order for a professional to be able to gradually withdraw his or her support and move on to help other participants, he or she must teach family members, friends, or volunteers how to assist the participant on a regular basis.

Less assistance over shorter periods of time will be sufficient for some participants. Some experts (e.g., Goodall, 1992) have labeled this type of support "transitional" or "consultative." "Transitional support" implies that the CLF will ultimately be able to phase out his or her support as the participant learns to attend an activity independently or with the support of other participants. Consultative support usually entails attending an activity only once or simply meeting with the activity leader to provide instructions, make introductions, or suggest adaptations.

Providing Family Support

The CLF works in a variety of ways to empower families[1] to help their children gain access to community recreation services that by law must accommodate all citizens (Ray, 1991). Many people may be unaware that their family member who has a disability has a right to participate in regular community activities, or that the Ameri-

---

[1]The term "families" will be used throughout this chapter and includes siblings, parents, legal guardians, significant others, friends, extended family, and residential housing staff.

Table 1.   Common situations that CLFs face and supports that they provide

Situation	Supports
Participant needs transportation.	Arrange for person being supported to carpool with other participants.
	Work with organizations to initiate a carpool procedure for all participants during activity application process.
	Provide travel training (e.g., instruction on how to bike, walk, use public transportation, or travel with a peer).
	Utilize family and friends.
	Assist organization in procuring transportation (vehicles and/or services) for all participants. Utilize foundations and community civic organizations such as the Kiwanis and Knights of Columbus for funding.
	Use school transportation for all participants.
	Note: Whatever transportation is available to other participants should be available to participants with disabilities. Likewise, transportation available to participants with disabilities should be available to all participants.
Participant does not have prerequisite skills for a particular activity.	Modify or adapt activity (e.g., with rule modifications, assistive devices).
	Provide support (e.g., utilize volunteers to assist with activity or to help the person with a disability improve his or her skills).
	Educate provider regarding the benefits of partial participation.
	Emphasize the need for interdependence and mutual support.
	Work with the organization to change policies regarding required skills.
	Assist the organization to offer similar activities without prerequisites.
Activity is too expensive.	Many activities offer scholarships; ask.
	Apply to civic or religious organizations for assistance (e.g., Knights of Columbus, Rotary Club).
	Assist organization in applying for funds so they can provide scholarships or subsidize fees.
	Encourage sliding-scale fees for all participants.
	Encourage schools to offer programs for *all* children and to share the cost with the recreation department; likewise, encourage the recreation departments to offer inclusive programming and share the cost with schools.
Full-time support is not available.	Utilize natural supports (e.g., other program participants, program leaders).
	Locate peers who enjoy the same activity.
	Identify volunteer organizations (e.g., United Way, college and high school groups) and recruit volunteers from among members.
	Ask a school principal, assistant principal, or counselor to identify potential student volunteers.

(*continued*)

Table 1.   (*continued*)

Situation	Supports
Child goes to school out of district, so meeting friends and arranging for transportation become more difficult.	Arrange for person to participate in after-school activities in his or her neighborhood school.
	Assist activity organizers in changing times to accommodate lateness in returning from school.
	Identify peers in neighborhood to participate in activities or hang out.
	Assist individual and family in learning about and understanding community options so they can make informed choices.
	Encourage parents to send child to neighborhood school.
Program organizers are concerned about liability.	Inform organizers that programs are no more liable for an individual with a disability than they are for individuals without disabilities.
Participant has no informal relationships (e.g., friends).	Call neighborhood school and talk to principal, vice principal, or counselor, in order to identify kids interested in hanging out.
	Locate older students to provide role-model/peer support.
	Organize a local friendship club.
Attitudes of others are negative (e.g., program does not accept people with disabilities).	Provide awareness training.
	Model positive attitudes/behavior (go to the activity with the person).
	Focus on the individual's abilities and strengths.
	Remind program organizers that it is illegal to bar people with disabilities from participating according to the Americans with Disabilities Act (ADA). Contact your state Executive Office on Discrimination.
Activity site is not accessible.	Become familiar with the rules and regulations of Title III (Public Accommodations) of the ADA.
	Help make site accessible (e.g., help procure funding for modifications).
	Provide physical support (e.g., assistance moving wheelchair over dirt path).
	Become familiar with local resources that provide low-cost modifications (e.g., grab bars, ramps).
	Move site.

cans with Disabilities Act (ADA) requires that public and private facilities be accessible to all citizens (U.S. Department of Justice, 1991).

One of the most important ways to assist families may be to provide them with information on the recreation services, facilities, and events that the school and community provide (Dattilo & St. Peter, 1991). Chapter 3 describes a process and a format for collecting information on community resources that can then be disseminated to families.

Determining individual and family preferences concerning leisure participation is essential and should be one of the first steps in providing direct services to any person with a disability. In some cases, this may entail no more than a brief discussion with an individual and his or her family (see Moon et al., chap. 3, this volume, for a format for collecting information about leisure preferences). However, if an individual cannot communicate his or her own preferences, the CLF may need to observe him or her in a variety of activities until a preference can be determined.

Sometimes support entails a brief follow-up phone call or visit to reassure the family that their son or daughter is making progress and is having fun (Dattilo & St. Peter, 1991). Another support to families may involve assessing their satisfaction with their child's participation in a school or community activity.

Providing families with training in advocating for and maintaining their child's participation in inclusive activities is also essential. CLFs can model ways to accompany a person with a disability and participate in an activity, or they can train families in a workshop setting. Families should also be trained in how to advocate for more inclusive services in their communities. One way to do this is to include them in workshops with other key community leaders, such as school personnel, community recreation directors, and human services providers. Some of the topics on which families may need information and training include:

Converting therapeutic recreation programs into community-based, integrated services
Creating CLF positions in recreation and human services organizations
Ensuring legal rights to inclusive services under the ADA
Developing accessibility adaptations and modifications that enhance participation
Using the individualized education program (IEP)/individualized transition plan (ITP) process to gain access to inclusive recreation experiences
Developing ideas for age-appropriate activities
Understanding what's in and what's out (e.g., fashion, popular toys, hot hang-outs)
Realizing the importance of choice
Developing community supports (e.g., volunteer participation)
Working toward the goals of recreation (e.g., having fun rather than competing)
Working as a team with community service providers to change recreation programs.

Table 2 provides some tips for providing training to families.

Coordinating Programs Across Agencies

A CLF must be an accomplished team player who understands and can work with families, as well as with agencies and organizations that provide recreation programs. For example, if a local chapter of The Arc hires a CLF to work with children who have mental retardation, he or she will have to forge a relationship with school administrators and teachers in order to facilitate school-based activities such as friendship clubs, sports, classroom-based recreation, and extracurricular pursuits.

Working within schools to promote inclusive, enjoyable leisure activities is a crucial part of the CLF's role for several reasons. First, parents of students with severe disabilities rate friendship and social relationship development as being as important an educational priority as functional life skills or academic skills (Hamre-Nietupski, Nietupski, & Strathe, 1992). Second, a CLF should be a critical part of the education transition team who implements community leisure goals and objectives that are part of a student's IEP or ITP. In fact, the involvement of therapeutic recreation specialists (TRSs) has been mandated by the Individuals with Disabilities Education Act (IDEA), allowing educators to rely on these professionals to assess leisure

Table 2. Tips for working with families

Parents are much better convincers of other parents than professionals. Ask families who have already experienced inclusive recreation to tell their personal stories.	Develop and provide handouts on community resources; include phone numbers and contact persons.
Use audiovisual presentations (e.g., slides, videos); they make great success stories.	Demonstrate a willingness to meet one-to-one with parents and provide lots of follow-up (e.g., letters, phone calls).
Encourage recreation providers to discuss their programs during training.	Be sensitive to the history of segregated programs and to the fear of inclusion.
Leave plenty of time for answering questions and expressing concerns.	Remember, many parents have a history of others' rejecting their child with a disability and are fearful it will happen again.
Be reassuring; constantly repeat your offer of support.	While encouraging inclusion, do not discourage segregated activities. Remember, the bottom line should be choice and opportunity.
Give concrete examples and specific ideas (e.g., where to find activities and how to access them). Do not use lingo and do not "preach" to families.	Provide food (e.g., coffee and donuts)
Provide transportation to training sessions, if possible.	

needs, assist with participation in school and community recreation activities, and provide leisure education as part of the student's curriculum.

Finally, for people with disabilities below the age of 22, the school is the key service provider and link to all other vital resources. School personnel have a great deal of information on each student's background and personal preferences; have access to families, general educators, and peers without disabilities and can lend credibility to any inclusion effort (Ray, 1991), all of which can be indispensible to CLFs, especially in fullfilling their responsibility for coordinating programs across agencies.

Leisure education can be provided to students and their families as part of the school curricula so that they are systematically taught to use available resources. This can be a part of every student's transition plan and can be formalized when included in the form of transition goals in the IEP or ITP. Leisure education can be designed to improve self-determination, choice making, social interaction, and knowledge of or access to community resources. Models such as those proposed by Bullock, Bedini, and Driscoll (1991) or by St. Peter (1991) can be adapted for use in most school programs.

The CLF will also have to maintain a close working relationship with all other organizations that provide programs, facilities, monetary assistance, or other forms of support to individuals in the community. For example, the CLF who worked for The Arc described in Chapter 11 of this text had to work with professionals from seven organizations, including the YMCA, City Parks and Recreation Department, Boys and Girls Club, Girl Scouts, local Arc, and public school system, in order to integrate the summer camps in her town.

Some professionals may find interagency agreements valuable in establishing working relationships with outside agencies. It is often helpful to capture the energy of interagency cooperation by putting agreements in writing to ensure full understanding and accountability regarding the responsibilities of all parties. Interagency agreements are written formal contracts that promote cooperation among agencies.

They are often simple to develop and should include the following key elements: 1) the names of agencies involved, 2) the names of contact persons, 3) detailed lists of each agency's responsibilities and the specific persons to be held accountable, 4) timelines for completion of activities, and 5) desired outcomes. Once the agreement is placed in writing and all parties have had the opportunity to work out any specific concerns, cooperation is more secure and progress almost inevitable.

Training and Technical Assistance

Formal and informal information sharing and education in the form of workshops, hands-on technical assistance, or classes are important ways of helping others to assist people with disabilities to participate in community recreation. Just as providing information to families in various formats is an essential role of the CLF, training and working with other professionals is also important. Professionals will benefit from training on most of the same topics listed for families earlier in this chapter. Other ideas for workshops include: 1) volunteer recruitment and management, 2) developing interdependent groups and natural supports within recreation activities, 3) fostering parent and community involvement, 4) funding sources, and 5) resources for program modifications and adaptive equipment. Tips for working with professionals can be found in Table 3.

Inservice programs must be developed according to the specific requests or needs of individuals or groups at any given time. There are, however, some general guidelines that CLFs should follow as they prepare presentations and materials on various topics. One good source for such information is the *LIFE Resource and Training Manual* (Bullock, Wohl, Webreck, & Crawford, 1982). Training materials and sessions have been designed to provide individuals with information on how to gain access to community recreation through the LIFE program. Some training sessions center on encouraging agencies to refocus mission statements to reflect a commitment to the integration of persons with disabilities. In addition, staff are trained in techniques and strategies for making simple adaptations for inclusion. And finally, participants are instructed in how to set up multi-agency councils that promote collaborative processes for including persons with disabilities in community activities. The LIFE materials are easily implemented and are applicable in a wide variety of recreation settings.

Another approach, designed by Brown (1989), focuses on helping the individual with a disability empower him- or herself to choose and then have access to community leisure activities. This program model highlights a training process whereby free choice, elimination of barriers, and access are combined. Four 1½-hour training modules were developed, focusing on teaching individuals about their rights and responsibilities, and improving their decision-making and problem-solving abilities. Individuals with disabilities were exposed to leisure case studies and asked to make their own decisions about leisure lifestyles based on the scenarios presented. The participants were found to demonstrate changes in their leisure activities while in the community as a result of the training programs.

THE PROFESSIONAL CLF

Professional CLFs can function within advocacy groups such as Arcs, YW/YMCAs, parks and recreation departments, residential programs, schools, sheltered workshops, adult activity centers, local United Cerebral Palsy organizations, mental

Table 3.   Tips for training and working with professionals

Research and gather information on all community agencies (e.g., schools, parks and recreation, Parent Advisory Councils, Arcs) with whom you are involved. This should be an ongoing process.

Encourage the sharing of resources between agencies.

Be careful not to compromise your standards/philosophy to work with an agency, but be able to adapt enough to get things done.

Identify or develop one or two people/positions in each agency as primary contacts for you and others.

Have respect for the agencies' programs and territories. Give them lots of credit for any amount of help.

Always give plenty of notice about meetings. Send personal letters and follow up with phone calls. Meet at times mutually acceptable to all.

Getting the first child involved may take some time. Remember, effort invested will have long-term benefits for others who wish to become involved.

Professionals who do not work with people with disabilities may need a basic introduction to a variety of specific conditions.

Give concrete examples of how to modify specific activities (choosing examples that are relevant to your audience).

Utilize a panel of professionals. People may listen to their colleagues more readily than to you, an outsider. If you are not able to locate individuals for a panel, work with a few people individually and then invite them to sit on your panel.

Be sensitive to the fear of people who have never worked with individuals with disabilities. Encourage questions and answer them openly and honestly.

Address liability issues; remember they are the same for all participants regardless of ability.

Address concerns that professionals may have about the other participants (e.g., they will not be accepting of individuals with disabilities, the individual with a disability will take too much attention away from other participants).

Discuss laws (e.g., the ADA)

Professionals who work with people with disabilities may fear loosing their jobs; demonstrate how jobs may change with inclusion but will not be lost.

Share ideas on policy modifications (e.g., eliminating prerequisite skills).

Provide food (e.g., coffee and donuts).

health and mental retardation agencies, religious organizations, nonprofit organizations that provide other services to adults with disabilities (e.g., employment training), and state vocational rehabilitation independent living centers.

Converting an Existing Position

Converting an existing position to a full-time CLF position has many advantages. The proposed CLF may already be familiar with the community and its agencies and services, as well as with the particular people with disabilities who may utilize such services. However, the change in position may also cause nervousness and tension for the new CLF. The individual moving into the CLF position may feel that his or her job or the services that he or she provides are threatened. In this case, it is important to emphasize that the services being provided will not be lost, merely changed. A recreation professional who offered special programs for people with disabilities will now offer his or her support to those same individuals in other community activities. Additionally, families may fear losing services for their children. These fears may be addressed by introducing the family to others in the community who have already experienced the process of integration, as well as by giving them plenty of individualized attention.

Securing Funding for a New Position

There are several avenues for seeking additional funds for a CLF position if there is no internal funding source available and no existing position that can be converted. State and federal grant money from the Office of Special Education, Vocational Rehabilitation Services, or Developmental Disabilities Planning Councils can be used to create a CLF position, although internal funding will eventually have to be found. Private funding from foundations such as the Mitsubishi Foundation, Ben and Jerry's, or the United Way can also be sought. Several agencies within a limited locale can also share resources in order to support a CLF position in much the same way that education, vocational rehabilitation, and development disabilities agencies have cooperated to support job coaching (Wehman, Moon, Everson, Wood, & Barcus, 1988).

Characteristics of a Professional CLF

Most people desiring to work as a CLF will not have had specific formal training for this position. However, many with a background in therapeutic recreation, physical or special education, rehabilitation, service coordination, or advocacy will already possess the characteristics that make a good CLF, including: 1) a belief in the inclusion of all people, regardless of skill level; 2) a belief in the right of all people to have fun; 3) the ability to communicate with parents and other professionals; 4) experience in providing training; 5) knowledge of human services delivery (both the advantages and pit falls) to people with disabilities; and 6) the experience or presence that will enable others to view the CLF as an authority or expert.

Furthermore, according to Buswell and Schaffner (1992), in order to provide friendship support in inclusive settings, a CLF needs to have: 1) a strong belief that friendships between people with and without disabilities are both possible and important, 2) an understanding of the development of friendships, 3) the ability to solve problems and be innovative, 4) a willingness to create new solutions when new challenges arise, 5) the ability to focus on strengths, and 6) the ability to be unobtrusive and to know when to fade support. Figure 1 shows an advertisement that one organization used to recruit two CLFs.

THE VOLUNTEER CLF

Volunteers have long provided support for persons with disabilities, not only in recreation programs, but in employment, home, and educational programs as well (Taylor, Biklin, & Knoll, 1987). A number of programs specially designed to allow volunteers to help children and adults with disabilities experience leisure and friendship have been documented (Calkins, Dunne, & Kultgen, 1986; Cooley, 1989; Voeltz et al., 1983).

Most successful volunteer programs have several factors in common, which Cooley and her colleagues at the Oregon Research Institute have been particularly successful in delineating and describing (Cooley, Singer, & Irvin, 1989). In fact, Cooley (1989) has developed an excellent manual that provides step-by-step instructions, lists of materials, and necessary forms for implementing a volunteer program that fosters friendships between community members and children with disabilities. Although it is beyond the scope of this chapter to describe in detail how

COMMUNITY LEISURE FACILITATOR: POSITION OPEN IMMEDIATELY TO CO-ORDINATE 3 YEAR PROJECT to assist school aged children and adolescents with severe disabilities to participate in regular community and school leisure activities in the Boston area. We are looking for highly energetic people who can work very flexible hours, want direct involvement in inclusive leisure programs, and can produce written products, and provide inservice training in a variety of formats. Bachelor's or Master's degree with 3 years experience in assisting persons with severe disabilities or in therapeutic recreation and at least 2 years experience in inclusive or community-based programs for people with severe disabilities; must also demonstrate ability to provide technical assistance and produce written products. Salary and benefits competitive. Please send letter of interest and resume to: Sherril Moon, Gardner 6, 300 Longwood Ave., Children's Hospital, Boston, MA 02115. (617) 735-6914.

Figure 1. A print ad aimed at recruiting CLFs.

to establish a volunteer program, some of the elements most critical to volunteer CLFs are discussed here.

A volunteer CLF must be a competent individual who understands the person and family whom he or she is assisting. The volunteer must also fully understand the project or activity, the context in which he or she is providing support. Furthermore, he or she must be able to inspire confidence and gain the trust of those with whom he or she is working. This is a tall order for anyone, but particularly for a new or younger volunteer. Nurses, therapists, special or physical educators, recreation professionals and other volunteers with formal education or experience who are already familiar with school or community programs will quickly be able to serve in a volunteer CLF capacity with a minimum of problems. Families and community or school program sponsors are likely to trust an experienced volunteer's ability to support a child with a disability, and volunteers such as those mentioned above won't need much formal training in medical procedures, behavior management, or family support. However, he or she may need training or information on the integration of recreation programs or on specific programs (e.g., requirements for participation in a community softball league).

Less experienced volunteers will need extensive, continual, formal training in a number of areas; the specific amount of training will depend on the volunteer's age, experience, and the role he or she will be expected to fill. For example, a teenage volunteer who will be working with other volunteers under a competent supervisor will not need as much training as a volunteer college student who, alone and unsupervised, is going to provide transportation and support over an 8-week period for a child playing on a soccer team.

Some programs, such as that organized by the parks and recreation department described by Wagner, Wetherald, and Wilson in Chapter 10, entail professional CLFs recruiting, training and supervising volunteers. Especially experienced and adept volunteer CLFs can also serve in training or supervisory capacities. In short, there is really no right or wrong way to include volunteers in a program, as long as participants, families, and program supervisors enjoy and appreciate their involvement.

Recruitment and Training

Volunteer CLFs can be recruited from high schools, colleges, churches, fraternities and sororities, volunteer referral agencies, and professional or advocacy groups, or they can be recommended by individuals who themselves assist persons with disabilities. An array of media, including radio and TV advertising, fliers, and organization newsletters, can be used for recruiting, as can presentations and simple word of mouth. The age and experience of the targeted recruits and, thus, the choice of recruitment source and method will be determined by the role that the volunteer is to fill. It is critical to fully understand the exact purpose of using volunteer CLFs before trying to recruit them. If friendship is the goal, then same-age peers should be recruited. If assistance in taking swimming lessons or playing soccer is the goal, then age won't be as important as the ability to actively participate in these activities.

After inviting persons to become volunteers, some type of screening procedure must be employed. Examining written application forms, conducting interviews, and checking references are all good ways of confirming the interests, experience, and commitment of potential volunteers. A simple form for obtaining this kind of information is provided in Figure 2. Cooley (1989) provides guidelines and forms for the screening process in her manual, *Fostering Friendships*. Other data collection methods are provided by Schleien and Ray (1988), who outline the process and provide forms to be used in initiating, implementing, and evaluating volunteers' participation. Volunteer CLFs very rarely need specific skills or a background as a disability professional; the main objective in selecting recruits is to choose people who are committed, reliable, and energetic.

Volunteer CLFs will sometimes need specific training or prior experience if they are to assist persons who need extensive support, or have multiple disabilities, behavior disorders, or medical or physical disabilities that necessitate the use of specialized adaptive equipment. Professionals and parents are typically happy to provide special training sessions on these topics, and close, regular, on-site supervision by a professional CLF or a volunteer coordinator can help to put the volunteer, participant, and family at ease. Volunteer CLFs should never be expected to provide total support for people with extensive needs; being comfortable in such a situation requires training, practice, and modeling by skilled and experienced individuals.

One of the best ways to train volunteers is to arrange for them to visit the homes and classrooms of the persons with whom they'll be working. This allows for observation, information gathering, and practice in interacting. It is also helpful for the volunteer coordinator, the volunteer, and the person being supported to spend some time together prior to integration into the program. This allows everyone to ask questions and get to know one another before larger groups enter into the picture. More-formal training sessions can also be planned for groups of CLFs, along with other recreation professionals, volunteers, community groups, and families. Some topics that are almost always relevant are inclusion philosophy and strategies, working with the general public in including people with disabilities, communication and listening skills, practical behavior-management strategies for community settings, assisting people with particular physical and medical disabilities, using partial participation strategies, and communicating with parents.

Probably the most important things to remember when including volunteer CLFs in a program is the need to match their interests with those of the participants

VOLUNTEER QUESTIONNAIRE

Name:_____ Date:___/___/___

Address (Home):_____

Telephone Number (Home):_____(Business)_____

Birthdate:___/___/___   Gender: ☐ Female   ☐ Male

1. Are you currently in school?   ☐ yes   ☐ no
   If yes, please write the name of the school/college and grade/class you are in below:
   Name of School/College_____ Grade/Class_____

2. What special skills, talents &/or interests do you have?_____
   _____
   _____

3. What do you like to do best during your free time? Please describe:_____
   _____

4. Have you had any volunteer experience?   ☐ yes   ☐ no
   If yes, please describe_____

5. Have you had any experience with people who have cognitive or physical disabilities? ☐ yes ☐ no
   If yes, please describe_____

6. Do you prefer to participate with an individual of a specific age or gender? Please check all that apply.
   ☐ Child   ☐ Teenager ☐ Adult   ☐ Male   ☐ Female   ☐ Don't Care

7. If you are in school, would you be willing to take a student with a disability to any of your nonacademic
   classes or school sponsored activities (e.g., school athletic teams/games, clubs)?
   ☐ yes   ☐ no   ☐ not sure   ☐ I do not participate in these activities.

8. Do you have your own transportation?   ☐ yes   ☐ no
   If yes, would you be willing to transport a person with a disability to an activity? ☐ yes ☐ no

9. Would you be willing to travel to a nearby community to meet with a project participant?
   ☐ yes   ☐ no

10. How many hours per week would you be able to participate? Please circle the correct number.
    1   2   3   4   5   6   7   8

11. Please circle the best day(s) for you to participate.
    Monday   Tuesday   Wednesday   Thursday   Friday   Saturday   Sunday

12. What are the best times of day for you to participate?_____

Figure 2.   A questionnaire can be a good initial step in the screening process for volunteer CLFs.

and to look for special expertise or experience in cases in which one or the other is needed. Careful planning, continued recruitment, a good training program, and constant supervision will make the program a success.

Supporting Volunteers

Most volunteers who provide support to people with disabilities in community or school activities will need some form of supervision. The type and amount of supervision will depend on the experience of the volunteer, his or her familiarity with the activity and its participants, and the strengths and limitations of the person who is being assisted. Many programs employ a volunteer coordinator on a full- or part-time basis to oversee volunteers. Cooley (1989) has listed a number of duties for which this professional is responsible, including the recruitment, screening, and training of volunteers; maintaining family contact; finding suitable activities; accompanying volunteers and participants on their first outings; and keeping necessary records.

Cooley and her colleagues also discuss the importance of the coordinator being immediately available to a volunteer in case a problem arises. She stresses the importance of having a supervisor attend all first outings and then maintain regular weekly contact with the volunteer. She also suggests scheduling monthly meetings to share ideas, problem solve, and conduct more formal training on particular topics. A supervisor must also visit the locations where volunteers provide assistance, in order to maintain contact with on-site professionals such as teachers, recreation directors, or coaches. Such visits will also allow the supervisor to answer questions and address the concerns of other adult participants or parents of young participants who do not have disabilities.

A REAL VIEW OF A CLF

The Training and Research Institute for People with Disabilities at Children's Hospital in Boston received a 3-year grant from the United States Department of Education, Office of Special Education, to coordinate community- and school-based recreation services for students with severe disabilities in three suburban Boston communities. This grant provided funding for two professional, full-time CLFs for 3 years. The goal was to demonstrate the variety of training and direct service accomplishments that a professional in this position could achieve. Table 4 provides a listing of the various organizations and activities in which the CLFs were involved.

The two CLFs, one from the field of therapeutic recreation, the other with a background in supported employment and secondary special education, kept daily time records of their work. These data were then organized into annual and then 24-month summaries to demonstrate the amount and kinds of work that a full-time CLF can do. Table 5 shows the total hours and numbers of people the CLFs worked with and the number of projects that they completed during their first 2-years in this position. In summary, the two CLFs worked directly with 148 students with extensive support needs and their families, as well as providing a variety of training formats for families, professionals, and kids. They also worked with 1,503 peers without disabilities in a variety of capacities and produced 25 different printed

Table 4. Actual CLF activities

Organizations	Activities	Products

Elementary, middle, and high schools (20):
   10 elementary
   6 middle
   4 high
YMCAs (4):
   swimming
   basketball
   gymnastics
   karate
Boy Scouts (6)
Girl Scouts (1)
Community Recreation Programs (7):
   soccer
   skiing
   baseball card collecting
   woodworking
   swimming
   arts and crafts
   cooking
Horse Stables (1)
Theater Group (1)
4-H (1)
Summer Camps (10)
	Friendship Clubs
	Inclusive gym class
	Soccer
	Swimming
	Cooking
	Karate
	Gymnastics
	Woodworking
	Theater
	After-school care
	School activity period
	Summer friendship group
	Social inclusion in school (lunch/recess)
	Hanging out:
	   football games
	   arcades
	   mall
	   movies
	   town carnivals
	   shooting hoops
	   eating pizza
	   getting hair done
	Volunteering
	Horseback riding
	Sailing
	Basketball
	Baseball card collecting club
	School-based social group
	Gymboree
	Dance lessons
	Cross country skiing
	Arts and crafts
		Community Access Survey
		Community Recreation Survey
		Leisure Interest Survey
		Newsletter
		Satisfaction Survey Instruments
		Volunteer Questionnaire
		Data Keeping Forms
		Book chapters, articles, and monographs
		Interviews:
		   parents
		   people with disabilities
		Brochures
		A variety of training handouts

products, such as surveys, articles, newsletters, and other resources for families and communities.

CONCLUDING COMMENTS

The participation of a CLF or similar support person can be the determining factor in successfully making school or community leisure activities inclusive. This per-

Table 5.　Data for two full-time CLFs over a 2-year period

Number of students with disabilities served	148
Number of students without disabilities involved	1,503
Hours spent with students[a]	2,863
Number of families served	148
Hours spent with families	1,445
Number of community members involved	767
Hours spent with community members (including teachers, program leaders, agency members)	2,269
Hours spent on products (newsletters, journal articles, brochures)	521
Number of products	25
Office hours[b]	1,217
Travel hours	597
Hours spent giving presentations	108

[a]Includes time spent with combined groups of students with and without disabilities.

[b]Includes time spent generating written correspondence, making phone calls, and preparing presentations.

son can provide support in any number of ways, including personally accompanying a participant to an event or finding someone else to do so, providing information and assistance to families, and teaching other community members about the importance of including citizens with disabilities. The role of the CLF is even more important since the ADA mandated that citizens with disabilities have access to all public recreation programs.

One benefit of CLF support is the low cost. Professionals hired for other purposes or other positions can easily assume the role of CLF, and volunteers can often function in CLF capacities. Finally, practically any organization can hire a CLF or convert an existing position. As the data in this chapter indicate, one or two full-time CLFs can provide services to a surprisingly large number of individuals, families, and organizations. As the remainder of this text indicates, the possibilities for this position are virtually limitless.

REFERENCES

Brown, P. (1989). Effects of self advocacy training in leisure for adults with severe physical disabilities. *Dissertation Abstracts International, 49,* 12A.

Bullock, C., Bedini, L., & Driscoll, L. (1991). *The Wake leisure education program.* The center for Recreation and Disability Studies Curriculum in Leisure Studies and Recreation Administration, University of North Carolina at Chapel Hill.

Bullock, C., Wohl, R., Webreck, T., & Crawford, A. (1982). *LIFE resource and training manual.* Chapel Hill: Project LIFE, University of North Carolina.

Buswell, B., & Schaffner, B. (1992, Spring). Building friendships: An important part of schooling. *OSERS News in Print, 5,* 4–8.

Calkins, C., Dunne, W., & Kultgen, P. (1986). A comparison of preschool and elderly community integration/demonstration projects at the University of Missouri Institute for Human Development. *Journal of The Association for Persons with Severe Handicaps, 11*(4), 276–285.

Cooley, E. (1989). *Fostering friendships: A manual for implementing a volunteer program that pairs community members with children with disabilities.* Eugene: Oregon Research Institute.

Cooley, E., Singer, G., & Irvin, L. (1989). Volunteers as part of family support services for families of developmentally disabled members. *Education and Training in Mental Retardation, 24*(3), 207–218.

Dattilo, J., & St. Peter, S. (1991). A model for including leisure education in transition services for young adults with mental retardation. *Education and Training in Mental Retardation, 26*(4), 420–432.

Goodall, P. (1992). *Integrated leisure options for individuals with severe traumatic brain injury* (Special Topical Report #1). Richmond: Virginia Commonwealth University, Medical College of Virginia.

Hamre-Nietupski, S., Nietupski, J., & Strathe, M. (1992). Functional life skills, academic skills, and friendships/social relationships development: What do parents of students with moderate/severe/profound disabilities value? *Journal of The Association for Persons with Severe Handicaps, 17*(1), 53–58.

Lord, J. (1983). Reflections on a decade of integration. *Journal of Leisurability, 10*(4), 4–11.

Moon, M.S., Inge, K.J., Wehman, P., Brooke, V., & Barcus, J.M. (1990). *Helping persons with severe mental retardation get and keep employment: Supported employment issues and strategies.* Baltimore: Paul H. Brookes Publishing Co.

Ray, T. (1991). *SCOLA leisure activity guide.* St. Paul, MN: Association for Retarded Citizens.

Rynders, J., Schleien, S., & Mustoven, T. (1990). Integrating children with severe disabilities for intensified outdoor education: Focus on feasibility. *Mental Retardation, 28*(1), 7–14.

Schleien, S.J., & Ray, M.T. (1988). *Community recreation and persons with disabilities: Strategies for integration.* Baltimore: Paul H. Brookes Publishing Co.

Stierer, C. (1988). *Community integration of persons with disabilities through recreation leisure participation and their acceptance by nondisabled peers.* Unpublished manuscript.

Taylor, S., Biklen, D., & Knoll, J. (Eds.). (1987). *Community integration for people with severe disabilities.* New York: Teachers College Press.

U.S. Department of Justice. (1991). *The ADA: Questions and answers.* Washington, DC: U.S. Government Printing Office.

Voeltz, L.M., Hemphill, N., Brown, S., Kishi, G., Klein, R., Fruehling, R., Levy, G., Collie, J., & Kube, C. (1983). *The special friends program: A trainer's manual for integrated school settings.* Hawaii Integration Project, College of Education, University of Hawaii. (ERIC Document Reproduction Service No. ED 256 128)

Wehman, P., Moon, M.S., Everson, J.M., Wood, W., & Barcus, J.M. (1988). *Transition from school to work: New challenges for youth with severe disabilities.* Baltimore: Paul H. Brookes Publishing Co.

~three~

Strategies for Successful Inclusion in Recreation Programs

M. Sherril Moon, Cheri L. Stierer, Patricia Johnson Brown, Debra Hart, Cheska Komissar, and Robin Friedlander

A number of steps must be taken in order to ensure the successful inclusion of people with disabilities in recreation activities. For some individuals these steps may include things as simple as identifying preferences and then providing the phone numbers of programs that can provide a preferred activity. For others, the steps might include not only identifying preferences, but also creating entirely new options, educating program sponsors and participants, accompanying the person to events, planning activity adaptations, and evaluating participant satisfaction. The most effective way to determine which steps should be taken for an individual is to determine his or her own needs and preferences and those of his or her family, the possibilities that exist in a particular community, and the integration practices that can best be used to help the individual take advantage of these opportunities.

Schleien, Green, and Heyne (1993) identified a set of recommended integrated-recreation strategies or practices that can be used to facilitate the inclusion of people with disabilities in school or community programs; these include: 1) individual needs and preference assessments, 2) guidelines for choosing activities, 3) environmental analysis, 4) collateral skill development, 5) adaptations, 6) ability awareness orientations and friendship training, 7) cooperative grouping arrangements, and 8) program evaluation. The purpose of this chapter is to describe how to implement these and other commonly used and effective strategies for facilitating inclusion.

Development of this chapter was supported through a grant from the Office of Special Education and Rehabilitative Services of the United States Department of Education (#H086U00030) to the Training and Research Institute for People with Disabilities at Children's Hospital, Boston, Massachusetts.

IMPLEMENTING CHANGE WITHIN AN ORGANIZATION

A number of preliminary steps are necessary in order to implement change within an organization. Educating yourself about current practices and recent legislation affecting the inclusion of individuals with developmental disabilities in community leisure and recreation activities and programs is a crucial first step. A thorough evaluation of the services offered by the agency or organization with which you are concerned is another essential step in the preparation process.

Educating Yourself

It is important for those who are going to facilitate relationships and supervise/ sponsor the integration of individuals with disabilities into recreation or leisure programs to ground themselves in a philosophy that supports their actions and to validate the techniques, grouping strategies, and activities that they plan to try. This can be achieved by reviewing the research and program descriptions in the literature on friendship development and integrated leisure, recreation, and physical education programs. This research will also eliminate the need to reinvent the wheel as you tackle the logistics of starting or expanding a program. A number of individuals and organizations have published articles and books that include strategies for integrating community leisure activities. Other organizations, such as ERIC, have set up databases that allow access to written materials or organizations that can help with specific recreation topics.

Eliminating Segregated Activities

Changing the philosophy that underlies traditional, separate therapeutic recreation programs offered by organizations such as city and county parks systems, schools, churches, local chapters of The Arc of America, YMCAs, and YWCAs remains a challenge. Trying to make use of existing resources while eliminating segregated programming can be a difficult undertaking, depending on such factors as how long a program has been in place, its past success, and the expectations of participants and their family members.

Because parents, residential program staff, and program managers may be unfamiliar with the concept of integrated recreation and leisure activities for individuals with disabilities, it may be best to approach change cautiously and desegregate programs gradually. Once several persons with disabilities have been integrated into a particular program or activity, and participants and staff have had a chance to become comfortable with the idea of integration, it will be much easier to increase the number and variety of persons who are included. It is also important to recognize that no matter how successful integration is, people tend to feel safest and most accepted among those who are most similar to themselves.

An alternate, more radical approach, which may be highly successful in certain circumstances, is to make a clean break, drastically altering the philosophy behind a program and immediately offering only integrated activities.

Regardless of which method is chosen, furnishing opportunities for individuals with disabilities to interact with others who face the same challenges concerning accessibility and to develop friendships with persons who do not have disabilities should remain of the utmost importance. The suggestions below, which have proven successful for others facilitating the integration of recreation and leisure programs, may be helpful to you as you initiate the process of change in your community.

Review Current Programs   Evaluate and review the programs currently available in the community, including such factors as locations, levels of accessibility, and participant cost. It is also helpful to determine whether people with disabilities have previously been involved in any of the current activities. Figure 1 is an example of a form that can be used in collecting this information from an agency that offers community recreation programs.

Determine Which Programs Would Be Suitable for Persons with Disabilities   Identify activities that are typically made available to persons without disabilities, have a high level of participation, and offer the greatest opportunity for social networking and interaction. These may include team sports, exercise or crafts classes, walk-a-thons, neighborhood recreation projects, and festivals. Highlight those programs that are suited to participants with a variety of skill levels. Aerobics classes, for example, allow for participants to move at their own pace and to move to a more basic step whenever necessary.

Begin to Eliminate Segregated Programs that Have Redundant Content   Assist people with disabilities to enroll in integrated activities that are similar to those offered in special programs. For example, a typical pair of overlapping programs would be a segregated bowling skills class for persons with developmental disabilities and a separate bowling class for their novice peers. Another would be an adaptive aquatics class for persons with disabilities and a regular beginning swimming class. It will be necessary to be supportive of each individual and to provide assistance for the transition to the integrated neighborhood community. In this context, being supportive can include a variety of tasks: providing assistance with registration, arranging for transportation, meeting with other participants during the first session, visiting the facility prior to the start of the program, meeting and talking with the facility staff, and determining the level of accessibility at the facility and the need for adaptive supports.

Provide Support and Set a Good Example for Agency Staff   Integration may be accomplished by combining special and general staff and providing training on integration and instructional strategies to all those involved. If leaders of general programs seem skeptical, immediately provide suggestions and offer assistance to allay any fears or misconceptions. The CLF can often handle these types of situations graciously, without divulging personal details about the participant's disability, by focusing instead on the person's strengths and abilities. Always keep in mind that *everyone* has different abilities.

Staff members themselves can also be a good source of new ideas for activities; they will already have interests and skills in activities that the CLF may not have considered. Planning meetings for new activities are also perfect opportunities to encourage staff to get to know the individuals with disabilities with whom they will be working.

Teach Self-Advocacy and Recruit Assistance from Individuals Who Are Empathetic to Your Cause   In every social network, there are individuals who are related to or acquainted with a person with disabilities. Such individuals can often serve as good role models during the change process. Consider contacting volunteers or paid staff who come from cultural backgrounds similar to those of the participants, or who come from the same neighborhoods.

Consumer advocacy groups or clubs in the nearby community, such as the Jaycees, local chapters of The Arc, Knights of Columbus, and fraternities or sororities can also be good sources of support. Local communities often have a commit-

RECREATION PROGRAM ANALYSIS

Name of Organization/Facility:_____

Contact Person & Role:_____

Phone Number (Voice):_____(TDD):_____

Transportation Alternatives : ☐a.Car   ☐b.Public Transportation   ☐c.Facility provided transport
Are b or c accessible? ☐Yes ☐No
Please describe the route between drop-off for b &/or c and facility (e.g., accessibility, busy streets)
_____

Activity/Group	Age of Participants	Gender	Number of Participants
1.			
2.			
3.			
4.			
5.			

Please make sure that information listed below corresponds to the above activities.

Date(s)	Day(s)	Time(s)	Membership Costs & Fees	Subsidy Available	Reduced Rate
1.					
2.					
3.					
4.					
5.					

Equipment/machines used : ☐Yes   ☐No   ☐ Facility owned   ☐ Participant owned
Type of equipment:_____
Special related rules (e.g., specific type of dress): _____
_____
Physical demands/medical considerations of site (e.g., temperature, lighting): _____
_____
Do people with disabilities currently participate in programs? ☐Yes ☐No ☐Integrated ☐Separate
Would staff like more information/training? ☐ Yes ☐ No
Accessibility Comments (use Community Accessibility Survey): _____
_____
_____
Other Information:_____
_____

Figure 1.   Form for evaluating recreational programs.

ment to being loyal and sharing ownership of programs within their own geographic area. Maintaining a positive attitude and building a support group for your consumers is always advantageous.

Self-advocacy in recruiting support is another method of facilitating the change process. Having persons with disabilities speak for themselves at public hearings on community recreation projects provides one such opportunity. Inviting individual participants and advocacy groups to make presentations at agency board meetings and at management team meetings is essential to the education of those who make decisions concerning budgets and programs.

Make Participation Success Oriented   The less rigid an activity and the fewer rules there are, the more opportunity there is for real success. Motivation is a critical factor in encouraging participation. Many individuals with disabilities have not experienced much variety in their recreational activities and so have only a limited repertoire of leisure skills. Some individuals have little motivation to participate, due to a lack of experience or to past failures. Every effort and contribution should be acknowledge by the leader of an activity. Establish the philosophy that winning itself is not the targeted outcome, but that participants should focus instead on their own personal improvement and accomplishments. Guided by this philosophy, participants can become more supportive of each other. Some activities that are well suited to this principle are individual sports, expressive arts, weight training and fitness programs, cultural fairs, and martial arts.

Ensure that Participation Is All-Inclusive   Every participant should have an important role in the project or activity; being a spectator is rarely an acceptable primary goal for a participant. Put your creative skills to the test by planning ahead to ensure that everyone can become involved to some degree. In some cases, however, simply interacting on some level with his or her peers without disabilities can be very important to a person with a disability. For example, in a team sport a manager might take care of the water, towels, and sports equipment, but wouldn't actually play on the team.

Provide Opportunities for Freedom of Choice and Control   Making choices is vital to building self-esteem and a sense of responsibility, and individuals who can take control of their leisure time and select activities that interest them are more likely to feel empowered. Thus, teaching decision-making skills and responsibility are important parts of every activity. When individuals make the wrong choice and experience negative consequences, it is important to take the time to discuss the outcome, the feelings that the individual has about what has happened, and how he or she might do things differently in the future.

Consider, for example, an individual who desperately wants to go scuba diving and discusses with the CLF the possibility of signing up for a course. This is a high-risk activity, and the individual has only limited swimming experience, as indicated by his house supervisor. After attending the first 2 weeks of classes, the individual discovers that he does not currently have the lung capacity to remain under water for more than 15 seconds without panicking. His decision to take the course has now become problematic, since he will be required to practice in a pond after the next session. At this point, it is important for the CLF to take the time to discuss what course of action the individual participant wishes to take, to work through the problem-solving and decision-making process with him. Talking about the situation, exploring options, taking time to think about these options, and then making a choice about how to proceed is crucial to the participant. In this particular case, there are several options that may be available. The first might be for the participant to practice breathing exercises at home with the assistance of support staff. The second might be for the individual to continue with the course in a limited capacity, assisting others in their diving experiences and practicing in the shallow end of the pond. A third option would be for him to enroll in a swimming class in order to gain more confidence and skill in the water.

Use Naturally Occurring Environments as Training Sites   Generalization of skills across different environments can sometimes be difficult for individuals with disabilities. Training and support in such areas as decision making, using community facilities, strengthening friendship skills, and using public transportation should be taught, as necessary, to the participants as the activity is actually occurring. In other words, practice is best done in the community. For example, when an individual wishes to make new friends, the best time to practice self-introductions is at a recreation activity that he or she is attending for the first time, when all participants typically introduce themselves.

Always Build on Relationships   When individuals with disabilities meet new people who are accepting and considerate, try to allow them the opportunity to participate in activities with these potential friends; help to foster the building of relationships. Recreation activities known as "ice breakers" can provide opportunities for just this type of interaction and can be adapted to any program. Some examples of ice breakers are paper and pencil games, hug tag, famous-people games, and *New Games* (see chap. 4, this volume)—all activities in which cooperation and interaction are keys to success.

DISCOVERING THE POSSIBILITIES IN YOUR COMMUNITY

One of the first steps in supporting people with disabilities in their leisure pursuits is getting to know the people and organizations in the community that sponsor recreation activities. Some may have extensive experience in including people with disabilities, while others may lack experience but have plenty of interest in starting integrated programs. Others may need a certain amount of time, assistance, or formal training before opening their programs to everyone. The best way to determine how suitable a facility is for inclusion is to visit the site and conduct an environmental analysis to determine strengths and needs. For example, you may find that the local YMCA offers two beginning swimming classes each Saturday and that one of the instructors has worked with children with disabilities and is most interested in integrating her class as long as she has some support from another adult who either has taught swimming or has had experience with children with special needs. This kind of information should influence what you tell families about the availability of inclusive swimming lessons, as well as the kind of support you arrange for anyone who desires to attend swimming classes.

It is impossible to assess some logistical and physical barriers to participation without actually visiting programs and talking to people. For example, the cost of an aerobics class at the YMCA may be $75.00 for nonmembers, while a similar class may cost only $25.00 at the county parks and recreation center. If visits to the two sites proved them to be equally accessible and in the same neighborhood, then cost could be the deciding factor.

It is also helpful for families, as well as school and human service personnel, to have access to a "resource bank" or database of community recreation options

(Falvey & Coots, 1989). Gathering such information and distributing it to the appropriate organizations is one of the key functions of a recreation facilitator. The resource bank should be compiled after visits to all relevant programs and, in addition to listing the activities that are available, should also contain information on costs, accessibility, locations, registration procedures, and integration histories. Data bases should be updated annually.

The form provided in Figure 1 can be used to gather any of the information mentioned above, whether for the purpose of gauging the attitudes of people running existing programs, of investigating the logistics (time, cost, equipment, accessibility, location) of programs, or of compiling a recreation resource bank.

KNOWING WHAT PEOPLE OF DIFFERENT AGES DO FOR FUN

One of the most socially valid ways of determining what leisure activities are appropriate for kids or adults with disabilities is to determine the preferred leisure pursuits of their same-age peers without disabilities (Brown, Branston, Hamre-Nietupski, Pumpiana, Certo, & Gruenewald, 1979; Moon & Bunker, 1987; Voeltz, Wuerch, & Bockhaut, 1982). York, Vandercook, and Stave (1990) summarize their survey of a group of midwestern middle school youth to collect data on favorite independent activities, things to do with friends, games, music, magazines, sports, and at-home activities. They also provide implications of these results for training, modifications, and future local surveys of this sort.

Figure 2 is an example of a survey that can be used to discover what kids or adults in a particular locality like to do for fun. This form was used by some of the authors of this chapter to survey the leisure interests of children and young adults in the Boston area. The results of this survey and more details about its use are provided in the appendix at the end of this chapter.

Collecting survey information while simultaneously analyzing formal recreation programs (see Figure 1) can serve a number of purposes. First, looking at both sets of data may help the CLF to determine whether formal programs such as sports leagues or informal activities such as hanging out at the mall are most popular among those of a particular age in a given community. Depending on the interests of peers without disabilities and on the availability of certain programs, involvement in *both* formal and informal activities can be a goal for some individuals. Secondly, these data can lead to improvements in community programs for all citizens, not just those who are disabled. It may be found, for example, that existing programs do not at all match what people are most interested in doing. This kind of information could persuade influential persons such as PTAs, teachers, business and civic leaders, and recreation professionals to lobby for better and more varied formal recreation options for all citizens.

When implemented by the authors, the peer interest survey described in Appendix A identified a wide array of recreational activities available to young people today. The variety of activities is striking (see Figure 8 and Table 2, in the appendix at the end of this chapter), especially when compared to the limited selection, in most communities, of "special" programs specifically designed for people with disabilities (e.g., adapted aquatics, bowling, Special Olympics). Enabling people with disabilities to choose to participate in the same activities as their nondisabled peers not only improves their decision-making skills, but also their chances of developing social networks that will extend into other life domains. As profession-

PEER INTEREST SURVEY

School you attend: _____

Birthday: _____ / _____ / _____   ☐ Male   ☐ Female
              month   day   year

1. What do you do for fun or in your free time? Please list the activities you do most often, second most often & third most often.

    1. _____

    2. _____

    3. _____

2. When you are doing something for fun, is it usually by yourself, with 1 to 3 other people, or in a group of people larger than 3? Please check the answer that most often applies.

    ☐ 1. In my free time I usually am by myself.

    ☐ 2. I spend most of my free time with 1 to 3 other people.

    ☐ 3. I spend most of my free time with a group of people larger than 3.

3. What musical instruments do you play (including singing)? Please list them below. If you do not sing or play any musical instruments please write "none" and go on to question #4.

    1. _____

    2. _____

4. What sports or physical activities do you most enjoy doing? Please list your favorite, in order, below. If you do not enjoy participating in sports or physical activities, please write "none" and go to question #5.

    1. _____

    2. _____

    3. _____

    4. _____

Figure 2.   The Peer Interest Survey administered by the authors.

5. What sports or physical activities do you most enjoy watching? Please list your favorite three, in order of preference. If you don't enjoy watching sports/physical activities please write "none" and go on to question # 6.

    1. _____

    2. _____

    3. _____

6. What kind of music do you enjoy listening to? Please list your favorite styles, performance artists, groups or composers, in order of preference. If you do not enjoy listening to music please write "none" and go on to question #7.

    1. _____

    2. _____

    3. _____

    4. _____

    5. _____

7. Do you have any hobbies? Please list any that you enjoy, in order of preference. If you do not have any hobbies please write "none" and go to question #8.

    1. _____

    2. _____

    3. _____

    4. _____

8. Are you a member of any organized groups, organizations, clubs, teams, or do you take any lessons? Please list any of these in order of preference. If you do not participate in any organized groups, please write "none" and go to question # 9.

    1. _____

    2. _____

    3. _____

    4. _____

    5. _____

Figure 2. (continued)

9. How do you get to activities that you do for fun when you have to leave home to do them?
   Please check the answer that most often applies .

   ☐ My parents   ☐ Public transportation (bus, train)

   ☐ My bike   ☐ My friends parents

   ☐ I walk   ☐ I drive myself

   ☐ Other_____

10. What games/toys do you enjoy? Please list the games/toys you enjoy in order of preference. If
    you do not enjoy games/toys please write "none" and go on to question # 11.

    1. _____

    2. _____

    3. _____

    4. _____

    5. _____

11.a) Would you consider inviting a person with a disability to join you in "having some fun" if
      there were such a person who was looking to make new friends ? Please check the response
      that best identifies how you feel.

      ☐ YES   ☐ NO   ☐ NOT SURE

   b) Would your group of friends consider inviting a person with a disability to join you
      in "having some fun" if there were such a person who was looking to make new friends?
      Please check the response that best identifies how you feel.

      ☐ YES   ☐ NO   ☐ NOT SURE

Figure 2. (continued)

als or volunteers assisting youth with disabilities, we need to look at the entire array
of recreation activities available in the community, rather than only selecting special programs offered by school recreation departments, Easter Seals, or local chapters of the Arc.

When investigating less-formal activities (e.g., hanging out at the mall or listening to music) one may want to pay attention to the size of the group participating in
the activity. Although some people do spend their free time in groups larger than
three, the low percentage of those surveyed who chose this option illustrates that
large groups of people with disabilities spending leisure time together is not typical
(see Figure 9 in the appendix at the end of this chapter).

Transportation is also a concern for *all* youth and families. Separate transportation systems that are provided solely for citizens with disabilities have been established in many communities throughout the country (e.g., transportation to and

from school, the work place, doctors' appointments). Unfortunately, this often creates the expectation that transportation will be available for all facets of an individual's life, including recreation activities. When this does not occur, a youth often loses the chance to take part in an activity because his or her parents or guardians have come to expect that special transportation will be available.

Although no one would argue with the assertion that it would be more convenient if transportation to an activity were always available, this is a rare occurrence (see Figure 10 in the appendix at the end of this chapter). Additionally, if acceptance as "just another one of the gang" is the desired result of integration, then people with and those without disabilities must have similar transportation options. This highlights the need to teach students with disabilities to travel independently and with their peers. The difficulties of arranging for transportation are experienced by all parents, not just those of children with disabilities. If the organization conducting the activity cannot provide transportation, one alternative would be to speak with parents and participants about initiating a carpooling system.

Additional implications of these data revolve around the low interest in playing music and the high interest in participating in sports and organized activities. Although 42% of those surveyed in this case played at least one instrument, 93% listed at least one sport and 67% listed organized activities (excluding the 3% of people who listed only music lessons in this last category). The fact that only 7% of those surveyed failed to list enjoyable sports/physical activities illustrates the importance of participating in sports throughout childhood and into adulthood.

Also striking was the number of different organized activities in which kids participated. There were 156 different activities and, surprisingly, many were offered through the community rather than the schools. These included a wide array of activities, ranging from scouts to Vietnamese lessons. Although this survey is demographically representative, it does not characterize all parts of the country. This is especially meaningful for a student who attends school outside of his or her community. Participating in a community-based organized activity can be an important way for those with disabilities to make friends in their neighborhood. See Tables 2, 3, 4, and 5 and Figures 8, 9, and 10 in the appendix at the end of this chapter for more specific information on what kids preferred to do.

Once the individual has chosen an activity and the transportation issue has been resolved, fear often becomes the biggest barrier to participation. Parents and professionals often demonstrate a resistance to integration based on the rationale that youth without disabilities will not want to become friends with youth with disabilities, or, even worse, that people with disabilities will be mistreated by their peers. However, the survey conducted by the authors showed that most young people are very open to participating in recreation activities with kids their own age with disabilities (see Table 6 in the appendix at the end of this chapter); the majority of students indicated an interest in getting to know others better, regardless of ability.

MATCHING INDIVIDUAL AND FAMILY INTERESTS WITH PEER PURSUITS AND COMMUNITY PROGRAM AVAILABILITY

One of the most important elements in providing appropriate school or community services is finding out exactly what a person with a disability and his or her family want or need (Turnbull, Turnbull, Bronicki, Summers, & Roeder-Gordon, 1989). Of course, the first step in this process is to speak directly with the person whom you are assisting to determine his or her preferences, dislikes, and support needs. When a person with a disability cannot speak for him- or herself or is very young, the family is usually the best source of information. A family-oriented interest survey such as that shown in Figure 3 can be used for a number of purposes.

First, family members can be surveyed to determine if their interests match available community programs; many may not be aware of existing inclusive activities. A facilitator can present this kind of information to families after he or she has surveyed them (see Figure 3) and has compared their expressed interests with a community program analysis (see Figure 1). Second, this is a first step in determining major support needs for groups of families. One facilitator, for example, may find that transportation considerations are the major factor for older adolescents and their families. Another, who is working with young children and their families, may find that families are willing to provide transportation for their children, but are also more concerned about the complex physical or medical needs of their sons or daughters.

Finally, such a survey can also detect whether family interests match what their child's age-peers without disabilities actually do for fun. These data, along with those collected from peer-interest surveys (see Figure 2) can be used to educate family and teacher organizations about age-appropriate leisure participation.

ENJOYMENT—THE GOAL OF PARTICIPATION

One of the nicest discoveries that the authors have made in recent years is that even people with very significant disabilities and few recreation skills can still enjoy any number of activities. For example, kids using wheelchairs can play on soccer teams; adults with no acting experience, or even any verbal communication ability, can participate in theater groups; and teens with autism or Down syndrome can serve as camp counselors along with their peers. The successful participation of people who are not as skilled or prepared as the majority of participants depends on many factors.

First, it is helpful to inform the leader or instructor of an activity ahead of time about the skill level of the person with a disability. It can also be helpful for the leader to then prepare other participants for the involvement of a person with a disability and to meet with the support person ahead of time, which creates an opportunity for some informal disability awareness training to occur. The support person can also observe the activity and participants and begin to devise modifications or watch for individuals who may be particularly helpful to or fearful of the new participant. Continual positive communication with participants aimed at helping them to understand the skill and behavioral limitations of the participant who is disabled is essential.

Second, ongoing support from a skilled peer, volunteer, or recreational professional can make up for a participant's lack of skill. Therefore, arrangements have to be made for someone to provide support for as long as is necessary. Families and others cannot just assume that people with disabilities should be accepted into all recreational situations, especially those that involve competition or specialized motor skills or artistic talents. Chapter 2 provides information on how a CLF can provide support.

Third, skill development can be accomplished through various outside means. Families and teachers can work with a participant on an activity during school

RECREATION INTEREST SURVEY

Student Name_____
               First   Last

Student Date of Birth ___/___/___ Gender: ☐ Male ☐ Female Grade _____

School Student Attends_____
                              Name   City/Town

Parent(s) Name_____
               First   Last

Address _____
              Street   City/Town   Zip Code

Phone Number (Home) _____ (Work)_____

RECREATION EXPERIENCES:

1. Are you interested in having your son/daughter participate in recreation activities with children who are nondisabled? ☐ Yes ☐ No ☐ Don't know

2. Do you feel that the recreation facilities in your community are physically accessible for your child (e.g., swimming pool, movie theaters, bowling alleys)? ☐ Yes ☐ No ☐ Don't know

3. What sources do you use to find out about recreational activities for your child? *Please check all that apply.*
   - ☐ Newspaper(s)   ☐ Friends   ☐ Information from school
   - ☐ Special publications from recreational providers   ☐ Other *(please explain)*_____

4. How does your son/daughter currently spend his/her time when they are not in school? *Please check all that apply.*
   - ☐ Listening to music   ☐ Watching T.V.   ☐ Spending time with friends
   - ☐ Going out to eat   ☐ Shopping   ☐ Spending time with family
   - ☐ Going to the Movies   ☐ Hobbies   ☐ Reading
   - ☐ Other *(please explain)*_____

5. What types of organized recreational activities is your son/daughter currently involved in? *Please check all that apply.*
   - ☐ Organized Sports   ☐ Boy/Girl Scouts   ☐ Church/Temple Groups
   - ☐ Social Clubs   ☐ Music Lessons   ☐ In School activities
   - ☐ None   ☐ Other *(please explain)*_____

Figure 3. A family-oriented recreation interest survey.

Figure 3.   *(continued)*

6. Have you ever enrolled your child in a community recreation activity?

☐ Yes   ☐ No

(If yes, please check which activity. If no, please explain why.)

☐ Organized Sports   ☐ Boy/Girl Scouts   ☐ Church/Temple Groups

☐ Social Clubs   ☐ Music Lessons   ☐ In School activities

☐ Other   *(please explain)*_____

Comments _____

7. Which of the above activities did your child enjoy the most and why?

☐ Organized Sports   ☐ Boy/Girl Scouts   ☐ Church/Temple Groups

☐ Social Clubs   ☐ Music Lessons   ☐ In School activities

☐ Other   *(please explain)*_____

Comments _____

8. The following is a list of activities that are commonly offered by local recreation deapartments.   Please place a check mark next to the 5 activities you think your son/daughter would most enjoy.

*RECREATION ACTIVITIES

☐ Aerobics	☐ Ballet & Tap	☐ Basketball
☐ Beading & Knotting	☐ Karate	☐ Creative Movement
☐ Piano Lessons	☐ Puppet Making & Show	☐ Quilting
☐ Basic Sewing	☐ Skiing: Cross Country	☐ Skiing: Downhill
☐ Fashion Design	☐ Golf	☐ Guitar Lessons
☐ Gymnastics	☐ Art Workshop	☐ Standard First Aid
☐ Swim Lessons	☐ Volleyball	☐ Yoga
☐ Baseball	☐ Canoe Lessons	☐ Soccer
☐ Lifeguard Training	☐ Sailing	☐ Windsurfing
☐ Summer Day Camp	☐ Tennis	☐ Emergency Water Safety

*These activities will depend on what is provided by your local school or parks and recreation department

9. Are there any other types of recreational activities that you think your child would enjoy?

☐ YES   ☐ NO

*(If YES, please describe)*_____

_____

_____

Figure 3.   (*continued*)

SUPPORT NEEDS

10. Please place a check mark next to each area where your child may have particular support need(s). If the supports are related to a specific activity, or equipment is necessary for your child to participate, please be sure to include this information. Please mark all that apply & use the comments section for specific detail.

A. PHYSICAL CONSIDERATIONS

☐ Mobility   ☐ Hearing

☐ Dexterity   ☐ Communication

☐ Vision   ☐ None

☐ Other (please explain)_____

Comments_____

_____

B. MEDICAL CONSIDERATIONS

☐ Diabetes   ☐ Seizures

☐ Allergic Reactions   ☐ Medication

☐ None

☐ Other medical condition which could restrict participation

Comments_____

_____

C. SOCIALIZATION CONSIDERATIONS

☐ Interacts well with peers   ☐ Does not interact well with peers

☐ Interacts well with adults   ☐ Does not interact well with adults

☐ Prefers large groups   ☐ Prefers small groups

☐ Prefers to be alone

Comments _____

_____

D. FAMILY SUPPORT CONSIDERATIONS

TRANSPORTATION ISSUES

☐ Family member or friend will transport   ☐ Child can transport self independently

☐ No transportation available   ☐ Other_____

ACTIVITY COST CONCERNS (*please explain*) _____

_____

SCHEDULING NEEDS (*please explain*)_____

_____

THANK YOU FOR YOUR ASSISTANCE IN COMPLETING THIS SURVEY!

hours or at home in the evenings or during weekends. Volunteers can also be recruited to spend extra time practicing with the participant. The authors have found that many people from classes or sports teams will express a desire to spend extra time with someone who has a disability. For some activities it may be necessary to develop partial participation methods or rule or equipment adaptations. Chapter 6 provides information on adapting activities.

EVALUATING THE EFFECTS OF INCLUSIVE PARTICIPATION

It is important to find out how each person who participated in an integrated leisure program benefited from the experience. Only by directly asking or observing the individual or by asking a person who knows her or him well—such as a parent, sibling, or roommate, can we find out if the leisure activity was fun for the person participating. This is also the best way to learn whether there is a need to alter the support being provided. The results of participant, family, and provider surveys are also the most objective way for a recreation facilitator to evaluate his or her own effectiveness on the job.

Figures 4 and 5 provide examples of participant and family satisfaction surveys that can be used to evaluate the success of individual support/inclusion efforts. In some cases, only the participant survey would be used. For example, an older adolescent with a significant physical disability but no cognitive impairments should be able to express his or her satisfaction without assistance from others. Of course, the manner in which the survey is administered will depend on the communication capabilities of the individual. In another situation, such as one in which the participant is much younger and has mental retardation, the family survey information, as well as observational data, will be just as important as the participant survey data.

The third type of satisfaction data that may be used to evaluate program effectiveness is that provided by community recreation program personnel. These data will particularly affect how leisure facilitators interact with other professionals in the future, and should also influence training and inservice efforts for particular programs. Figure 6 provides a form for evaluating program-provider satisfaction. This particular format allows one to get feedback on the integration effort in its early stages so that changes can be made while the child or adult with a disability is still participating.

The fourth type of evaluation data is the recreation or leisure facilitator's own feelings about the success of the activity. This is a form of "self-evaluation," but is also useful for determining the CLFs support needs. Figure 7 provides a sample survey form for the CLF.

CONCLUDING COMMENTS

This chapter describes a variety of strategies that can be used to help people with disabilities successfully participate in community leisure activities. The first strategies described revolve around exploring existing options. Organizations that provide leisure services and citizens who use such services should look closely at what is currently being offered in order to eliminate segregated or duplicate programs. This kind of self-evaluation may also lead to the initiation of new activities that are more conducive to participation regardless of skill level and that emphasize cooperation among participants, rather than competition or skill development.

PARTICIPANT SATISFACTION SURVEY

Name of Child: _____

Support Staff Involved:_____

Name of Activity:_____ Date:____ /____ /____

		YES	NO
1.	Was the recreation facilitator helpful in finding activities in which you were interested?	☐	☐
2.	Did you get chances to express your preferences before activities were identified for you?	☐	☐
3.	Did you enjoy the activity/program in which you participated?	☐	☐
4.	Was the recreation facilitator helpful in assisting you to participate in the activity to your fullest ability?	☐	☐
5.	Did you make any new friends while participating in the program/activity?	☐	☐
6.	Did you develop any new interests as a result of participating in this program/activity?	☐	☐
7.	Were the other participants and program staff/volunteers friendly and helpful?	☐	☐
8.	Will you continue to participate in this activity or another similar one?	☐	☐
9.	Would you like more support in participating in this or another similar activity?	☐	☐

Recommendations & Comments:

Figure 4.   A participant satisfaction survey.

Family Satisfaction Survey

Name of Child: _____

Support Staff Involved: _____

Name of Activity: _____ Date: ___/___/___

	YES	NO
1. Was the support staff helpful in identifying recreation activities for your son/daughter?	☐	☐
2. Did staff give you ample opportunities to express your choice in leisure activities for your son/daughter?	☐	☐
3. Has staff assisted you in identifying transportation to & from the activities if needed?	☐	☐
4. Does your son/daughter enjoy the activity in which he/she is participating/has participated?	☐	☐
5. Was the support staff helpful in teaching you how to assist your son/daughter in participating in recreation?	☐	☐
6. Have opportunities for social interaction or friendship increased for your son/daughter since he/she began participation in this leisure activity?	☐	☐
7. Have you noticed any changes in your son/daughter as a result of his/her participation in the activity (e.g., new friends, skills)?	☐	☐
8. Do you feel that participating in integrated activities has helped improve the overall quality of your son's/daughter's life?	☐	☐
9. Will your son/daughter continue to participate in the integrated activity or similar activities?	☐	☐
10. Would you recommend this kind of activity or similar program participation to other parents/significant others?	☐	☐

Recommendations & Comments:

Figure 5.   A family satisfaction survey.

Program Provider Satisfaction Survey

Name of Program/Activity: _____

Name of Participant(s) with Disabilities: _____

Name of Person Completing Survey: _____

Time 1 Date:____ /____ /____   Time 2 Date:____/____ /____   Time 3 Date: ____/____ /____

	Time 1	Time 2	Time 3
1. Did support staff provide sufficient assistance to integrate the participant with a disability into your program?	YES ☐ NO ☐	YES ☐ NO ☐	YES ☐ NO ☐
2. a. Was any information provided on working with people who have disabilities?	YES ☐ NO ☐	YES ☐ NO ☐	YES ☐ NO ☐
b. If yes, was the information adequate & understandable?	YES ☐ NO ☐	YES ☐ NO ☐	YES ☐ NO ☐
3. Was any feedback adequate & helpful?	YES ☐ NO ☐	YES ☐ NO ☐	YES ☐ NO ☐
4. Do you feel comfortable about having a student with a disability in your program?	YES ☐ NO ☐	YES ☐ NO ☐	YES ☐ NO ☐
5. In the future, do you feel you could work with other people with disabilities in your program?	YES ☐ NO ☐	YES ☐ NO ☐	YES ☐ NO ☐
6. Have you noticed any changes in the individual as a result of their participation in the activity?	YES ☐ NO ☐	YES ☐ NO ☐	YES ☐ NO ☐
7. Have interactions between the participant with a disability & other participants increased since the beginning of the program?	YES ☐ NO ☐	YES ☐ NO ☐	YES ☐ NO ☐
8. Have you noticed any changes in other participants as a result of having a fellow participant with a disability in the program?	YES ☐ NO ☐	YES ☐ NO ☐	YES ☐ NO ☐
9. Would you recommend this kind of support to other recreational programs?	YES ☐ NO ☐	YES ☐ NO ☐	YES ☐ NO ☐

Recommendations & Comments:

Figure 6.   A program provider satisfaction survey.

Community Leisure Facilitator Survey

Name of Participant:_____

Name of Facilitator:_____

Activity:_____

Time 1 Date:____ /____ /____   Time 2 Date:____/____ /____   Time 3 Date: ____/____ /____

	Time 1	Time 2	Time 3
1. Is the participant still part of the activity? If no, please explain_____	YES ☐ NO ☐	YES ☐ NO ☐	YES ☐ NO ☐
2. Did support need to be reinstated by project staff after initial pullout? If yes, please explain_____	YES ☐ NO ☐	YES ☐ NO ☐	YES ☐ NO ☐
3. Does the participant need continuing support in order to participate in the activity? If yes, who is providing the support?	YES ☐ NO ☐	YES ☐ NO ☐	YES ☐ NO ☐
4. Has the participant begun other activities as a result of this activity? If yes, what is the name of the new activity & who initiated this participation?_____	YES ☐ NO ☐	YES ☐ NO ☐	YES ☐ NO ☐
5. Has anything occurred outside of the activity as a result of the activity (e.g., new friends)? If yes, please explain_____	YES ☐ NO ☐	YES ☐ NO ☐	YES ☐ NO ☐
6. Have there been any problems with participation? If yes, was a solution found & who identified the solutions?_____	YES ☐ NO ☐	YES ☐ NO ☐	YES ☐ NO ☐
7. Is further intervention needed?	YES ☐ NO ☐	YES ☐ NO ☐	YES ☐ NO ☐

Recommendations & Comments

Figure 7. A Community Leisure Facilitator survey.

Other strategies involve systematically identifying community leisure options and family and individual interests so that choices can be matched with existing options. This process also allows the creation of new activities based on direct input from those who would actually participate.

Finally, a variety of program evaluation strategies are described and simple record-keeping forms provided for collecting evaluation data to assess participant, family, provider, and facilitator satisfaction.

~Appendix~

The Peer Interest Survey

The peer interest survey shown in Figure 2 was completed by 619 youth (338 females and 281 males) of ages 3–22 (see Table 1), randomly selected from a variety of general education and recreation settings in metropolitan Boston, Massachusetts, including child care centers, public schools, summer camps, and universities. The sample included children and young adults from diverse socioeconomic backgrounds. The majority of respondents completed the survey independently during school or camp hours. Parents of students in child care centers completed the surveys in their homes and three project staff administered the survey verbally to those students in kindergarten and 1st and 2nd grades who were not able to read. Written and verbal assurances were given that all survey answers would remain confidential.

The survey (see Figure 2) included general inquiries about free time, as well as more specific questions on sports, music, individual activities, organizations, and so forth. The questions included in the survey were chosen based on current research regarding the types of activities that kids participate in (Smith, 1990; York et al., 1990). Below is a sampling of questions from the Peer Interest Survey and a brief discussion of the findings related to each.

What do you do for fun or in your free time?

Participants were given three blank spaces to complete this open-ended question. Table 2 shows those activities most frequently chosen in response to this question for males and females, organized by age group. The variety of responses received for this question included over 200 different activities. Therefore, the students' specific narrow responses (e.g., rugby) were analyzed and placed into 10 broader categories, which included The arts, Clubs/organized activities, Friends/family, Individual activities, Events, Play, Sports, Toys, Work, and Other. The most frequently chosen activity categories included Individual activities and Friends/family.

Table 1. Survey participants by age and gender

Age group	Males	Females
3–5	33	24
6–8	54	64
9–11	65	71
12–15	67	51
16–18	40	90
19–22	22	38

Table 2.   Most frequently chosen activities in three categories in response to the question "What do you do for fun or in your free time?" on the Peer Interest Survey

Toys		Sports		Individual activities	
Activity	Number of respondents	Activiy	Number of respondents	Activity	Number of respondents
Nintendo	68	Sports	65	TV	101
Play games	16	Basketball	58	Read	83
Computer	14	Baseball	55	Listen to music	45
Toys	13	Bike	53	Listen to radio	14
Video games	11	Swim	42	Sleep	14
Figures	11	Football	20	Pets	12
Dolls	9	Soccer	20	Eat	9
Board games	6	Skateboard	16	Drugs	6
Barbies	6	Exercise	15	Collect comics	4
Blocks	5	Hockey	13	Read comics	3
Cards	4	Tennis	9	Get nails done	2
Gameboy	4	Rollerskate	8	Make airplanes	2
Puzzles	4	Bowl	7	Motorcycle	2
Squirt guns	3	Gymnastics	7	Plant	2
Toy cars	3	Run	6		
Legos	3	Tag	6		
Monopoly	2	Swing	5		
		Track	5		

The Toys and individual activities categories include all toys/activities that had more than one response. The Sports category includes all sports hat had more than five responses. All numbers are real numbers, not percentages.

Individual activities   This category includes, but is not limited to, what are usually described as hobbies. Although these activities may be done in a group, the people who mentioned them considered the activity itself, rather than the other participants, as the focus. Examples include collecting, driving, eating (not "going out to eat"), listening to music, reading, making models, taking care of a pet, sunbathing, and watching television.

Friends and family   This category includes activities that involve friends or family members (e.g., "hanging out with friends" and "talking to cousins"). Activities such as "going to the mall with friends" were also included in this category, since they specifically describe the activity as being done with others (as opposed to just "going to the mall," which would be placed in the events category). Also included are responses such as "playing with a sibling," "hanging out," "having sex," "going to parties," and "talking on the phone."

Sports   This category includes physical activities (excluding those found in other categories, such as ballet [The arts])—both organized games (e.g., basketball, baseball, kickball) and individual sports and exercises (e.g., aerobics, lifting weights, fishing, ice skating, running). For younger children, activities that require physical exertion (e.g., running around, climbing rocks, jumping rope, climbing trees) are also included in this category.

Toys   Surprisingly, items in this category were named by all age groups surveyed, although frequency did decrease as age increased. Included in this category are activities involving any items that one might find in a toy department or store (e.g., action figures, video games, blocks, board games, cards). Responses indicated that at the youngest age, boys are interested primarily in toys, then gradually shift toward sports as they grow older. Sports remain by far the most frequently named activity for boys ages 9–22 (see Figure 8). Girls ages 3–5 chose sports as their primary interest, and then did so again from ages 9 to 11. They were primarily interested in individual activities between the ages of 6 and 8, and from ages 12 to 22 they were involved primarily with friends and family.

There were a total of 1,732 responses to the question "What do you do for fun or in your free time?" (each participant being permitted up to three responses). Table 2 provides a listing of some of the most frequently picked activities from the most frequently picked categories. The Toys and Individual Activities categories include all toys/activities that had more than one response. The Sports category includes all sports that had more than five responses. All numbers are real numbers, not percentages.

When you are doing something for fun, is it usually by yourself, with one to three other people, or in a group of people larger than three?

In response to this question, participants were asked to check the answer that most often applied and were given three choices: 1) by myself, 2) with one to three other people, or 3) with more than three people. Figure 9 depicts the responses of all participants. No significant differences were found between the various age groups. As expected, most people did not spend their "fun" time alone; only 11% of the females and 17% of the males chose this option. Instead, the majority of respondents (62% of the females and 53% of the males) said that they engaged in recreational activities in small groups that included from one to three other people.

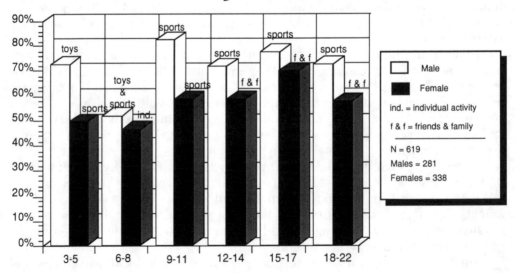

Figure 8. Categorized response rates to the question "What do you do for fun in your free time?" on the Peer Interest Survey.

When you do something for fun, how many people are usually with you?

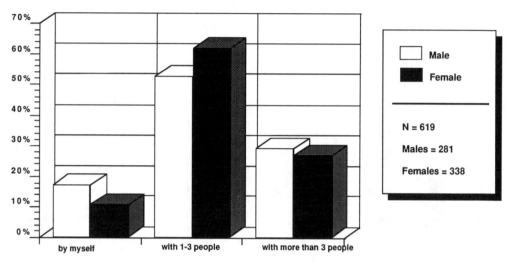

Figure 9.   Response rates to a question on the Peer Interest Survey concerning whether children engage in recreational activities alone or with friends.

How do you get to activities that you do for fun when you have to leave home to do them?

Participants were given seven possible responses to this question (i.e., my parents, my bike, I walk, public transportation, my friends' parents, I drive myself, other) and asked to check the answer that most often applied to them. Figure 10 depicts the results of this question. The data clearly show that through age 14, parents are the primary mode of transportation and walking the number two mode. From age 15 through age 17 these two reverse positions—walking becomes the most used mode of transportation (perhaps because it becomes "uncool" to be seen with one's parents). Finally, from ages 18 to 22, driving oneself becomes popular, but walking remains the number two choice for 35% of the participants.

What sports or physical activities do you most enjoy doing?

Participants were given four blank spaces to complete this open-ended question. Out of 619 participants, only 7% failed to list at least one sport. A total of 1,576 responses were given, which included over 100 different answers. Table 3 indicates the four most frequently chosen sports/physical activities for each age group, organized by gender. For example, 53% of the 12- to 14-year-old females surveyed enjoy basketball and 25% enjoy softball; 65% of the 6- to 8-year-old males enjoy baseball. Because participants were able to list four choices, there was some duplication across the responses; hence the percentages for any given age group may equal more than 100%.

What type of transportation do you use?

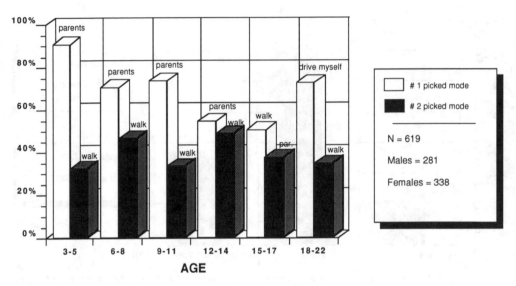

Figure 10.   Response rates to a question on the Peer Interest Survey pertaining to transportation to and from recreational activities.

Do you sing or play any musical instrument?

Participants were given five blank spaces to complete this open-ended question. Responses were divided into six categories (i.e., brass, keyboard, percussion, voice, string, and wind). Table 4 indicates the percentage of participants, organized by age, who play instruments in these categories. Forty-two percent of participants played at least one instrument. Thirty-six instruments and types of singing were listed by participants; the most popular being singing, piano, violin, guitar, and recorder.

Table 3.   Most frequently named preferred sports/physical activities for each age group

Age	Females	Males
3–5	Swimming (29%), running (25%), playground equipment (21%), bike (17%)	Baseball (36%), soccer (30%), basketball (27%), playground equipment (21%)
6–8	Swimming (34%), soccer (27%), baseball (20%), kickball (13%)	Baseball (65%), basketball (43%), soccer (41%), football (20%)
9–11	Basketball (42%), soccer (41%), baseball (27%), swimming (24%)	Baseball (42%), soccer (28%), basketball (27%), hockey (18%)
12–14	Basketball (53%); soccer (31%); softball (25%); tennis, volleyball, swimming (20%)	Baseball (55%), basketball (42%), football (37%), hockey (18%)
15–17	Swimming (27%), softball (23%), basketball (21%), tennis (20%)	Basketball (53%), football (45%), baseball (43%), hockey (28%)
18–22	Swimming (26%), tennis (21%), softball (18%), tennis (20%)	Basketball (53%), football (45%), baseball (43%), hockey (28%)

Table 4. Survey responses to the question "What musical instruments do you play?" on the Peer Interest Survey

Age	Brass	Keyboard	Percussion	Voice	String	Wind
3–5	0%	9%	5%	37%	11%	9%
6–8	0%	12%	3%	16%	8%	14%
9–11	6%	34%	6%	13%	13%	26%
12–14	1%	18%	4%	15%	13%	19%
15–17	2%	7%	2%	17%	7%	6%

Are you a member of any organized groups, organizations, clubs, or teams, or do you take any lessons?

Participants were given five blank spaces to complete this open-ended question. Responses to this question were categorized into seven different areas: The arts, Political, Social, Academic, Religious, Sports, and Other. These categories and the percentages of students who selected them are shown in Table 5. Table 5 also lists all of the different responses (a total of 159) given by the participants within each category.

Would you consider inviting a person with a disability to join you in "having some fun" if there were such a person who was looking to make new friends? Please check the response that best identifies how you feel.

Participants of ages 6–22 were asked to complete the above question and were given choices of "yes," "no," and "not sure." For the 3–5 age group, the question was worded a bit differently because parents were completing the survey on behalf of their children. In the youngest age group, parents were asked, "Would you like your child to have opportunities to interact and develop friendships with children who have disabilities?" They were given the same response options as were survey participants who were completing the questions themselves. Table 6 indicates the responses to this question, organized by age and gender, and includes a column for participants who failed to respond ("no answer").

REFERENCES

Brown, L., Branston-McLean, M., Baumgart, D., Vincent, B., Falvey, M., & Schroeder, J. (1979). Using the characteristics of current and subsequent least restrictive environments in the development of curricular content for severely handicapped students. *AAESPH Review, 4*(4), 407–424.

Falvey, M., & Coots, J. (1989). Recreation skills. In M. Falvey (Ed.), *Community-based curriculum: Instructional strategies for students with severe handicaps* (pp. 141–163). Baltimore: Paul H. Brookes Publishing Co.

Moon, S., & Bunker, L. (1987). Recreation and motor skills programming. In M. Snell (Ed.), *Systematic instruction of persons with severe handicaps* (3rd ed.). (pp 214–244). Columbus, OH: Charles E. Merrill.

Schleien, S., Green, F., & Heyne, L. (1993). Integrated community recreation. In M. Snell (Ed.), *Instruction of students with severe disabilities* (4th ed.). (pp. 526–555). New York: Macmillan.

Smith, M.D. (1990). *Autism and life in the community: Successful interventions for behavioral challenges.* Baltimore: Paul H. Brookes Publishing Co.

Table 5. Organized groups/lessons named in survey responses (sorted by category)

Sports (51%)	The arts (28%)	Social (18%)	Religious (10%)	Academic (5%)	Political (4%)	Other (2%)
Aerobics	Art class	4-H Club	Church	Academic decathlon	Alliance Against Discrimination	Burger King Kids Club
Baseball	Arts and crafts	Afterschool daycare	Church ensemble	Book club	Kadima Club	Club House Team
Basketball	Ballet lessons	Alcohol rehabilitation program (in school)	Friends meeting	Business coop	NAACP Youth Council	Mickey Mouse Club
Bowling	Band	Alcoholics Anonymous	Hebrew school	Chinese lessons	Naval Reserve Officers Training Corps (NROTC)	Model club
Cheerleading	Bass ensemble	Boy scouts	Monthly retreat	Computer lessons	Students Against Drunk Driving (SADD)	Nintendo Club
Coach sports	Chorus	Boys and girls club	Peer ministry	Cosmos science		Party time club
Color guard	Dance	Brownies	Religious after school program	Debate team		Pathfinders
Cross-country	Dance lessons	Camp	Sunday school	French club		Planting group
Exercise	Drama	Camp fire		Greek school		Quiet creek
Fishing club	Indian dancing	Chess		Homework club		Redmen
Fitness center	Jazz	Chumpers club		Italian school		Rocky Horror Picture Show Fan Club
Floor hockey	Knitting club	Class day committee		Police Explorers Club		Spy club
Football	Music	Class officer		Reading group		Spy war club
Golf	Music lessons	Cub Scouts		SAT preparation		Teddy Bear Chums
Gym class	Orchestra	Catholic Youth Organization (CYO)		Scholarship organization		Teenage Mutant Ninja Turtles Club
Gymnastics	Painting class	Day care		Speaking		War club
Gymnastic lessons	Role playing game club	Fraternity		Special education intern		WLVI Radio Station Kids Club
Hiking lessons	Singing group	Friendship club		Teach		Wrecking club
Hockey	Tap	Girl Scouts		Theory class		
Horseback riding	Theater	Honor society		Thomas Jefferson Forum		
Ice skating	Violin lessons	Jewish Community Center (JCC)		Vietnamese lessons		
Ice skating lessons	Woodworking lessons	Methodist Youth Fellowship				
Intramurals		Play group				
Karate		Portuguese Club				
Kickball		Prom committee				
Lacrosse		Sorority				
Parks and recreation		Student council				
Scuba diving		Summer camp				
Skateboarders club		Teen club				
Skating		Tiger Cubs				
Skating lessons		Volunteer				
Skiing		Yearbook committee				
Soccer		Youth group				
Softball						
Sports						
Stickball						
Stilting						
Street hockey						
Swim lessons						
Swim team						
Swimming						
T-ball						
Tennis						
Track						
Volleyball						
Water-skiing lessons						
Wrestling						
YMCA						

Percentages indicate the frequency with which activities in each category were named by respondents.

Table 6.   Survey responses to a question that asked if the respondent would consider inviting a person with a disability to join him or her in "having some fun"

Age	Yes	No	Not sure	No answer
3–5	59%	16%	18%	7%
6–8	62%	13%	24%	1%
9–11	55%	4%	39%	2%
12–14	54%	5%	35%	6%
15–18	56%	2%	40%	2%
19–22	68%	2%	27%	3%

Turnbull, H.R., Turnbull, A.P., Bronicki, G.J., Summers, J.A., & Roeder-Gordon, C. (1989). *Disability and the family: A guide to decisions for adulthood.* Baltimore: Paul H. Brookes Publishing Co.

Voeltz, L., Wuerch, B., & Bockhaut, C. (1982). Social validation of leisure activities training with severely handicapped youth. *Journal of The Association for Persons with Severe Handicaps, 7,* 3–13.

York, J., Vandercook, T., & Stave, K. (1990). Recreation and leisure activities: Determining the favorites for middle school students. *Teaching Exceptional Children, 22*(4), 10–13.

~four~

Finding or Creating
Fun in Your Community

M. Sherril Moon,
Cheska Komissar, Robin Friedlander,
Debra Hart, and William Kiernan

The purpose of this chapter is to identify several programs and specific types of leisure activities that children, adolescents, and young adults with and without disabilities can enjoy together, regardless of their individual skill levels. The activities described below were chosen because none of them requires a special setting, large amounts of money, or staff with professional expertise. It should be relatively easy for a teacher, family member, recreation professional, or volunteer to initiate a program similar to any one of those that appear here.

Some of the activities and programs described here—such as the Girl Scouts and Boy Scouts of America and swimming and aerobics classes at the local YMCA—are readily accessible in many communities. Other programs, such as the friendship club or activity period, may have to be initiated by someone who is willing to invest some organizational and supervisory time in the early stages. Whenever possible, it is best to try to get people with disabilities involved in existing programs. Sometimes, however, enjoyable activities have to be created in order to bring people with and those without disabilities together. This is particularly true during difficult economic times, when funds for extracurricular programs at schools and for community activities have been curtailed. Our advice is to achieve what you can with what already exists and to create what you need to. The important thing is that the participants enjoy the program or activity.

You will probably find a number of programs in any given community that may be enjoyable for children, adolescents, and young adults with significant disabilities, including scout troops, 4-H clubs, school sororities or fraternities, YMCA classes, parks and recreation programs, and community sports programs such as youth soccer leagues. The information in this text should help prepare you to effectively approach school or community groups about a person with a disability join-

Development of this chapter was supported through a grant from the Office of Special Education and Rehabilitative Services of the United States Department of Education (#H086U00030) to the Training and Research Institute for People with Disabilities at Children's Hospital, Boston, Massachusetts.

ing these or similar activities. In most cases, confidence in the participant and a commitment to helping them get acquainted with the targeted program is all that's needed for successful integration. The case examples below show how some individuals have benefited from joining certain school or community classes, organizations, or teams.

PLACES AND WAYS TO HAVE FUN IN THE COMMUNITY

The Young Men's Christian Association (YMCA)

This organization, which is oriented toward meeting neighborhood and family needs, is open to anyone—regardless of race, creed, or religious affiliation—who can pay the initiation and yearly membership fees. There are branches all over the country, and most major metropolitan and suburban areas have several branches, each oriented to the particular neighborhood in which it is located. YMCA's typically include pools, workout areas, racquet courts, and classes in many individual and team sports. Many offer child care and after-school programs, summer day camps, and some programs for older citizens. Classes or field trips may be offered in cultural subjects, arts and crafts, or self-help areas. Nonmembers can usually register for classes (but at a fee higher than members would pay) and can often use the facility for a one-time fee.

Traditionally, YMCAs offer a few separate classes or programs for children with disabilities; however, the staff tend to be very open to including persons with disabilities in other programs when approached. If you have difficulty locating a YMCA near your home, contact National YMCA, Program Services Division, 101 N. Wacker Drive, Chicago, Illinois 60606.

A YMCA Case Study

Bobby was an 11-year-old diagnosed as having mental retardation and mild cerebral palsy. He would not communicate verbally, with the exception of asking for "more" and sometimes answering "yes" or "no." He was small for his age and had some difficulty walking. The special classes that Bobby attended were conducted in a town approximately 20 miles away from his neighborhood, and his commute to and from school took about an hour.

Bobby's teacher had heard about a project in which a leisure facilitator provided assistance to families in getting children with disabilities involved in after-school and weekend recreation activities. Through numerous discussions with Bobby's mother, the teacher had learned that Bobby's main activity outside of school was watching television. Both his teacher and mother agreed that Bobby would benefit both physically and socially from some sort of active recreation with other children in the community, so the teacher contacted the leisure facilitator for assistance.

In order to discover what activities Bobby most enjoyed, the facilitator met with his teacher, mother, and adaptive physical educator. The teacher identified those activities that Bobby seemed most eager to participate in during school and his mother pointed out those things that he seemed to enjoy doing with the family. The adaptive physical education instructor discussed Bobby's physical and motor strengths and preferences. Finally, the facilitator observed Bobby during and after school to determine what activities he seemed to enjoy most. Since he laughed constantly during his weekly class swimming trip, and a YMCA pool was located less than 10 minutes from his house, Bobby was asked by the leisure facilitator if he would like to go swimming with her sometime. The next three times she saw Bobby, he asked to go swimming by making a swimming motion with his arms, and, as a result, that was the activity chosen. At this point the facilitator, teacher, and mother worked out a "team strategy" for approaching the local YMCA.

Bobby's mother first contacted the YMCA and requested that a program brochure be sent to her. According to the brochure, there were two options for Bobby: he could become a member of the YMCA, allowing him to participate in open recreational swims (offered about nine times a week for children) and to pay reduced rates for group lessons, or he could enroll in the lessons only and pay a slightly higher fee. After Bobby's mother had several phone conversations with the pool director, and had assured her that the recreation facilitator or teacher would attend the lessons with Bobby, she registered him in a beginning swimmers' group that met once a week for a period of 8 weeks.

In the beginning, the swimming instructors were very nervous about having Bobby in their class of 12 children, who ranged in age from 7 to 11. There were two other classes, with approximately 10 students each, in addition to Bobby's, using the pool at the same time. The instructors had many children to watch and were afraid that Bobby, who could not hold his breath under water, would be in some danger; they requested that the teacher or facilitator be near him at all times. However, because they received reassuring answers to all of their questions and constant reminders of how much fun Bobby was having (the smile on his face being enough), the instructors very quickly became much more comfortable and the extra supervisor they had requested was able to move further and further away from the group. The teacher or facilitator stayed nearby only because of the large number of children in the pool during lessons. Everyone agreed that extra support would not have been needed during free swims, or if life-vests had been permitted.

After Bobby completed his lessons at the YMCA, his adaptive physical education instructor at school commented that he seemed to feel much more confident in the water and had become totally independent with the help of floaters (small life-preservers that fit around the arms or waist). Furthermore, he was no longer afraid to have his head underwater, something he had always avoided in the several years he had been swimming with his parents and physical education teacher.

After the lessons were completed, Bobby's mother expressed an interest in registering him for more lessons in the future. She was encouraged by the pool staff at the YMCA to get him an annual membership, which would allow him to take lessons at a discounted rate, as well as to use the pool with other children during free-swim times. Bobby's mother decided to purchase a membership for both Bobby and his sister, with the reassurance that the school, local Arc, and leisure facilitator would assist the family in locating volunteers to swim with Bobby. With the help of Bobby's swimming instructor from the YMCA, he was able to get a special notation on his membership that allowed him to bring someone in to swim with him at no additional charge (since he was not yet able to swim independently).

After observing Bobby on several occasions while he was swimming with a volunteer, Bobby's mother also expressed an interest in taking him swimming, something that they had not previously done together. Finally, because of their positive experiences with the pool staff, Bobby's parents began to consider registering him for summer camp at the YMCA.

The Boy Scouts and Girl Scouts of America

The mission of the Boy Scouts of America is to train boys and young men of ages 8–20 in the responsibilities of participating as citizens in the community. The program is divided into a progressive, three-part experience: Cub Scouting, Boy Scouting, and Exploring. Cub Scouting is a neighborhood- and family-centered program for boys ages 8–10. The 10-year-olds usually become Webelos Scouts, a group designed to help them make the transition to the more advanced Boy Scouts. Cub Scouts belong to small dens (usually 4–10 boys) and to a larger community pack, which meets less frequently and consists of many dens. Cub Scouts usually work on home-based projects such as arts and crafts. Boy Scouting is for boys ages 11–17 and is usually outdoor oriented, involving activities such as hiking and camping away from home. Boy Scouts meet in troops, which usually include 10–20 members. Finally, Exploring is for young men and women ages 15–20 and is largely directed away from the home. Explorer posts are organized to give members experience in special interests, usually professions, businesses, or hobbies, and the number of youths involved varies greatly among communities. There are also special Boy Scout troops for children who have disabilities, but the National Boy Scout Office encourages all children to join typical community troops.

The Girl Scouts' mission is similar to that of the Boy Scouts, and girls and young women ages 5–18 are invited to participate. However, Girl Scouts revolves around the members' own planning, and anything that is healthy, safe, and fun may be considered as a possible focus for any given troop. Therefore, although the badges that they work toward and certain national fundraising activities are universal, each group in each community may be largely unique.

Girl Scouts are divided into five levels, based on school grade or age. Girls in kindergarten join as Daisies, and those in grades 1–3 become Brownies. When girls join Brownies, they are encouraged to work toward "tryits," patches that members can earn by trying certain activities. At the Junior level of Girl Scouts (grades 4, 5, and 6) girls may begin working toward merit badges or patches earned for trying and actually succeeding, or showing improvement, in certain activities (e.g., the swimming badge requires learning certain strokes and safety procedures). Although girls are encouraged to work toward badges, it is not a requirement. Finally, girls in seventh through ninth grade become Cadettes, while those in tenth grade through the end of high school are Seniors.

Boy Scouts and Girl Scouts are national organizations that include thousands of volunteers on both the local and national levels. Both groups, especially in larger cities, employ field directors who ensure that scouting is offered to all children in a given local area. Leaders of the packs, troops, and posts are volunteers, usually parents, college students, or other members of the community. All receive support from the local office, which in turn receives support from the national level. Both Boy and Girl Scouts offer school-year programs that include weekly meetings; summer programs consist primarily of camps. Boy Scout camps are usually attended by the troop as a unit, but individual Scouts may also register. Girl Scout camps are usually attended by individual girls, even some who do not participate in Girl Scouts throughout the rest of the year.

To become involved in local scouting, if no listing for a local office can be found in the phone book, contact: Boy Scouts of America, 1325 West Walnut Hill Lane, POB 152079, Irving, TX 75015-2079 *or* Girl Scouts of the United States of America, 830 Third Avenue, New York, NY 10022.

A Girl Scout Case Study

Sarah was an 11-year-old girl diagnosed as having mental retardation and cerebral palsy. She was able to laugh or cry to indicate her level of enjoyment, used a wheel-chair, and, according to her teacher, could not really push herself anywhere without assistance.

Sarah's teacher contacted the regional scout office to see if she could join a local troop. She had noticed that Sarah responded well to students without disabili-ties when they came in to volunteer in her class. Several of these students were Girl Scouts and the teacher felt that Sarah might really enjoy participating in afterschool activities with them.

Sarah's parents were hesitant about having her join the Girl Scouts; initially, they did not believe that Sarah would benefit from such an activity and were wor-ried that it wouldn't fit into their own hectic schedules. But they were willing to give it a try.

Two teenage student volunteers were located through a local high school vol-unteer organization to accompany Sarah as she participated in a variety of activities twice monthly in order to discover which she enjoyed most and to provide her with the widest variety of choices possible. After attending approximately 10 activities offered in her community, Sarah seemed to enjoy Girl Scouts the most, as evidenced by her constant laughter during the weekly meetings. Once Sarah's parents heard the positive reaction of the leaders, saw how readily Sarah was accepted by the other girls in the troop, and witnessed her reaction to the meetings, they overcame their reservations about the activity, and Sarah became a Girl Scout. The troop, which included the volunteers from Sarah's school, had two leaders, one of whom was excited about having Sarah in the troop, while the other had reservations. The leader's hesitancy was addressed by Sarah's teacher, the local field director, and the other leader. Because so many people were certain that Sarah would fit in with the other scouts, the hesitant leader soon became comfortable with the idea.

Before Sarah joined the group, the leaders discussed disabilities in general, and Sarah's disabilities in particular, with the six other members, making sure that all their questions were answered and their fears laid to rest. Because some of the girls were still concerned that Sarah would change the troop and perhaps slow them down, Sarah's teacher attended a second meeting to discuss disability in more detail and to talk about inclusion and what it would mean for both Sarah and the troop. Sarah attended her first four meetings accompanied by her teacher, who was able to provide support by making sure that Sarah was included in activities and by encouraging the other girls to interact with her; after that, she attended every other meeting and discussed ways that the leaders and other troop members could help to provide support for Sarah. The teacher usually just spoke with individual troop members whenever she saw a simple thing that could be done to assist or in-clude Sarah.

The group noticed that during the meetings Sarah was able to push herself in her wheelchair without assistance. Often, Sarah would push herself toward the loud laughter and conversation of the other girls or approach them to observe an activity that the group was involved in. Furthermore, members who knew Sarah from school commented that she seemed to be much happier at Girl Scout meetings, where she was most often laughing or smiling, than she was at school, where she was more often crying than not. It became evident through her reactions that Sarah preferred the conversation and company of her peers without disabilities to that of her usual classmates, most of whom were nonverbal.

Eventually, Sarah moved to a school for older children that was much further from her own community and her scout troop. Although the troop offered to change their meeting times from after school to later in the evening so that Sarah would be able to attend, her parents felt that she would be too tired to go to a Girl Scout meeting after a full day of school and the long ride home. However, as a result of Sarah's positive experience with the troop, her parents began researching the possibility of her attending Girl Scout summer day camp. Attending camp during the summer enabled Sarah to see her old friends again and to meet new ones.

A Boy Scout Case Study

Erik was a 15-year-old eighth grader with Down syndrome. He attended junior high school in his neighborhood with his peers without disabilities. Although Erik had attended inclusive classes his whole life, the director of special education in his town was concerned that he had not been socially active with his peers outside of school. So the director, after securing permission from Erik's parents, asked the recreation coordinator of the local chapter of The Arc to help find an activity in which Erik could participate with other teenagers.

Several phone conversations were held with Erik and his parents to discuss what types of activities might interest him. Erik was interested in meeting with other people his own age, preferably males, in a more formal activity at least one time a week, without the assistance of his mother or father. Two activities that met most of these requirements were found in the vicinity, a Boy Scout troop and a junior high monthly social gathering. Erik decided to choose only one of these activities (and his parents agreed) because his Special Olympics training was keeping him quite busy and he did not wish to commit to too many after-school activities.

Through the regional Boy Scout office, the recreation coordinator was able to contact the leader of a Boy Scout troop that met quite close to Erik's house. Several conversations were held with the troop leader, and he requested that some information on disability awareness be provided to the 17 boys, ages 12–16, in his troop. The coordinator attended the meeting at which disabilities were discussed. The boys were encouraged to ask questions and voice any concerns that they might have about including a member who was different in some ways. Questions asked included the following: Will I catch it? Do we have to be nice to him? Why is he joining? What if he can't keep up? How should I talk to him? What do I do if he does something that bothers me? Several of the boys indicated that they knew Erik from school and were excited about having him as a new member.

The recreation coordinator attended the first two meetings with Erik to reassure the troop leader, who was somewhat nervous about Erik's inclusion with the other boys. Further support was offered to the leader, but after two meetings he felt confident about his and his troop's ability to include Erik as a full member. After the first meeting, Erik's parents informed the leader of the troop that Erik was on the International Special Olympics Swim Team, and they feared that there might be some conflict between swimming practice and the Boy Scout meetings. It was made clear to them and to Erik by the leader and a senior patrol member (an older Boy Scout) that the Boy Scouts expected a commitment if Erik decided to join, but that it was acceptable that Erik come half an hour late to each two-hour meeting if there was a conflict with swimming practice.

Erik attended five Boy Scout meetings before deciding not to join. Although he enjoyed the troop, it was taking up a substantial part of his time (a weekly 2-hour meeting, in addition to time spent working on badges), and he had to choose between Scouts and Special Olympics. According to his parents, this was the first time that Erik had made such a decision independently, and afterward they felt more confident about his ability to make informed choices concerning his leisure time. A year later, Erik again expressed an interest in becoming a Scout, and eventually joined the same troop after giving up Special Olympics.

4-H

4-H has traditionally assisted children and youths to learn life skills through agriculture. Today, however, 4-H offers a wider variety of activities for school-age children. Although they still maintain clubs that are primarily based around caring for and showing animals (e.g., horse clubs, sheep clubs, rabbit clubs), 4-H includes numerous activities oriented toward the needs of students within their own communities. Surprisingly, there are 4-H clubs in most urban, and even inner-city, settings. Some examples are clubs based around rocketry, computer science, double dutch (jump rope), gardening, home economics, arts and crafts, and public speaking. Each club is based around an adult volunteer leader and a small group of youths with an interest in a specific topic. Depending on their particular area of interest, the members may participate in both competitive (e.g., working toward showing animals in a county fair) and cooperative (e.g., performing science experiments as a group) activities. In addition, 4-H may provide leadership training or other short-term workshops to local high school students within the schools.

If you cannot find a listing for 4-H in the phone book, the National 4-H Center will assist you in finding a group, starting a group, or working on a 4-H project within your own family. You can contact the National 4-H Center at 7100 Connecticut Avenue, Chevy Chase, MD 20815.

A 4-H Case Study

Freddy was a 11-year-old girl diagnosed as having significant developmental delays. She was able to laugh or cry to indicate her level of enjoyment and used a wheelchair. Freddy attended a school in her own community, but was in a separate class for students with significant disabilities.

Her teacher contacted a community recreation liaison to see what Freddy's options were for joining a community activity. After discussions with Freddy's teacher and parents, it was decided that it would be best to arrange for her to experience a wide variety of activities in order to see if she expressed a preference for certain types of events.

The 4-H club in Freddy's town ran a small farm with sheep, cows, goats, and rabbits. The members of the club ranged in age from 5–18 and took full responsibility for the care of the animals. Each member set up his or her own contract outlining when he or she would care for the animals. After several phone discussions between the 4-H director and the recreation liaison, the director decided that the best time for Freddy to participate (at least initially) would be on Saturday mornings, when all 20 of the other members participated as a group. The director was initially quite skeptical about Freddy's ability to participate, but was reassured by the fact that high school volunteers would be available to assist Freddy so that she could be an active participant along with the other students. He also requested that either a parent or the recreation liaison attend the first Saturday meeting.

Freddy attended three 4-H meetings, at which she was able to help feed and groom the animals as well as socialize with the other children, who were very eager to include her. Although Freddy seemed to enjoy the 4-H Club, the animals, and the other children, her parents decided that they wanted her to try other activities and come back to 4-H if it seemed to be the one that she enjoyed most. Freddy did not join 4-H that year, as several other activities were found that were more convenient for her family. Because of the experience, however, the leaders of the club realized that children with disabilities could participate in the group and began to encourage other such children to become members. And after trying out several other activities, Freddy herself joined 4-H later that year.

Parks and Recreation Programs

Departments, commissions, and offices of parks and recreation can be found in many municipalities or counties across the country. These offices are usually supported by the city or town with state and/or federal funds. They are often affiliated with the National Recreation and Park Association (NRPA), which is a national, nonprofit service organization dedicated to promoting parks and recreation and to ensuring that all citizens have an opportunity to participate in satisfying leisure activities. Recreation departments vary in size, depending on the ability and commitment of the locality to provide recreation services; they may be responsible for a variety of activities—from maintaining local parks to offering year-round programs, including summer camps and child care. Departments may employ professional recreation personnel or utilize other paid or volunteer staff to operate particular programs.

Because city parks and recreation departments are so diverse, it is impossible to list all of the possibilities for every office in every locality. However, if one looks in the blue pages in the phone book or calls a local governing office (e.g., a city/town hall or chamber of commerce), one will be able to learn whether there is a recreation office in their own community. Even if a department itself does not run programs, they often have schedules of city-sponsored events (e.g., parades, concerts, park events), especially those that take place on public property. Many departments have pools and provide swimming classes and recreational swim opportunities, and they can often, at relatively low costs, organize sports and exercise teams and classes, arts and crafts lessons, field trips, and a variety of self-help activities.

Larger parks and recreation programs employ specialists trained in therapeutic recreation services who manage a variety of programs for people with disabilities—from separate camps and classes to fully inclusive programs such as summer day camps, swimming lessons, and aerobic classes. More progressive programs may have recreation liaisons or facilitators who can assist citizens with disabilities in locating integrated, community leisure activities. Chapter 10 provides a model for integrating parks and recreation department programs.

You can contact the National Recreation and Park Association at 2775 South Quincy Street, Suite 300, Arlington, Virginia 22206-2204 to identify programs that are available on a local, regional, or national level.

Community Soccer Leagues

The world's most popular sport, soccer, has become the sport of choice for many school-age children across the United States. It has caught on for several reasons: both boys and girls can play; it is not as dangerous as some other popular sports, like football; nearly all kids can participate in the game, regardless of their skill level; and it is appropriate across all ages. Soccer leagues have sprung up everywhere; they are sponsored by school systems, parks and recreation programs, churches, YMCAs, and private organizations. Soccer leagues may include a variety of programs, from competitive teams at different age levels to skill-building clinics. Because this is one of the major after-school activities for young children, it is a great place for elementary school–age students with disabilities to "play" with kids without disabilities.

One large suburban soccer league in Maryland, Montgomery Soccer, Inc., opened its doors by inviting all children ages 6–9 with disabilities to participate in its spring clinic, which is held over four Saturdays in April and May. The league board composed a letter to parents that was distributed in all special education classes during January. Those who were interested returned the letter, and the special education coordinator helped the board determine which clinic or team each child with a disability should be assigned to. Assignments depended on where the family lived, the physical and motor characteristics of the child, and the openness of particular team or clinic instructors. Several volunteers, primarily special education teachers, agreed to provide extra support during the clinics. A special education professor at a local university agreed to provide some disability-awareness training to the league's executive board and coaches and recruited several college students to volunteer on Saturdays as facilitators for the players with disabilities.

A Parks and Recreation/Soccer Case Study

Sam was a 5-year-old with autism who had a difficult time playing with children his own age. He attended a segregated preschool program, but spent 1 hour, 2 days a week in a regular kindergarten class. Sam's teacher and parents wanted him to spend more time in active play with children who were not disabled. Sam loved outdoor activities, had well-developed motor skills, and was good at running, kicking, and throwing a ball.

Sam's teacher told his parents about the city recreation department's soccer program, which ran for 10 weeks. The program consisted of teams that were each made up of 15 kids, ages 5–8. The first two sessions involved skill instruction and the remaining sessions consisted of team play.

Sam appeared to enjoy playing soccer, as he would talk about it during the week. However, he had some difficulty picking up the basic skills, such as dribbling, passing, and figuring out who his teammates were, although these were common problems for most of the 5- and 6-year-olds. Sam's parents felt that he could use a little tutoring to help him acquire these skills, so a high school student who was on the soccer team and was interested in working with Sam was contacted. The student volunteer met with Sam once a week, and they worked on a variety of skills. They got along well together and Sam made significant progress. The student volunteer felt that it would be helpful if Sam had other kids to practice with, so Sam's parents contacted other parents involved in the city recreation soccer program to determine if they would be interested in having their child participate in this type of activity once the organized soccer program ended. Several expressed an interest, so a group was organized that met once a week at a local high school after the league had ended for the season. The team was coached by the student volunteer and was made up of 12 children without disabilities, Sam, and two other children with disabilities. At each session, the team spent a half hour on skill-building games and exercises, followed by a half hour of team play. The group met for 2 months through the summer, and Sam made progress in both his soccer game and in socialization. He seemed to be at ease with his teammates, and when the recreation department's soccer program began again Sam was able to participate without any extra support.

Community Theater Groups

There are organized theater groups in many communities across the country. Productions generally run throughout the year, with children's groups meeting during the summer. Membership in the theater group usually doesn't require previous experience. Community members of all ages participate in these productions— either on stage or behind the scenes working on props, scenery, or costumes. Theater groups depend on the community for both membership and financial support for the show. As a result, community participation by any interested citizen is strongly encouraged. Participation in community theater groups can be fun for an individual of any age with a disability, but it can be an especially appropriate activity for young adults, whose formal recreation options become limited when they leave school. You can find out about local theater groups by calling the drama department at the local public school or by checking in the local paper for community events and organizations. Many parks and recreation departments also sponsor or work with community theater groups.

A Theater Group Case Study

Maggie was a 22-year-old with mental retardation and visual impairments who had just graduated from a special public school for students with significant disabilities. She enjoyed watching TV, as well as a variety of arts and crafts that she did with her mother and older sister. Maggie did not have a job and missed seeing her friends from school. She enjoyed attending church on Sundays, and often talked to other members about TV shows that she had viewed during the previous week. One of these people happened to be an actor in a local amateur theater group and thought that Maggie might enjoy going with her to rehearsal during the next several weeks. Maggie's mom knew that this would be a great opportunity for her to spend some time out of the house and away from the family.

A local special education teacher who also acted in the company provided some disability-awareness training to the cast and crew and agreed to model appropriate ways to interact with Maggie. Some of the things she showed them were how to tell Maggie to stay behind the scenes when necessary and how to give her instructions or correct any errors that she made. Maggie was also given the chance to talk to the cast and crew about her disability. Everyone understood that the most important thing for Maggie was just to hang out and feel that she was part of the group. Maggie soon began getting involved in set changes and wardrobe prep, and, eventually, she even acted in some group scenes.

Programs Sponsored by The Arc

The Arc (formerly The Association for Retarded Citizens of the United States) is a national advocacy organization that protects the rights of citizens with disabilities.

The Arc provides education and information to people with disabilities and their families, as well as some direct services, including vocational and recreational counseling. Most local chapters of The Arc have an executive director, professional staff, and a governing executive board. Funding comes from government and private sources, and fees may be charged for some activities or programs, such as summer camps. State and national offices of The Arc help local affiliates meet their programmatic objectives.

Some local chapters of The Arc have hired leisure specialists like those described in Chapter 2 to initiate integrated recreation programs in their communities. A variety of opportunities may be sponsored by a local chapter of The Arc, from after-school child care, Saturday sports programs, and summer camps (see Chapter 11), to programs that send community liaisons to families to help identify the activities for which individual children are best suited. Local chapters of The Arc are great sources of support in finding volunteers and creating peer-support networks. They usually also have information on other local service providers, volunteer agencies, and general community organizations. Their main job is to help citizens with disabilities and their families get the support they need, whatever it may be.

The national Arc is very involved in the promotion of integrated recreational and educational opportunities. For example, along with the National 4-H, they cosponsored the publication of *Together Successfully*, a manual providing strategies and guidelines for integrated recreation. This manual, edited by John Rynders and Stuart Schleien, is available from The Arc and is an excellent resource for starting integrated activities. For this manual or other information, write to: The Arc, Publication Department, P.O. Box 1047, Arlington, TX 76004.

Volunteering

Volunteerism has always been a part of the American way of life. However, citizens with disabilities have historically been viewed as persons whom others volunteer to assist in some way, rather than as committed volunteers in their own right. With the increasing emphasis on the full citizenship of people with disabilities, as embodied in the 1990 Americans with Disabilities Act (ADA), the opportunity for persons with disabilities to volunteer is both timely and self-affirming. Volunteerism provides a unique opportunity for people with disabilities to meet friends, learn a variety of skills, and network with people who may be potential employers. As a practical matter, young adults with disabilities are often unemployed or underemployed and have an abundance of free time to commit to community service.

Volunteer opportunities are abundant in most communities and include many activities, from working in a local public library, hospital, or youth center, to assisting people who are aging, ill, or homeless. Activities may include ongoing commitments, such as working in a soup kitchen every Sunday evening, or one-time events, such as community clean-ups. The time involved and the type of activity should be matched to an individual's preference and schedule. People can volunteer by contacting a local service agency such as the United Way or by joining a community service organization, such as the Knights of Columbus or Kiwanis Club, or any number of religious, high school, or college organizations dedicated to community service. Volunteer opportunities and organizations can be located by calling a local newspaper, Chamber of Commerce, United Way, Bureau of Visitor Affairs, high school guidance counselor, college student activity office, or religious organization.

Any individual or group responsible for facilitating integrated leisure participation can help a person with a disability become a volunteer. It usually requires making contacts, describing to several people the unique needs of the person with a disability, and accompanying the person to one or more of the volunteer activities until he or she is comfortable.

Project REC at Boston Children's Hospital (Moon et al., chap. 2, this volume) received a grant from the Mitsubishi Electric America (MEA) Foundation to assist individuals with disabilities in finding volunteer opportunities. Project REC, with the support of MEA, has discovered volunteer opportunities in the Boston area by exploring a variety of avenues, including: 1) contacting volunteer or service groups at local high schools and colleges, even when the volunteer with a disability is not enrolled in that school; 2) joining corporations or other groups such as churches in their ongoing volunteer activities; and 3) going directly to an organization such as a shelter, youth center, or nursing home to see if volunteers are needed in any capacity at that facility.

A Volunteer Case Study

Kevin was an 18-year-old with mental retardation who attended a school about 40 minutes from his home town and was looking for ways to become involved in his community. His mother heard about the project sponsored by MEA and contacted Project REC, whose representatives met with Kevin and presented him with several volunteer options. One was volunteering together with "Club Orange," a community service organization based at the high school. It was thought that this would be a good way for Kevin to meet local students his own age, as well as become involved in the community. Upon closer examination, however, it was found that for the most part this group volunteered to assist individuals with disabilities, which was not something in which Kevin was interested.

Kevin's second option was volunteering together with a local college service organization. However, it was soon discovered that although the group claimed to participate in special service projects every other week, they actually took part in only two or three per year and did not get together socially at other times. Since Kevin's goal was to become more involved in the community, preferably on a regular basis, this situation turned out to be less than ideal.

Finally, Kevin was put in contact with Horizon Research, Inc., a locally based subsidiary of Mitsubishi, a company with a corporation-wide commitment to providing service to the communities in which its facilities are located. With encouragement from the Mitsubishi Foundation, a small group of individuals at this company got together a minimum of twice a month, once to plan the type of service in which they would become involved and once to provide the service itself. When approached by Project REC staff, the Horizon staff welcomed the opportunity to increase their numbers, as well as provide any support that Kevin might need.

In the beginning, the employees of Horizon Research were hesitant to include Kevin in the planning meetings; they had no difficulty "taking him along" to volunteer, but were not sure what his contributions might be at the preparatory meetings. However, after their first experience volunteering with him (painting and repairing the home of an elderly man), they came to understand that he could also make decisions about what he enjoyed or did not enjoy doing.

Kevin participated in several events with the employees at Horizon Research before he and his family moved to another community. During the volunteer experience he met and became friendly with Max, another participant who happened to live in a town near Kevin's new neighborhood. Kevin and Max continued to volunteer together once in a while, but also went out to eat together occasionally. Thus, through his volunteer experience, Kevin not only learned how to contribute to the community, but also made a friend.

WAYS TO HAVE FUN AT SCHOOL

Over the years we have discovered a number of ways for young children and teenagers with and without disabilities to socialize, play, and just hang out together. Specific instructional strategies and curricular adaptations (Rynders & Schleien, 1991), the role of families and professionals (Hamre-Nietupski, Nietupski, & Strathe, 1992), and even research showing how social interactions can best be facilitated (Stainback & Stainback, 1987) have all been documented. The effects of peer tutoring, cooperative learning, disability awareness training (Meyer & Putnam, 1986), and specific types of media, such as books and movies, have also been shown. We know it works, and we know that most of the time it is not even that hard to do. It simply takes some leadership on the part of people who are committed to bringing kids together. The main elements include using common sense, getting permission from the right "authorities," such as parents and school personnel, being aware of all the medical and physical needs of the students with disabilities, and providing some basic training to participants on what to do in certain emergency situations.

There is no best way to bring kids together. The strategy chosen should be based on the numbers of students, experience of the leaders and participants, desires of the families, resources available in the school and community, and philosophy underlying the general and special education programs. If your main purpose is simply to give students the chance to get to know each other and have a little fun, almost any activity can be a success. Trust the kids—they usually know what to do! If, however, you're still looking for some specific suggestions or a framework for school-based leisure programs, the following activities may suit your needs.

Regular Extracurricular Activities

Most schools sponsor a variety of after-school activities: sports teams; musical groups such as band and chorus; clubs centered on science, environmental, and foreign language interests; student government bodies; and service groups such as sororities or fraternities. Students with disabilities should be given the opportunity to join these activities and have every right to do so.

If students with disabilities, their families, or certain special educators are hesitant about inclusion, or if the students without disabilities or their activity sponsors have doubts, a number of steps can be taken. First, some disability awareness training can be implemented to help the typical students and their teachers understand the strengths, desires, similarities, and rights of the students with disabilities (see Zigmunt, Larson, & Tilson, chap. 12, this volume). Simultaneously, students with and without disabilities can get to know each other through specially designed activities such as friendship clubs or other programs discussed in this chapter. As students become more comfortable with each other, those without disabilities can be encouraged to invite those with disabilities to join typical school programs. Finally, special education professionals can enhance inclusion by becoming sponsors or co-sponsors of general school activities. This provides natural opportunities for modeling appropriate interaction, disability awareness training, and supervision as needed.

Friendship Clubs

Friendship clubs are composed of typical students who are interested in becoming involved in various ways with students with disabilities. This type of program can become part of an existing club or can be easily initiated as a new club in most schools (see Figure 1). It provides a natural environment for promoting friendships between students with disabilities and their typical peers.

The club can be organized by students, teachers, or responsible persons outside the school, and can include students from elementary school through college ages. The teachers or other adult sponsors can promote the club in the same manner as other extracurricular activities. Figure 1 shows one school's initial advertisement for members. Other information on starting a club is provided in Chapter 12 (Zigmunt, Larson, & Tilson, this volume) which shows how one large school system approached this activity.

Club members should be involved in choosing the type of relationship they want to develop: big brother/big sister, in-school peer support provider during integrated nonacademic classes, participation in afterschool athletics and clubs, support during organized community activities, or informal "hanging out" in the community. Members who wish to develop relationships with students their own age must understand that these students are to be treated as peers and not as younger children; The organizing adult or student can involve teachers who work with younger students if club members are specifically interested in developing big brother/big sister relationships. Students may also need more-formal disability awareness training or a couple of sessions on being friends during which they are taught about the strengths or possible limitations of students with disabilities. They will typically need direct adult supervision or support in their initial meetings so that they can ask questions or get help in areas such as behavior management or physical/medical issues.

A Friendship Club Case Study

A teacher from a high school special education program was interested in getting her students more involved in nonacademic activities that occurred in the school. Her class was composed of eight students, age 13–16, who had mental retardation. The students spent most of their day in the classroom and community working on functional academics, such as budgeting, shopping, and recognizing certain words by sight, as well as on a variety of community-access and vocational skills. The classroom teacher first met with the physical education teacher, who was very adept at including students with disabilities in his program. Both teachers felt that a peer support network could assist the students with disabilities in being included in classes and activities without much difficulty or any need for extra staff support. The classroom teacher then spoke with her students about attending inclusive classes and discovered that all but one were interested.

The classroom and physical education teachers decided to start a "Friendship Club" that provided peer support. After getting clearance from the principal, they put up posters around the school advertising the club and a meeting date. Eighty students attended the first meeting; a core group of thirty students decided to join the club. These students provided the teachers with a list of their nonacademic

FRIENDSHIP CLUB

FRIENDSHIP IS AS LASTING AS THE MOON

The Training and Research Institute at Children's Hospital is working to get students with special needs together with other students for fun and friendship. Staff accompanies and assists all those involved so that everyone learns, grows and most importantly, has fun.

The following are some ideas on how you can participate. These ideas are based on the interests expressed by students with special needs from several communities. We would like you to read through these suggestions, think about any that would be of interest, and see if you can come up with any other things that you think would be fun to try.

A group that goes to concerts, movies, or the theater on a regular basis.

Spending one afternoon a week with a student hanging out, going to the mall, going out to eat, or participating with them in some sort of structured community programming like the programs offered through a local community recreation provider.

Going to a class with someone in your school or nearby school to act as a peer tutor.

Going with someone to an after-school activity that you already participate in like the band, chorus, or an organized sport.

An environmental group that organizes and participates in cleanups of areas in your community.

Acting as a big brother or big sister to a younger student in your community or surrounding area.

Does any of this look like fun to you? Can you think of other things that you think would be fun to try?

If this looks interesting to you, please call **Robin Friedlander or Cheska Komissar (735-6914)** or talk to your school representative.

Figure 1.   A poster used to recruit peers for a new friendship club.

classes and activities (e.g., physical education, art, home economics, and shop) in order to allow them to arrange the schedules of the students with disabilities accordingly. The majority of students elected to approach their classroom teachers to make sure that it was all right for a student with a disability to join the class. Two of the students did not feel comfortable doing this, so the teachers who had organized the club approached these teachers. All of the teachers approached proved to be very receptive to the idea.

Five of the students participated in at least one nonacademic class with a "friend," and two of the pairs of students also participated in afterschool sports programs (e.g., field hockey and soccer) together. Four of these relationships, between students who lived close to one another, developed into friendships that continued outside of school.

School Activity Periods

Some public schools give students an opportunity for further enrichment through nonacademic experiences led by the school faculty. Generally, these schools offer an activity period, usually on a weekly or bi-weekly basis, with opportunities to change activities each quarter. Each teacher is asked to offer one activity, which is usually hobby related (e.g., claywork, exercise, model building, a sport, creative writing, jewelry making), and each student is required to give his or her first, second, and third choices for these nongraded activities. Students are then matched to activities; every attempt is made, of course, to give as many students as possible their first choices, taking into account the limits that the teachers have set on the number of participants. Finally, once a week, or once every 2 weeks, the day is accelerated (e.g., classes are held to 40 minutes, rather than the usual 50) to create an extra period at the end of the day, during which students attend their activities. This is an ideal time for students to gain and improve lifetime leisure skills, as well as to get to know teachers and new students on a more social basis than usual.

Often, special education students are excluded from these kinds of activities, or a visit to a special education class may be offered as a "disability awareness" activity. However, it has been found that students with disabilities can participate fully in these activities along with their typical peers. This level of interaction provides the typical student with more than a lesson on disability awareness: it provides a situation in which he or she can meet and get to know someone with a disability on a more equal level, since everyone is being introduced to a new activity at the same time.

An Activity Period Case Study

The Cole Middle School was the site of a special education class of five students, ranging in age from 10–14. These students had all been diagnosed as having significant multiple disabilities. Three of the students were able to communicate by saying or signing "yes" and "no" and by pointing to pictures representing emotions, activities, and items. The other two students had symbol communication systems that allowed them to indicate whether they enjoyed something or not. Three of the students were able to move about independently, while two were able to walk with assistance. Because this class was part of a regional collaborative program, the students lived 45–60 minutes away from the school.

The teacher of the class contacted a CLF to ask for her assistance in socially integrating some of her students with other children in the school. Although she understood that the likelihood of friendships carrying over to after school was low due to the distance that most students lived from the school, the teacher felt that it was important for the students in her class to develop relationships with their peers and to experience more normalized participation in school activities.

Once a week, the students at Cole participated in an activity period. One of the activities that they could chose was "Disability Awareness." During this activity, which was limited to five participants, students would come into the special education class and be paired, one-to-one, with a student with a disability. The pairs would then participate in activities that often included tasks related to daily living (e.g., sweeping, washing dishes). Although the students were able to interact with each other, it was on a trainer–trainee basis, and for the students in the special education class, the activities were nothing new or different.

After receiving input from the CLF, the special education teacher decided that she would try to have her students participate in the same activities as their peers without disabilities. However, she found that there were only a limited number of activities in which her students were able to participate, as many were academically oriented (e.g., silent reading for fun), or physically competitive (e.g., advanced basketball competition). However, some of her students were able to participate in activities such as wreath making, bowling, and aerobics classes.

The special education teacher decided to change her own activity from disability awareness to "Games for Fun," which consisted of New Games (Fluegelman, 1976, 1981). New Games are actually activities that have been around for years but have been redesigned so that anyone can participate. The goal of these games is to have fun and play hard, not to win. New Games are built around softwar (contained, refereed conflict or fighting), creative play, trust, and cooperation. They can include from two to hundreds of players and can be altered through rule changes and changes in player functions. The games often include the use of equipment such as pillows, parachutes, earthballs, and boffers (foam-rubber swords) that can be used in various ways. New Games have been used to facilitate inclusion and cooperation among groups of people of all ages, races, and ability levels.

During the first quarter, Games for Fun was offered to 10 typical students from the school, along with four students from the special education class (the fifth student participated in another activity, with the help of an aide.) By the third quarter, the special education teacher had opened the activity to 20 students without disabilities in addition to all five of her own students. Although word did "leak" out to some extent, most of the typical students who had signed up for the activity did not know that they would be participating with students who had disabilities. These students' interactions with the students in special education were more natural and spontaneous than those of classroom volunteers or of students who had previously participated in the Disability Awareness activity.

Subsequently, several students who participated in the Games for Fun activity began to eat lunch with the students from the special education class and to interact with them during class breaks. Games for Fun became one of the most popular activities in the school, with many students having to be turned away because of limits on student–teacher ratios.

Lunch Buddies

One of the most natural times for school-age youths to socialize is at lunch. Learning how to eat a meal at the usual time while chatting quietly with others is also an important prerequisite for participating in independent adult settings such as work sites or restaurants. School lunch periods provide the perfect atmosphere for kids with and without disabilities to learn important social skills and to get to know each other.

One way to start this process is to recruit a group of volunteer students who are interested in getting to know kids with disabilities. Some instruction on the importance of including kids with disabilities in social settings is usually helpful. It is also a good idea to give these students some information on the specific person with whom they may be spending lunchtime. This will, in part, enable them to react appropriately to any behavioral outbursts or medical emergencies. Having an adult within earshot to answer questions is also a good idea. Groups of from one to four typical students for each student with a disability have worked well.

As students grow more comfortable with each other, arrangements can be made to have them visit restaurants together on occasion. This gives all the kids a chance to leave campus and provides a natural community-based skills training opportunity for the students with disabilities. One or two teachers or other adults can accompany several groups of students, usually up to 15, on an off-campus lunch outing. Whenever possible, students should not be required to pay more for lunch than they would at school. Using classroom materials funds, extracurricular monies targeted to clubs, or funds from charitable sources such as Knights of Columbus projects or a PTA bake sale would be appropriate in such cases.

Summer Friendship/Outing Groups

Many students with disabilities attend school year round. Going to school during the summer months can be a real barrier to recreation program participation, since most youth programs are conducted between June and September. One strategy for getting kids together during the summer is to recruit students without disabilities to participate in summer school programs as part of the leisure domain or physical education curriculum. Students can be recruited during the school year to allow time for schedules to be arranged around jobs, camp, and family vacations. Brochures, or "letters to home" for younger children, can be helpful recruiting tools, since parents are often looking for summer activities to keep their kids healthfully occupied. Enabling kids without disabilities to enroll in a special class for week-long sessions during which they serve as peer supporters or buddies can provide much needed child care for some parents and a perfect source of companionship, peer modeling, and fun for the kids with disabilities.

It can be helpful to obtain extra funding or rearrange funding so that the participants spend a significant amount of time in community settings. For example, eating lunch at a variety of fast food restaurants, swimming at city or YMCA pools, and learning to read real safety signs in buildings and on the street are all practical and natural ways to provide education and therapy. This way, kids can learn from peer models and both the kids and staff can get out of the classroom. Older kids can do things that are less structured, such as going to movies or hanging out at the mall. More formal outings can include arranged visits to explore future vocational possibilities or trips to learn the local subway or bus system.

Case Study—Day Trippers, A Summer Friendship Group

Six students of ages 16–19, each diagnosed as having multiple disabilities, participated in this activity. Two of the students used wheelchairs, one used a walker, and all but one had difficulty communicating. All of these students had 12-month IEPs and attended the same special education class at a high school that was a 15–60 minute commute from their home communities. Ten months of the year, the school was occupied by other high school students; in the summer, it was empty except for two classrooms used for a camp for children 6–12 years old.

Several of the high school students who volunteered in the special education classroom expressed an interest in getting involved in summer activities with some of the students with disabilities whom they had gotten to know during the school year. They asked the special education teacher if they could take the students on day trips to nearby beaches, amusement parks, and other attractions in the city of Boston. Because the students with disabilities had to attend school all summer, the volunteer students initially thought that these types of activities would be out of the question.

But the special education teacher was quite excited about the prospect of her students visiting some of the local summer "fun spots." However, she had some logistics to take care of first. She needed to make certain that the students' parents would be supportive of such activities, so she sent information slips and permission forms home with each student. All the parents were excited about their children being included in these activities, and a new group, Day Trippers, was formed. Consulting with the teacher about what the students with disabilities liked and disliked, and utilizing their own knowledge about the students, the high school student volunteers planned one trip per week for a period of 6 weeks. An adult chaperon was present at each of the outings, but always made an effort to stay in the background.

The teacher of the special education class has since made Day Trippers a regular part of her curriculum, and although the participation process has become more formalized, the students themselves initiate each trip, as they always know best what is "in" for teenagers at any given time.

School Sports Teams

Most public, private, and post-secondary schools have an intramural sports program. Intramural sports leagues are composed of different teams from the same school who compete against each other for fun and exercise. They tend to be less competitive and less structured than most other school sports teams (e.g., playing sites and times may vary, coaching and practices are less formal. Intermural (also known as extramural) teams exist primarily on the college and secondary school levels and are made up of participants from the same school who compete against teams from other schools. These teams tend to be more competitive and more organized. All of these types of teams may provide opportunities for an individual with a disability to participate.

Similar opportunities are available to the student who is older (age 17–21) and to adults in the community. Many local churches and businesses, such as bars and restaurants, sponsor sports teams, as do many employers, and such teams will often accept individuals who are not associated with a specific company. Some community recreation providers (e.g., YMCAs, recreation departments) also offer a variety of leagues that all community members can participate in. These teams are an excellent way for an individual with a disability to have a good time while also developing a social network in their community.

A School Sports Team Case Study

Michael was a 16-year-old diagnosed as having significant mental retardation. He attended a special class in a high school about 40 minutes from his home. The school had a prominent athletic program with an especially strong basketball team that had won the state championship. Michael had expressed an interest in making friends and his teacher was able to assist him in meeting students both in his home town and at school. Several of the students that he became friendly with were on the basketball team at his school and he repeatedly expressed to both his new friends and his teachers an interest in participating on the team.

Michael's high school had two interscholastic basketball teams, a varsity and junior varsity, which were both highly competitive. Unfortunately, less-competitive intramural teams were not available at his school, and his teacher felt that it would be impossible for Michael to participate on either of the existing teams. Although Michael understood many of the rules of basketball and was able to shoot baskets, he did not possess the speed or agility to participate in the very competitive games. However, several of Michael's new friends were on the junior varsity team, and they felt that there must be a team somewhere that would allow him to play basketball. They decided to approach their coach about finding another team on which Michael could play.

At the same time Michael's peers were talking to the coach, Michael began discussing with his adaptive physical education (APE) teacher his desire to play basketball. The APE teacher then contacted the coach and the two of them arranged a meeting with Michael. They discussed the possibility of him playing on a less competitive team in his home town at the local YMCA, but found that Michael really wanted to be on the junior varsity team with his new friends. Several days after meeting with Michael, the coach and APE teacher met again and began discussing strategies that would enable Michael to attain his goals.

Transportation immediately arose as a problem. Michael's program coordinator was very hesitant to try to arrange alternative transportation for Michael, as he was nervous that other students would demand it as well. Michael's grandmother was contacted and stated that she would be willing to forego Michael's transportation twice a week and pick him up instead. The second barrier was the scheduling of basketball practice; the junior varsity team did not always practice right after school, so most team members sometimes went home and then returned for practice. Michael was able to quickly resolve this problem by asking a member of the team if he could hang out with him until practice (e.g., at his home, at the school store). Finally, the coach met with Michael and explained to him that he would be able to participate with the team only during warm-up exercises, which took place during the first half hour of each practice. He also explained to Michael why he would not be able to play in the games or during the remaining hour of each practice. They talked about try-outs for the team, and Michael understood that there were many students who wanted to play on the team but were not skilled enough to make the cut.

After the first two practices, it became evident that Michael did not want to leave after the half hour warm-up. The coach began giving him odd jobs when the warm-ups were over (e.g., handing out towels and water). These responsibilities were gradually increased, and Michael eventually became a co-manager of the team, along with another student. In this way, Michael, who was not good enough to be a *playing* member of the team, found an alternate method of team participation that allowed him to be accepted as an integral part of the team at both practices and games.

Programs for Older Students (Ages 18–22)

Students receiving special education can stay in school until they are 22 years old, while their peers without disabilities and some schoolmates with disabilities requiring only moderate support leave school at 18 or younger. Therefore, older students probably do not really have "same-age" peers at school with whom they can socialize or develop friendships. For these young adults, it is important to look outside the high school environment for age-appropriate relationships.

College fraternities and sororities typically conduct projects that can include working with youth with disabilities, and many are open to participating in some kind of friendship program with a local school. Such a program can be initiated on a college-wide basis by working through the school's "Greek" governing council or by approaching individual fraternities or sororities, and the process usually takes some organizational effort by a teacher or someone very familiar with the older student with disabilities. This person can assist by providing some training and information to the college students on integration, communication, transportation, behavior management, and student history or preferences. Families can assist by providing financial or transportation assistance and all relevant health or medical information. Providing feedback on their son's or daughter's enjoyment of the activity can also be helpful.

Participation in activities can occur in both group and one-on-one situations. One or more adults who know the students with disabilities may need to help initially to match the students with a college partner. However, whenever possible, each student should have the freedom to choose his or her own partners and activities. Slovic, Ferguson, Ferguson, and Johnson (1987) provide some excellent guidelines for starting this kind of social or friendship alliance.

CONCLUDING COMMENTS

The programs, activities, and case studies described in this chapter are only samples of what can be found in most areas of the country. Of course, the specific kinds of leisure alternatives that are available in a community will depend on a variety of factors, including population density, tax or income base, and geographic region. The only way to discover exactly what may be available or what can be created is to use some of the simple techniques described in Chapter 3 of this volume.

You may find that some individual or group has already done a thorough job of seeking out the leisure alternatives in your area. There may also be people who are serving as CLFs through advocacy, school, parks and recreation, or private organizations. These professionals or volunteers can help individuals and their families match their leisure preferences with particular activities. One way to discern whether the groundwork for integrated leisure participation has been done is to inquire in several places, including the local chapter of The Arc, the state Developmental Disabilities Council, the local school system's special education department, and the nearest county or town parks and recreation office's therapeutic division.

When it appears that no group or individual has as yet identified the possibilities for leisure participation in a particular community, this text should be helpful in finding or creating activities (or contacting someone who can do this for you), getting and keeping people involved, and making sure that a variety of integrated activities become available for citizens of all ages and ability levels. The remaining chapters in this text provide specific tools and models that can be used to either create or improve leisure options.

REFERENCES

Fluegelman, A. (1976). *The "New Games" book.* New York: Doubleday—The Headlands Press, Inc.

Fluegelman, A. (1981). *More "New Games."* New York: Doubleday—The Headlands Press, Inc.

Hamre-Nietupski, S., Nietupski, J., & Strathe, M. (1992). Functional life skills, academic skills, and friendship/social relationship development: What do parents of students with moderate/severe/profound disabilities value? *Journal of The Association for Persons with Severe Handicaps, 17*(1). 53–58.

Meyer, L.H., & Putnam, J. (1986). Social integration. In V.B. VanHasselt, P. Strain, & M. Hersen (Eds.), *Handbook of developmental and physical disabilities.* New York: Pergamon Press.

Rynders, J., & Schleien, S. (Eds.). (1991). *Together successfully: Creating recreational and educational programs that integrate people with and without disabilities.* Arlington, TX: Association for Retarded Citizens.

Slovic, R., Ferguson, D., Ferguson, P., & Johnson, C. (1987). G.U.I.D.E.S. aid transition for severely handicapped students. *Teaching Exceptional Children, 20*(1), 14–18.

Stainback, W., & Stainback, S. (1987). Facilitating friendships. *Education and Training in Mental Retardation, 22*(1), 18–25.

~SECTION TWO~

LEGAL AND TECHNICAL SUPPORTS

Since the mid-1970s a number of federal laws have been passed that when enforced ensure that people with disabilities can enter school or community recreation programs. It is crucial that families, advocates, and program providers understand the implications of laws, especially those such as the ADA, IDEA, and the Tech Act, which speak directly to the opening of community and school recreation programs to any interested participant. Chapter Five introduces federal legislation that has helped open the door to school and community activities for people with disabilities.

Technology, due in large part to recent legislative mandates, has also provided wider access to recreation programs. The authors have learned how to include more people by making a variety of physical or programmatic adaptations to an activity's rules, procedures, equipment, or physical environment. Chapter Six discusses some of the most easily implemented adaptations and provides accessibility standards that have been mandated by the ADA.

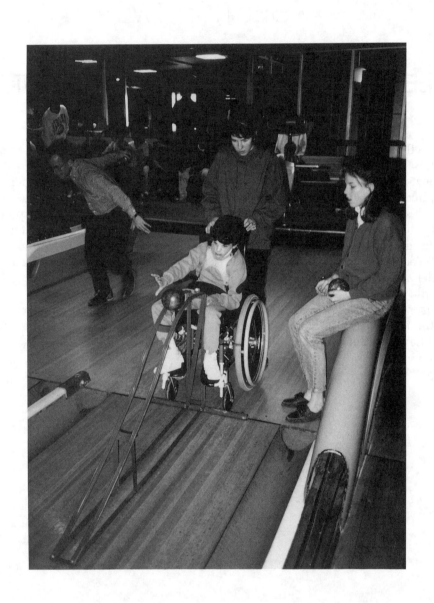

~five~

The Impact
of Federal Legislation
on Recreation Programs

Rikki S. Epstein,
John McGovern, and M. Sherril Moon

Since the 1960s, a number of federal laws have been enacted that either directly or indirectly affect the daily lives of citizens with disabilities. Most of these laws relate primarily to education, vocational rehabilitation, employment, health services, housing, income maintenance, social services, and basic civil rights, and some of them are specifically concerned with the provision of or access to recreation services.

The Americans with Disabilities Act (ADA), PL 101-336, is probably the most significant federal legislation to date in the area of recreation services. The ADA, which was signed into law by President Bush in 1990, is a far-reaching civil rights law that prohibits discrimination against people with disabilities in all public and private organizations. Because of the significance of this law to recreation programming, the majority of this chapter is devoted to it. But before the ADA is discussed, the impact of several other important pieces of legislation is outlined below.

THE INDIVIDUALS WITH DISABILITIES EDUCATION ACT (IDEA), PL 101-476

The Individuals with Disabilities Education Act (IDEA), the 1990 reauthorization of PL 94-142 (the Education for All Handicapped Children Act of 1975), mandates that a free appropriate public education in the least restrictive environment be provided for all children with disabilities. The law guarantees public education services for children from birth through 21 years of age and requires that secondary students' individualized education programs (IEPs) include transition plans. These plans must include annual statements of needed transition services for the move into postsecondary education, vocational training, integrated employment, continuing

---

Several of the laws discussed in this chapter are being considered for reauthorization as this volume goes to press. The reader should consult agencies affected by these laws at the local, state, or federal level in order to obtain the most up-to-date information on legislation.

adult education, adult services, independent living, and community participation. The first transition document must be written no later than a student's 16th birthday and should delineate interagency responsibilities and linkages to outside agencies that must be established before the student leaves school (Wehman, 1992).

IDEA encompasses previous amendments, including PL 99-457—the 1986 reauthorization, that mandated service provision to infants, toddlers, preschoolers, and their families—and also changes the language of the old law from "handicapped children" to "children with disabilities." IDEA also adds two new categories, autism and traumatic brain injury, to the list of those disabilities specifically mentioned in the legislation and adds assistive technology to the list of service needs that can be requested and provided through the IEP process.

IDEA addresses the provision of both physical education and therapeutic recreation as related or supportive services that can be requested and delivered as part of the IEP requirement for students with disabilities. Specifically, physical education must be provided in a general program unless the student is enrolled full-time in a separate facility or needs a specially designed physical education program that is prescribed in the IEP. Specially designed programs do not necessarily mean separate classes, but can involve peer or adult assistance, rule modifications, or special equipment. Whenever possible, a specialist in adapted physical education should help design this program (Sherrill, 1993). It is also helpful that the law mandates the provision, through the IEP process, of assistive technology whenever it is needed to allow a student to participate in physical education or recreation activities. There are a number of resources for helping students with disabilities participate in general physical education; the reader is referred to Block, 1994; Block & Krebs, 1992; and Sherrill, 1993.

IDEA also identifies recreation as a necessary service and outlines the proper steps in the assessment of leisure and recreation, the provision of recreation programs in schools and community agencies, and the initiation of inclusive leisure education (Reynolds, 1993). The transition-plan component of IDEA mandates that if recreation programs are needed by a student as he or she moves from school to adulthood, then the providers of these services in the community must be invited to participate in the development of that student's IEP. Adding community recreation plans to a secondary-age student's IEP is definitely a primary way of facilitating a successful transition from school to adult community participation and independent living (Wehman, Moon, Everson, Wood, & Barcus, 1988).

In summary, advocates and family members of students with disabilities should be aware that according to the provisions of IDEA, the IEP process can be used to ensure that the development of community recreation skills and participation in physical education classes are included in a student's educational program.

DEVELOPMENTAL DISABILITIES
ASSISTANCE AND BILL OF RIGHTS ACT OF 1990 (DDA), PL 101-496

The Developmental Disabilities Assistance and Bill of Rights Act (DDA), PL 101-496, which was reauthorized in 1990 and is once again being considered for reauthorization in 1994, provides formula grants to states for planning, coordination, advocacy, and the training of personnel to work with people with developmental disabilities. In addition, the law authorizes: 1) a formula grant program to fund the operation of state protection and advocacy systems; 2) a project grant program to support university affiliated programs (UAPs) for persons with developmental disabilities; and 3) national significance grants to support projects aimed at increasing the independence, productivity, and inclusion in the community of persons with developmental disabilities (OSERS, 1992).

Each state must establish a Developmental Disabilities (DD) Planning Council, which is responsible for using a formula grant of at least $350,000 for improving services to the state's citizens with developmental disabilities. Each DD Council can use its grant allotment to fund educational, advocacy, or community organizations that provide inclusive employment, community living, child development, or community education programs. It should be possible for schools or community agencies to apply for small grants from any state DD Council that promotes the establishment of inclusive leisure services.

Many states also have a UAP that is based at a university or teaching hospital. These research and training programs have the capacity to obtain state, federal, and private-foundation grants that can be used to fund inclusive leisure services within schools and communities. Community service providers, advocates, families, and educators should contact such programs in their states to explore UAP involvement in community leisure research, training, and model-program development.

TECHNOLOGY-RELATED ASSISTANCE FOR INDIVIDUALS WITH DISABILITIES ACT (TECH ACT), PL 100-407

The Technology-Related Assistance for Individuals with Disabilities Act (TECH Act), PL 100-407, enacted in 1988, established several new grant programs to facilitate the development of assistive technologies for use by persons with disabilities (OSERS, 1992). The main purpose of the law is to help people gain access to all types of assistive devices or aids that can help them to lead more productive lives and to close the gap between technological innovations and practical applications of such technology. The law has resulted in 31 state grants, awarded on a competitive basis by the U.S. Department of Education, that have been used to fund consumer-responsive, comprehensive, statewide technology-assistance programs. Most of these states have set up information networks, technical assistance programs for schools and families, and avenues through which individuals who need assistive technology can obtain the proper equipment or services. The law also authorizes a number of nationwide grant programs, contracts, and cooperative agreements that may be awarded on a competitive basis to both nonprofit and for-profit entities, and are to be used to develop, demonstrate, disseminate, and evaluate assistive technology products and services.

Assistive technology can often help persons with disabilities to participate in appropriate leisure and recreation activities (see Moon, Hart, Komissar, Sotnik, & Friedlander, chap. 6, this volume, for more information), so families, advocates, and service providers should make it a point to contact entities in their state that have been funded through PL 100-407. Those who are not familiar with the services available in their particular state can contact the Technical Assistance Project, associated with RESNA, an interdisciplinary association for the advancement of rehabilitation and assistive technologies, which serves as liaison between the U.S. Department of Education and funded programs. The number is (703) 524-6686 Voice/TDD, and they are located in Suite 1540, 1700 N. Moore St., Arlington, VA 22209-1903.

REHABILITATION ACT AMENDMENTS (REHAB ACT), PL 102-569

This law, first enacted in 1973 and reauthorized in 1992, affects a wide range of rights and services, including vocational training and employment, independent living (including recreation services), and basic civil rights. Individuals, advocates, and families should contact their state vocational rehabilitation agency for more specific information on how each state administers programs funded through this law.

Title V (particularly in Section 504 of the original Rehabilitation Act of 1973 and then as amended in later reauthorizations) contains a number of provisions that safeguard the rights of individuals with disabilities. The law basically protects against discrimination in all federally assisted programs and activities and mandates that these programs be made accessible to persons with disabilities. The Americans with Disabilities Act (ADA) extends the reach of Section 504 by making similar nondiscriminatory demands of both private and public entities. Section 504 provisions require that public school programs, including interscholastic athletics and extracurricular activities, allow qualified students with disabilities the opportunity to participate. The statute also requires that schools include students with disabilities in general education settings whenever possible, regardless of whether the student has an IEP. This is particularly important when the student has a disability that is not specifically listed in IDEA (King, 1992). This law has thus far been underutilized in ensuring equal access to school and community activities, including recreation alternatives.

THE AMERICANS WITH DISABILITIES ACT (ADA), PL 101-336

The Americans with Disabilities Act (ADA), PL 101-336, is a landmark piece of legislation. Signed into law on July 26, 1990 by President Bush, this civil rights law has the clearly defined purpose of eliminating discrimination against people with disabilities and guaranteeing access to every critical area of American life. The ADA creates an unprecedented opportunity to eliminate barriers to independence and productivity for the 43 million people with disabilities living in the United States, who are often unable to secure such basic services as education, transportation, housing, employment counselling, and recreation.

The ADA defines an individual with a disability as one who: 1) has a physical or mental impairment that substantially limits one or more major life activities, such as seeing, hearing, speaking, walking, caring for oneself, working, learning, or participating in recreation; 2) has a record of such an impairment (e.g., a person who has been treated in the past for a mental illness); or 3) is regarded as having such an impairment (e.g., a person who has extensive scars from burns). This broad definition includes individuals with vision impairments, hearing impairments, mental retardation, cerebral palsy, multiple sclerosis, cardiac disorders, chronic health disorders, rehabilitated drug and alcohol problems, or HIV infection, to name just some of the disabilities covered.

Other disability rights laws preceded the ADA. The Architectural Barriers Act of 1968 (PL 90-480) required that all facilities built in part or in whole with federal funds be accessible to individuals with disabilities. The Rehabilitation Act of 1973 required that programs conducted by agencies that received federal funding be accessible to persons with disabilities. But these earlier laws were limited in both scope and impact compared to the ADA, which extends protections to the private sector and applies whether or not federal funds have been received.

General Provisions of the ADA

Title I   Title I of the ADA prohibits employers from discriminating against "otherwise qualified individuals with a disability" in any employment action. This applies to hiring and firing, raises and promotions, job training, and insurance and other benefits. Employers must also provide reasonable accommodations for employees with disabilities, including modification of work stations and equipment, unless this would cause undue hardship for the company.

Title II   Title II prohibits state and local governments and agencies (e.g., school districts, parks and recreation departments, and park districts) from discriminating against people with disabilities in the provision of services, programs, and activities. Title II also prohibits discrimination by providers of public transportation.

Title III   Title III prohibits private entities from discriminating against people with disabilities. This includes such establishments as restaurants, health clubs, YMCAs, theaters, private schools, hotels, banks, parks, zoos, museums, and shopping centers that provide public accommodations (goods, services, and facilities).

Title IV   Title IV requires that telecommunications relay systems be made available to individuals with hearing and/or speech impairments.

Overall, the ADA protects the civil rights of people with disabilities through a system of enforcement that permits both administrative claims and civil actions. The Equal Employment Opportunity Commission (EEOC) handles employment claims, and regulations issued by the Department of Justice (DOJ) outline the procedure for filing complaints against businesses and government entities under Title II and Title III.

Impact on Community Recreation Programs

Schools, YMCAs, parks and recreation departments, and other organizations that provide recreation programs cannot exclude potential program participants from services, programs, or activities on the basis of disability. The ADA describes a potential program participant as a qualified individual with a disability, meaning that the person meets the essential eligibility requirements for program participation. These requirements must be the same for persons with and without disabilities, and may include residency, ability-to-pay program fees, willingness to abide by the rules of conduct for the program, and compliance with registration procedures. Other factors may include age requirements and minimum levels of skill for competitive programs.

The ADA requires the consideration of three types of accommodations when an individual with a disability meets essential eligibility requirements:

1. *The agency should modify rules, policies, or practices, as necessary, to enable an individual's participation.*   Many parks and recreation departments require in-person registration for popular programs such as day camps, sports leagues, child care programs, and swimming lessons. A reasonable modification in this case would be to change the procedure to permit phone-in or mail-in registration. Another example would be changing rules that bar animals from a recreation center, which would be discriminatory against a person who is blind and

uses a guide dog. Another example would be changing the playing rules in a particular sport (e.g., tennis players who use wheelchairs could be allowed two bounces before returning the ball).

2. *The agency should remove architectural, transportation, and communication barriers to enable an individual's participation.* The ADA requires that physical barriers be removed if this is readily achievable (e.g., a health club might need to widen doorways for people who use wheelchairs; a recreation center might need to install grab bars in the restrooms and construct ramps at entrances to the building). The ADA does not require the immediate removal of all architectural barriers in existing facilities, but it does require that any programs conducted within the facility be made accessible. This may be accomplished by moving the program to an accessible location (e.g., relocating a Girl or Boy Scout troop meeting from the third floor to the first floor of a building to accommodate a child who uses a wheelchair). If, however, an existing facility is unique (e.g., the only ice skating rink or the only indoor swimming pool in a particular community), then any architectural barriers must be removed. The ADA also requires that newly constructed facilities or areas be free of architectural barriers. Chapter 6 of this volume (Moon et al.) provides a simple survey for evaluating architectural barriers in most facilities.

   Vehicles purchased or leased for use in the transportation of recreation program participants must also be "readily accessible." This entails, at a minimum, wheelchair lifts, interior passenger securing systems, and other similar modifications. In certain circumstances, recreation agencies can be required to provide transportation for participants with disabilities to and from programs at the agency's expense.

   All agency communications, including fliers and program brochures, must be available in a format that is accessible to people with hearing and/or vision impairments. Agencies should also acquire a TDD (text telephone) or access to a telecommunication relay system that will enable telephone communication with individuals who use TDDs.

3. *The agency should provide auxiliary aids or services as necessary.* For example, if a participant with a hearing impairment registers for an arts and crafts program and requires instructional assistance, a reasonable accommodation might be the provision of a sign language interpreter. For individuals with cognitive impairments, the agency may consider furnishing additional staff or volunteers who can serve in a variety of capacities, such as instructor, facilitator, partner, or peer advisor.

Program Requirements

Programs, services, and activities provided by community recreation agencies must be available in the most inclusive setting possible; ideally, this means people with and without disabilities participating side-by-side in the same program. Accommodations must be made to ensure that leisure participation is as effective for persons with disabilities as it is for everyone else.

Community recreation agencies can still offer separate, specialized recreation programs for individuals with disabilities, but these individuals also have the right to chose to participate in a general program. For example, the YMCA can offer recreation programs specifically for children with mental retardation, but it would be a violation of the ADA if the YMCA refused to allow children with mental retardation or other disabilities to participate in any of its other recreation programs.

The ADA regulations also outline several other acceptable accommodations. These include adding staff and providing for home visits for any individual who, because of a disability, cannot attend activities outside of his or her residence. Often, additional staff supervision can make the difference for a person with a cognitive impairment who is capable of developing a skill or enjoying an activity, but simply requires additional assistance. Reasonable accommodations also include the use of adaptive equipment and auxiliary aids. Adaptive equipment might include a bowling ball with a recessed handle, a computer for playing games, or other similar devices. Examples of auxiliary aids include sign language interpreters, assistive listening devices, readers, taped texts, materials in braille, and large-print materials. See Chapter 6, this volume, for additional information on making accommodations in recreation programs.

Community recreation agencies may not, under any circumstance, pass on the cost of ADA compliance to a participant with a disability. Costs associated with accessibility must be absorbed by *all* participants or by the agency itself.

Of course, not every individual with a disability will require accommodations or modifications, and many individuals with disabilities already participate in community recreation programs without any form of assistance. However, when assistance is necessary, the ADA requires an agency to make reasonable accommodations. Some common questions and answers about accommodations are presented in Appendix A at the end of this chapter.

Community recreation agencies are responsible for examining their own programs, services, and facilities to determine whether or not they comply with the ADA. Through this self-evaluation process, each agency can clearly determine where barriers or discriminatory practices, if any, exist and how they can best be removed.

Park and recreation departments, girls' and boys' clubs, scout troops, and school districts pride themselves on offering a wide range of creative, challenging, and worthwhile programs and services for individuals of all ages and ability levels in their communities. Sports leagues, after-school activities for children and teenagers, summer camps, fitness and exercise classes, cultural arts, and special events are just a few of the programming options that are available.

Community recreation providers who use their creative problem-solving talents every day are in an excellent position to come up with innovative solutions to accessibility problems. With the passage of the ADA, the opportunity now exists for recreation service providers to play a significant role in educating the public about including people with disabilities in every aspect of community life.

~Appendix~

Some Common Questions
and Answers about the ADA

Question 1. If a potential program participant has a severe behavior problem, such as a tendency to become physically aggressive toward other people, does the agency have an obligation to provide accommodations?

Answer: Yes. The existence of such behaviors signals the agency that "reasonable accommodations" must be made. These may include, but are not limited to: providing a one-to-one staff to participant ratio; providing training for staff so that they can structure activities in such a way as to avoid incidents that might escalate into physical altercations; providing training that will enable staff members to reinforce the positive behaviors and discourage the inappropriate behaviors of the participant; making home visits if the participant's behavior is such that participation in the usual program format is unworkable; and consulting with behavior specialists and professionals in other environments (e.g., schools) where appropriate plans for accommodating such behaviors may already be in use. If, however, accommodations for a person with a disability fail, and the safety of others is at risk, then a participant may be removed from the program.

Question 2. Can an agency require a participant who exhibits unusual behavior or who has severe physical disabilities to bring a personal care attendant along to an activity.

Answer: No. An agency cannot require that a personal care attendant be brought to a program. However, an agency may suggest this as an option, and, if the participant agrees, this may be permitted as an accommodation.

Question 3. Does an agency have an obligation to accommodate a person who requires personal services in order to participate in a program?

Answer: No. Agencies are not required to provide "personal services" for participants. Generally, the agency is not responsible for providing assistance with such tasks as eating, using the bathroom, or changing clothes. If a participant has difficulty in these areas, an agency should consider suggesting that a participant bring a personal care attendant, family member, or friend along to an activity.

Other personal services include the provision of wheelchairs, eyeglasses, or hearing aids. While these are not required, some facilities voluntarily provide wheelchairs and other assistive devices for use by those with limited mobility.

Question 4. If an agency provides only inclusive recreation programming, is it required to develop segregated programs if participants or their parents request them?

Answer: No. Generally, an inclusive recreation opportunity is enough to satisfy ADA requirements. The possible exception would be cases in which such a program was poorly planned, was staffed with persons with no training in working with persons with disabilities, or created a hostile environment (e.g., one in which a person with a disability was teased or taunted by the other participants); in such situations, the inclusive program might not be considered appropriate under the law.

Question 5. What effect will the ADA have on extramural school programs such as sports teams, debate teams, and science clubs?

Answer: The opportunity to participate in extramural programs will continue to be contingent upon the candidate's possession of skills essential to the activity. If any 16-year-old tries out for a volleyball team, and it is found that he or she cannot serve, set, or spike, then he or she won't make the team. The same criteria would be applicable to a person with Down syndrome or any other disability. But staff members should be sure not to jump to conclusions. For example, it might seem at first that a person who could not speak would be unable to participate on a debate team, but the determining factor should be whether the person is as good at formulating logical and persuasive arguments as the others trying out for the team. If a person with a disability proves to be talented in debate, then those sponsoring the team could hire a sign language interpreter or purchase a voice synthesizer to work around any communication difficulties.

Question 6. Are organizations such as Girl Scouts or the YMCA subject to the same requirements under the ADA as a public park and recreation agency?

Answer: The groups mentioned are private organizations that are open to the public. Therefore, the ADA does apply to their operations; the relevant requirements are found in Title III, the part of the law that applies, for example, to grocery stores, gas stations, law offices, banks, hotels, and similar entities. While Title III requirements differ slightly from those applicable to a parks and recreation agency (which would be covered under Title II) they are generally similar.

Question 7. Are recreation programs sponsored by a religious organization, such as a church, covered by the ADA?

Answer: No. All services provided by religious entities are exempt from the ADA. Religious organizations need only comply with the employment provisions of the ADA. However, many state laws that prohibit discrimination because of a disability do apply to churches. Furthermore, it should be noted that many religious organizations are voluntarily complying with the ADA requirements.

Question 8. Can a person with a physical disability who wishes to participate in community groups such as soccer or little leagues be barred from participation because, for safety reasons, it would not be practical to include players who use braces or wheelchairs?

Answer: No. An organization must first conduct a personalized assessment of the real risk of injury in the program, and attempts must be made to accommodate that risk. For example, if a six-year-old who uses crutches were to play tee ball, there would probably be a risk of injury. Therefore, the team should ask if a coach or buddy can be on the field and assist such a person during play; or the rules should be changed to allow someone else to bat for the child; or he or she could bat, but a substitute runner could be used; or the child could play the outfield, where contact with other fielders and with runners would be less likely. In the absence of an approach that identifies actual individual risk and attempts at accommodation, such a rule would be discriminatory under the ADA.

REFERENCES

Americans with Disabilities Act of 1990 (ADA), PL 101-336. (July 26, 1990). Title 42, U.S.C. 12101 et seq: *U.S. Statutes at Large, 104,* 327–378.

Architectural Barriers Act of 1968, PL 90-480. (August 12, 1968). Title 42, U.S.C. 4151–4157 et seq: *U.S. Statutes at Large, 82,* 718.

Block, M.E. (1994). *A teacher's guide to including students with disabilities in regular physical education.* Baltimore: Paul H. Brookes Publishing Co.

Block, M.E., & Krebs, P.L. (1992). An alternative to least restrictive environments: A continuum of support to regular physical education. *Adapted Physical Activity Quarterly, 9*(2), 97–113.

Developmental Disabilities Assistance and Bill of Rights Act of 1990 (DDA), PL 101-496. (October 31, 1990). Title 42, U.S.C. 6000 et seq: *U.S. Statutes at Large, 104,* 1191.

Education of the Handicapped Act Amendments of 1986, PL 99-457. (October 8, 1986). Title 20, U.S.C. 1400 et seq: *U.S. Statutes at Large, 100,* 1145–1177.

Individuals with Disabilities Education Act of 1990 (IDEA), PL 101-476. (October 30, 1990). Title 20, U.S.C. 1400 et seq: *U.S. Statutes at Large, 104,* 1103–1151.

King, C. (1992, September). Fact sheet: Resolving disputes involving the education of children with disabilities. *The PEATC Press,* p. 3.

Rehabilitation Act of 1973, PL 93-112. (September 26, 1973). Title 29, U.S.C. 701 et seq: *U.S. Statutes at Large, 87,* 355–394.

Reynolds, R. (1993). Recreation and lifestyle changes. In P. Wehman (Ed.), *The ADA mandate for social change* (pp. 217–233). Baltimore: Paul H. Brookes Publishing Co.

Sherrill, C. (1993). Advocacy, the law, and the IEP. In C. Sherrill (Ed.), *Adapted physical education, recreation, and sport: Cross disciplinary and lifespan issues* (pp. 75–98). Madison, WI: WCB Brown and Benchmark, Publishers.

Technology-Related Assistance for Individuals with Disabilities Act of 1988, PL 100-407. (August 19, 1988). Title 29, U.S.C. 2201 et seq: *U.S. Statutes at Large, 102,* 1044–1065.

U.S. Department of Education, Office of Special Education and Rehabilitative Services (OSERS). (1992). *Summary of existing legislation affecting people with disabilities.* (Publication No. ED/OSERS 92-8). Washington, DC: Clearing House of Disability Information.

Wehman, P. (1992). *Life beyond the classroom: Transition strategies for young people with disabilities.* Baltimore: Paul H. Brookes Publishing Co.

Wehman, P., Moon, M.S., Everson, J., Wood, W., & Barcus, M. (1988). *Transition from school to work: New challenges for youth with severe disabilities.* Baltimore: Paul H. Brookes Publishing Co.

~ six ~

Environmental, Material, and Procedural Adaptations to Promote Accessibility

M. Sherril Moon, Debra Hart, Cheska Komissar, Paula Sotnik, and Robin Friedlander

The Americans with Disabilities Act (ADA), PL 101-336, mandates that all public accommodations, including facilities where recreation, exercise, and social services are provided, be physically accessible to persons with disabilities and nondiscriminatory in their rules, policies, and practices, and that reasonable modifications or adaptations may be required, if necessary, of public or private providers in order to meet these criteria. Accessibility and nondiscriminatory participation may also require the removal of architectural, communication, or transportation barriers, or the provision of auxiliary aides and services (*Federal Register*, July 26, 1990). Therefore, by law, all recreation providers must now become familiar with adaptations, physical accessibility requirements, and the array of assistive technology devices now available, both the complicated and the relatively simple.

The Technology-Related Assistance for Individuals with Disabilities Act (Tech Act), PL 100-407, defines an assistive technology device as: "any item, piece of equipment, or product system, whether acquired commercially off the shelf, modified, or customized, that is used to increase, maintain, or improve functional capacities of individuals with disabilities" (Sec. 2561 [3], 1988). Although the ADA does not specifically address the issue of assistive technology, many of the adaptations or modifications and auxiliary aids that the law does mandate as reasonable accommodations would fall under this category.

These two laws, PL 101-336 and PL 100-407, have made accessibility to recreation through adaptations, physical accessibility modifications, and assistive technology more of a reality in recent years. The purpose of this chapter is to show how modifications of a recreation facility or environment or of equipment, rules, and activities can enhance the inclusion of persons with disabilities in community programs. In this chapter the terms "adaptation," "modification," and "accommodation" are used synonymously to denote changes in or additions to facilities, equipment or materials, or rules and procedures that are designed to make them accessible to a wider range of people. Adaptations specifically applied to materials and equipment are also referred to as "assistive technology."

FACILITY OR ENVIRONMENTAL ADAPTATIONS

Until recently, many people with certain disabilities could not participate in community or school leisure activities because they could not gain access to or make use of the facilities in which programs were conducted. Narrow doorways and halls or lack of transportation or parking spaces for people using wheelchairs and lack of signage or listening systems for people with sensory disabilities are some examples of typical problems at facilities. However, as Rynders and Schleien (1991) point out, many of these problems are now being addressed through adaptations such as the installation of ramps for wheelchairs, braille signage, support bars in bathrooms, enlarged doorknobs, and extended handles on drinking fountains.

Public accommodations, including restaurants, hotels, theaters, retail stores, museums, schools, libraries, parks, community centers, malls, and child care centers will become even more accessible because of the standards and criteria mandated by the ADA. Such accessibility standards include physical modifications, removal of barriers, and alternatives to physical alterations, such as "in-store assistance" and "door-to-door delivery." It is important for families, educators, advocates, and leisure facilitators to make sure that leisure sites meet ADA accessibility standards. The survey provided in the appendix at the end of this chapter includes criteria established by the ADA and can be relatively quickly administered to determine whether a site is accessible. Efficiently determining a program's accessibiltiy is not only critical as a first step before a person with a disability can enjoy a leisure persuit, but is also crucial in enforcing compliance with ADA requirements.

If it is determined that a particular facility is not physically accessible, any number of adaptations to that site may need to be made—from major rebuilding and additions to simple rearrangements of furniture or equipment. Some specific facility adaptations that improve accessibility for everyone are outlined below.

Specific Adaptations

Paving   The surface of any area is important for people who have difficulty with mobility. Rugs with wrinkles in them can cause difficulty in maneuvering with crutches and wheelchairs, and they may cause people to trip, especially those with balance or vision difficulties. Walkways need to be clear and free of debris, and tree roots growing under the sidewalk must be removed, as these can cause fissures that make it difficult for someone using a wheelchair to negotiate the sidewalk. Sandy areas may cause similar difficulties. Although they are not always possible (e.g., on nature trails or playgrounds), hard surfaces such as cement and macadam are always preferable.

However, an unpaved area does not have to be inaccessible to anyone. Rocks and debris (e.g., fallen branches) should be cleared from nature trails on a frequent basis and certain "natural" covers should be applied when possible. Materials such as mulch are better than sand, and small stones are never advantageous, either in terms of safety or accessibility. Boardwalks are helpful in many areas, including forests and beaches. Just because an area needs to be accessible does not mean that it must lose its beauty. Pathways through large sanded areas, if designed properly, can curve naturally with the land and be aesthetically pleasing, as well as making access easier for a multitude of individuals, including mothers with strollers, older people, small children learning to walk, and people who use wheelchairs, crutches, or canes.

Curbcuts Curbcuts are important not only to allow access to a sidewalk, but also for allowing entry to businesses and activities adjacent to the sidewalk. Organizations and facilities offering recreational services should have curbcuts adjacent to their facilities at each corner of the block and directly in front of the facility at the drop-off/pick-up area. If a curb cut needs to be added to city-owned property, the proper authorities will have to be contacted. It is also helpful if someone at the facility is in charge of maintaining the curb cuts and surrounding sidewalks to ensure that they have proper drainage and are clear of snow (snow plows often leave mounds of snow right in front of curb cuts) and other debris. It is important to follow federal guidelines for curbcuts, allowing no more than a 1-inch rise for each 8 inches of length.

Barrier-Free Paths/Hallways and Handrails Halls and pathways should not contain tables, chairs, magazine racks, or any other items that are so large that they significantly narrow the width of the travel area. Furthermore, it is helpful to have at least one side of a hall or path free of any items that might be walked into by someone who has vision difficulty or is using the wall or the edge of the path as a guide. All paths, especially those outdoors, should have handrails. Handrails also need to be placed along ramps, as well as in restrooms. This is especially helpful for people who need to use the handrails for support to get into or out of wheelchairs, as well as for people who just need to hold onto something for balance.

Doorways Doorways should be a minimum of 32 inches wide in order to allow people using a standard-size wheelchair or other device to assist with ambulation (e.g., crutches or a walker) to pass through. Furthermore, doors should be either automatic or easy to open. If this is not possible in your facility, you may consider installing a doorbell—they are relatively inexpensive and easy to install and can be purchased at almost any hardware store. If you do plan to install a doorbell, remember that it must be accessible (e.g., not too high and not at the top of a set of stairs) and that someone must be available to answer it at all times.

Lever Doorknobs It is not always possible to have every door operate automatically. In the case of a typical manual door, it is helpful to consider the type of handle used. Large handles that can be hooked onto with an entire hand are helpful, but can only be put on doors without latches. One common solution to this problem is a large handle with a button that releases the latch, but, unfortunately, persons who need this type of large handle may not be able to push the button. Also available are levers that fit over regular doorknobs and enable a person to operate the door by simply pushing down on the lever and pulling or pushing the door, allowing independent access for some people who are unable to grip regular doorknobs.

Controlled Noise Levels People who have difficulty seeing often have trouble orienting themselves in a new setting. One of the things that can help alleviate this problem is controlling the noise level at a site. This may seem like a formidable task in some recreation settings, but even small changes can result in large improvements. For example, noisy classes should be conducted behind closed doors, when possible. Televisions and radios should be turned off when not in use; if staff is listening to music for entertainment, the volume should be kept low.

Contrasting Colors   Using contrasting colors in a recreation area and in materials is also helpful. If walls are painted yellow, doors should be a different color. Signs and posted notices should also be in contrasting colors. For items such as computer screens and signs, a background of black, blue, or green with yellow text is recommended. Colors for printed materials should also be chosen carefully; although one may love the look of a new brochure in purple or bright pink, it is always easiest to read black print on a white background. These are all important considerations if one wants to encourage people with visual impairments to participate in activities.

Pictorial Signage   Whenever possible, directional signs in a facility should use pictorial images (e.g., arrows). Printed materials should also include pictures; for example, a brochure might include a graphic representation of each activity next to its written description.

Sighted Guides   Upon hearing the words "sighted guide," people often immediately begin to worry about cost. Actually, anyone can act as a sighted guide, assisting a person who is blind or who has some other disability in becoming oriented to a new facility or in finding the specific location they are looking for. In fact, some recreation programs have other participants serve in this capacity during activities. The important thing is to be sure that all staff, as well as anyone else who might be called upon to assist a person with a visual impairment (e.g., a volunteer), have some training in mobility and orientation assistance. Such training may be available from an organization that supports people with disabilities, a local teacher who has experience with people who are blind, or an individual with a visual impairment.

Environmental Accessibility—A Case Study

Oxford is a small rural oceanside community. When residents with disabilities were polled as to what activities they would be most interested in, the majority mentioned that it was frustrating to live so close to the water, yet not be able to enjoy the beach because maneuvering over the sand was too difficult. The recreation director of Oxford was concerned with the results of this survey, as his department was in charge of beach maintenance. Over the course of a year, the director was able to secure permission from the city council to construct a boardwalk. Meanwhile, several local lumberyards donated the necessary materials or provided them at cost, and the shop class from the local high school, with the help of a local construction firm, began building the sections of the boardwalk. Upon the completion of the boardwalk, the town had a dedication ceremony that received a great deal of local publicity.

Several surveys were conducted at the beach throughout the next summer to explore how citizens felt about the boardwalk. The results indicated that the boardwalk was used by over half of the people who visited the beach. It was most popular among elderly citizens and mothers who had young children in strollers. Thus, although Oxford's efforts were initially made to assist people with disabilities, many other community members were also able to benefit from the newly accessible beach.

EQUIPMENT OR MATERIAL ADAPTATIONS (ASSISTIVE TECHNOLOGY)

Modified or special pieces of equipment, both those that are commercially available and those that are homemade, are probably the most common adaptations in leisure activities. This type of adaptation is most often referred to as "assistive technology" and can involve something as simple as Velcro sewn to a glove to make gripping easier or as complex as a complete environmental control unit (ECU) or hardware system for controlling appliances throughout an entire home.

There are a number of excellent resources that describe how to either modify existing materials or how to purchase and use special pieces of equipment in recreation settings (Adams & McCubbin, 1991; Burkhart, 1980, 1982; Dixon, 1988; Glennen & Church, 1992; Musselwhite, 1986). Periodicals such as *Parks & Recreation* and *Recreation: Access in the 90's*, both published by the National Recreation & Park Association, also contain helpful information on choosing, making, and buying assistive devices.

Gripping Gloves and Straps   Gripping gloves and straps are commercially available from a wide variety of sources. Some are all-purpose and can be found, for example, in occupational therapy catalogs. Others are activity specific and highly specialized; for example, there are gloves with special non-slip surfaces and special straps that assist the wearer in holding a tool such as a paddle, bat, or rake.

Built-Up Handles and Controllers   Handles and controls can often be "built up," or made bigger and easier to control, for people who have problems with grasping and dexterity. For example, hot glue can be applied to buttons on a tape recorder to make them easier to find and push. One advantage of hot glue is that it peels off relatively easily when it is no longer needed. Levers can also be used to control devices. In addition to the cost factor, another advantage of using built-up controls rather than special switches is that the device does not have to be internally altered in any fashion (this is especially important if it is under warranty). Paint brushes, pencils, and markers are examples of very thin tools that may need to be built up for people with difficulty grasping. Again, there are commercially available items (such as thick-handled paint brushes or paint-brush covers) listed in occupational therapy catalogs, but items such as pencil grippers (rubber triangles that fit over pencils), pipe insulation, and tape all work just as well, and at a fraction of the cost.

Switches   Numerous types of switches are commercially available in electronics stores such as Radio Shack and in a variety of catalogs. These can be connected to almost any device (e.g., toys, CD players) and can be modified to suit individual needs—for example, to be operated with a fist, foot, head, finger, or breath of air. Burkhart (1980, 1982) and Glennen and Church (1992) provide excellent advice on selecting and building inexpensive switches.

Dycem/Scoot Guard   Dycem and Scoot Guard, both typically available in hardware stores, are great for helping hold items stationary. For example, a piece of Dycem can be used to hold a cup of water still so that people who are only able to use one hand will be able to dip a paintbrush into it without having to hold it steady. Another adaptation might be to place a piece of Scoot Guard on a table to keep pens, pencils, beads, tiles, and other craft items from falling.

Velcro   Velcro, available in most sewing stores, can be very useful to people who have difficulty gripping recreational equipment. For example, if a person has difficulty holding a golf club, he or she might purchase an inexpensive pair of golf gloves; pieces of Velcro could then be sewn to each glove and attached (either with glue or self-stick backing) to the club in the proper positions.

Large Print, Braille, Audio Cassettes   All materials pertaining to the facility and activities should be available in large print and braille, as well as on audio cassette. This includes materials given out at the time of the activity, as well as brochures and advertisements. It is not enough to make materials available in only one of these forms (although one is better than none). The state or local office or commission for individuals with visual impairments should be able to assist in translating materials into braille. When putting materials onto cassette, they should be read in a clear speaking voice. In addition, difficult names (e.g., proper names, street names) should be spelled out. Finally, a facility needs to advertise the fact that materials are available in accessible formats; if people do not know that something is available, they will not be able to use it.

TDDs   Telecommunication devices for the deaf (TDDs) can be purchased and connected to any phone line. A TDD enables a person who is deaf to communicate on the telephone by typing and receiving typed messages. If your organization owns a TDD, it is important to make sure it is connected and that each staff member who might answer the telephone knows how to use it. Unfortunately, a TDD will frequently sit unused because no one at a facility knows how to operate it.

If you are not able to purchase a TDD, it is important to advertise that your organization can be reached through a relay operator, so that people with hearing impairments will know that they are welcome and encouraged at your facility. A relay operator acts as a translator between two people when one is speaking on the phone and the other is using a TDD. The operator will receive a typed message and relay it vocally; likewise, he or she will listen to a vocal message, type it, and send it to a person using a TDD. As each state has its own relay operators, you will need to call your local operator for the number. It is also recommended that you speak to the operator about how the system works before receiving your first call.

FM/Loop/Infrared Systems   There are several types of assistive listening systems that are especially useful in auditoriums, theaters, meeting rooms, and other spacious environments. When using an FM system, sound is fed through a microphone or existing PA system to an FM transmitter that relays the sound to individual receivers used by people with hearing impairments. An induction loop is a loop of wire that encircles the room and transmits the sound through magnetic signals. Infrared systems use light beams in the infrared range of the spectrum to carry sound to a special portable receiver worn by the listener. These systems can be used with existing amplification systems and are available through a variety of commercial dealers.

Other Adaptations for Hearing Difficulty   Just as it is important to offer materials in a variety of formats to people with visual impairments, it is also important to "translate" all spoken communication during an activity (e.g., instructions, discussion) into a variety of formats for people with hearing impairments. In addition, although it takes a great deal of training to become an interpreter, it would be helpful if staff members knew at least enough sign language to make an individual feel welcome. Interpreters can be expensive, but may be necessary in order for a person with a hearing impairment to fully participate in an activity. Once again, it is imperative that potential participants know that you are willing to be accommodating, but remember to always ask the participant him- or herself before making an accommodation.

ASL stands for American Sign Language, which is different from signed English in that it has a grammar and syntax of its own. ASL is the most commonly needed sign accommodation. Physically Signed English (PSE) is English signed into an individual's hand. This is typically used by people who are both hearing and visually impaired. CART stands for computer assisted real time reporting and basically consists of a stenographer who types what is being said into a computer and a program that translates the stenographer's shorthand into standard English, which can then be read by a person with a hearing impairment who cannot understand ASL.

Finally, for people with difficulty hearing, it is always helpful to have written materials (e.g., the instructions for a game or activity) on hand.

Verbal Instruction and Demonstration   It is always helpful to not only give verbal instructions for an activity, but to demonstrate the activity several times as well. In this manner, people who do not understand the instructions will know what is expected of them. In addition, an individual may want to observe an activity for a time before participating so that they can fully understand each step.

PROCEDURAL ADAPTATIONS

Sometimes an activity can be made more accessible by actually altering the manner in which the activity proceeds rather than by making physical changes to the environment or materials. Most activity adaptations can be categorized into two groups (Moon & Bunker, 1987; Rynders & Schleien, 1991): 1) rule or procedural changes, and 2) changes in skill sequence. Both types of change are described briefly below. A number of sources provide more detailed information on making activity adaptations, including Adams and McCubbin (1991), Dixon (1988), Jansma, Decker, McCubbin, Combs, and Ersing (1986), Rynders and Schleien (1991), Wehman and Schleien (1981), and Winnick (1990).

Rule Modifications

The intricate rules or specific procedures that are part of some recreational activities can prohibit many people with disabilities from participating. Often, however, rules can be changed or dropped altogether without changing the purpose or flow of the activity. For example, a participant who uses a wheelchair could be allowed to hit or throw a ball rather than kicking it. For another participant, two-handed dribbling could be allowed in basketball, or, in pool, all balls could be considered fair shots for a player who has trouble discriminating which ball to hit. During card games, a player who cannot discriminate between cards or who cannot understand the rules could have a silent partner to help him or her make decisions. As long as all participants can agree on rule changes for individuals or groups of participants during an activity, any number or variety of alterations can be made.

Rule Modifications—A Case Study

Katie is a 9-year-old with Down syndrome who has entered an inclusive community summer camp in her town. The emphasis at this camp is on arts, crafts, and sports. The sports include swimming, volleyball, kickball, softball, rowing/canoeing, and personal aerobics training.

Katie loves sports, but her level of activity is restricted because of a heart condition. She is not allowed to run or walk for long distances or participate for more than 10 minutes in any aerobic activity unless supervised by a parent or by medical personnel. Katie really wanted to swim, canoe, and play volleyball, softball, and kickball at camp, so her parents and head counselor decided to implement some activity adaptations that were discussed with all counselors and activity supervisors. On the first day of camp, all participants were told how the adaptations would be implemented, and volunteer partners were recruited. Nearly all the campers in Katie's group wanted to participate as partners, so a rotation system was set up to allow each of them to assist Katie at least once every day.

Some of the adaptations included the use of pinch runners for softball and kickball and a substitute for volleyball who rotated in every 10 minutes to allow Katie a break. No restrictions were necessary for swimming, except in the case of an occasional race. For these events, a number of campers, including Katie, were allowed to sign up as timers and starters rather than racers. These campers were then given the option of participating in a synchronized swim session in which the emphasis was on movement and stroke patterns rather than competitive racing. As it turned out, many of the campers preferred this class over the races, and what began as an alternative for Katie became a popular option among many other campers during swim periods.

Canoeing turned out to not be a problem for Katie. In reality, none of the campers had enough experience or strength to paddle for long periods, so the instructor devised a system in which two campers and a counselor manned each canoe, allowing the counselor to maneuver the boat as necessary. The emphasis was placed on technique and safety practices for all campers.

Skill-Sequence Modifications

Most of us learn a new recreational activity by breaking it down into its component parts and then learning these steps in some sort of sequential order (Rynders & Schleien, 1991). By analyzing the component steps or sequence of skills involved in an activity, one can determine the actual requirements of participation and the specific places where modifications can be made.

This type of analysis is particularly helpful in determining where and when persons with disabilities may need support from other participants. Having some people partially participate in certain areas of an activity is very appropriate in almost any recreational endeavor, as long as all of the participants understand why changes are being made. Some common skill-sequence adaptations include having a person pick up a bowling ball and hand it to a bowler with a disability, having someone hold a camera or push the button to photograph a shot that is set up by a person with a disability, and having a cooking partner to help stir, pour, or measure ingredients during a cooking class. The most important point is that the person with the disability should do as much as possible independently, but have assistance available when it's needed. Usually, a group of participants can come up with creative and unintrusive ways to enable someone to partially participate, and trial and error in learning how to do this should be encouraged.

CHOOSING SPECIFIC ADAPTATIONS

Several experts have provided guidelines for modifying recreation activities. Kennedy, Smith, and Austin (1991) provide a four-point guide: 1) change the outcome of the activity as little as possible; 2) involve all participants in the selection of adaptations; 3) try not to invent separate areas or parts of an activity that segregate participants; and 4) try to use the same rules for everyone, to the greatest extent possible. Rynders and Schleien (1991) provide five guidelines: 1) adapt only when necessary; 2) try to adapt only temporarily if a participant can eventually develop new skills; 3) adapt only on an individual basis; 4) adapt for normalization, so that the person does not stand out; and 5) make adaptations that are transferrable across settings and are cost efficient.

Although all adaptations must be made on an individual basis according to an analysis of the skills involved in an activity and the strengths and weaknesses of a specific participant, there are some more-general modifications that usually improve accessibility for all people with particular types of disabilities. These accommodations, outlined in Table 1 can be easily implemented in any facility and will help any site meet ADA accessibility requirements.

RESOURCES FOR DETERMINING ACCESSIBILITY AND ADAPTATIONS

Understanding accessibility requirements and then making the modifications necessary to ensure accessibility is a complicated and time-consuming process, and no single individual or agency is equipped to handle this type of decision making alone. Therefore, it is crucial that recreation providers seek assistance from a variety of sources. Understanding laws such as the ADA and the Tech Act (see Epstein, McGovern, & Moon, chap. 5, this volume) are also crucial.

The passage of the Tech Act has created new networks of assistance across the country. For example, Title I of the law awards grants of approximately $500,000 annually for up to 3 years to those states that qualify. The funds must be used to

Table 1. General adaptations for specific disabilities

Ambulation difficulty	Adequate paving
	Curbcuts
	Barrier-free pathways and halls
	Handrails
	Wide doorways
Grasping difficulty	Lever doorknobs
	Gripping gloves and straps
	Built-up handles
	Dycem/Scoot Guard
	Velcro
Low vision	Barrier-free pathways and halls
	Controlled noise levels
	Contrasting colors
	Large print, braille, cassette recordings
	Sighted guides
Hearing difficulty	TDDs
	FM units/loop systems
	ASL, PSE, CART, verbal assistance
	Written materials
Cognitive difference	Verbal instruction and demonstration
	Pictorial signs
	Rule adaptation
	Skill-sequence modification
	Partial participation

develop a statewide system of assistive technology services. Forty-two states had received funding as of 1993, and it is hoped that all 50 states will be funded by 1995.

RESNA, a multidisciplinary association for the advancement of rehabilitation and assistive technologies, provides technical assistance to all states funded under the Tech Act. RESNA can provide information on assistive technology and can refer individuals to local resources.

There are also a number of organizations that specialize in providing recreation experiences for people with disabilities. Most can provide the locations of accessible facilities for specific activities, as well as the names and addresses of local teams, organizations, and facilitators/advocates. Some organizations, such as *Wilderness Inquiry*, provide a variety of outdoor activities—canoeing, kayak touring, rafting, and dog sledding—to groups of varying skill levels. Regarding equipment, before purchasing commercially available materials, it is important to consider that these may not be the most normalized, temporary, or cost-effective adaptation. Get advice from groups such as RESNA or from individuals with disabilities and consult with professionals such as Park and Recreation personnel. Large, complex, and expensive adapted equipment may actually segregate participants with disabilities rather than enhance their inclusion in typical recreation activities.

~Appendix~

Community Access Survey

The survey that follows was developed by the chapter authors based on criteria established in the ADA; it was designed to be administered relatively quickly in order to determine whether a facility or program is accessible to potential participants with disabilities.

COMMUNITY ACCESS SURVEY

Name of Organization/Facility _____

Address _____

Telephone Number (Voice) _____ (TDD) _____

A. TRANSPORTATION	YES	NO
1. Accessible public transportation to organization/facility	☐	☐
2. Drop off directly in front of the organization/facility entrance	☐	☐
3. Organization/facility provides accessible transportation	☐	☐

Comments _____
_____

B. PARKING	YES	NO
1. Signage at entrance of lot directs toward accessible parking	☐	☐
2. Zoned area designated for drop-off/pick-up adjacent or near curbcut &/or accessible entranceway	☐	☐
3. HP space closest to accessible entrance	☐	☐
4. Parking spaces are at least 96" wide	☐	☐
5. Symbol of accessibility visible at each space	☐	☐

Comments _____
_____

C. PATHWAYS (Outdoors)	YES	NO
1. Pathways minimum width of 36" for 1 wheelchair or 60" for 2 wheelchairs	☐	☐
2. Pathway surface evenly paved & without interruption	☐	☐
3. Curbcuts located at the corner of each intersection	☐	☐
4. Curbcuts maximum 1" incline to 8" of length	☐	☐
5. Signage to areas of building in words	☐	☐
6. Signage to areas of building in symbols	☐	☐

	YES	NO
7. Signage to areas of building is tactile	☐	☐
8. Signage to areas of building is high contrast	☐	☐

Comments _____
_____

D. General Organizational Structure

	YES	NO
1. Staff with training regarding disabilities are available	☐	☐
2. Specific rules limit access (e.g., no dogs)	☐	☐
3. Staff available to assist with directions & questions	☐	☐
4. Staff available to assist with transfers	☐	☐
5. Staff available to assist with sign language interpretation	☐	☐
6. Adaptive equipment available on premises	☐	☐
7. Inclusive programming available	☐	☐
8. Specialized programming available	☐	☐

Comments _____
_____

E. Doors (*Public entrances are those which are not loading or services entrances*)

	YES	NO
1. At least one public entrance must be accessible	☐	☐
2. Accessible primary entrance width of 32" with door open 90 degrees	☐	☐
3. Distance between entrances no more than 3-minute walk for nondisabled person	☐	☐
4. Automatic opening doors in entranceway	☐	☐
5. Automatic opening doors in corridors	☐	☐
6. Automatic opening doors in rooms	☐	☐
7. Operating mechanism for doors is automatic	☐	☐

	YES	NO
8. Operating mechanism for automatic doors is user initiated	☐	☐
9. Operating mechanism for automatic doors is marked	☐	☐
10. Doors close slowly (minimum of 3 seconds)	☐	☐
11. Doors to individual areas minimum width of 32"	☐	☐
12. Thresholds do not exceed 3/4" for exterior sliding doors or 1/2" for all other doors	☐	☐
13. Door hardware mounted no higher than 48" above floor	☐	☐
14. Doors operable with one hand & do not require tight grasp	☐	☐
15. Signage for rooms is in words	☐	☐
16. Signage for rooms is in symbols	☐	☐
17. Signage for rooms is tactile	☐	☐
18. Signage for rooms is high contrast	☐	☐

Comments _____
_____

	YES	NO
F. RAMPS/LIFTS/STAIRS (Inside & Out)		
1. Slip resistant ramps maximum 12" incline to 12' length	☐	☐
2. Ramps have handrails on both sides extending 12" beyond the top & bottom of ramp	☐	☐
3. Ramp made of solid material with a minimum width of 36" measured at handrails	☐	☐
4. Ramps access same areas as stairs & are usable by standard & scooter (three wheel) style wheelchairs	☐	☐
5. Ramps have level areas to stop & rest at least every 30'	☐	☐
6. Stairs have solid risers	☐	☐
7. Stairs have handrails	☐	☐
8. Stairs have nosings that project no more than 1 1/2"	☐	☐

	YES	NO
9.Mechanical lift available	☐	☐
10.Lift operated by user	☐	☐
11.Lift operated by user after receiving a key from someone else	☐	☐
12.Lift operated by staff	☐	☐
13.Facility staff trained to operate lift	☐	☐

Comments _____
_____

	YES	NO
G. ELEVATORS *(required for buildings that exceed 3 stories or that exceed 3000 sq" per story unless it is shopping mall or office of health care provider)*		
1. Elevator(s) accesses same area(s) as steps & is used for passengers only	☐	☐
2. Elevator(s) accesses same area(s) as steps & is used for freight	☐	☐
3. Elevator(s) is self-operated	☐	☐
4. Height between car & floor landing is no greater than 1/2"	☐	☐
5. Elevator door opening minimum of 36"	☐	☐
6. Doors close slowly (minimum of 5 seconds)	☐	☐
7. Door equipped with electronic eye	☐	☐
8. Cab size minimum of 54" x 68"	☐	☐
9. Operating buttons no higher than 48"	☐	☐
10.Signage for floors & directional markings on operating panel are tactile	☐	☐
11.Audible & visable signals in elevator cab at each floor	☐	☐
12.Signage for floor location at each landing is tactile	☐	☐
13.Floor identification at the rear of each cab (e.g., mirror)	☐	☐
14.Emergency controls & telephone at bottom of operating panel	☐	☐

	YES	NO
15. Buttons touch sensitive & easy to push	☐	☐
16. Railing available for support	☐	☐

Comments _____
_____

H. CORRIDORS/LOBBIES	YES	NO
1. Minimum width for wheelchairs to pass is 60"	☐	☐
2. Turning radius of 60" x 60" (to allow 360 degree turn in wheelchair)	☐	☐
3. Corridors free of obstructions with 80" clear headroom	☐	☐
4. Permanent fixtures mounted on wall project maximum of 4"	☐	☐
5. Directory of building is in words	☐	☐
6. Directory of building is in symbols	☐	☐
7. Directory of building is tactile	☐	☐
8. Directory of building is high contrast	☐	☐
9. Corridors brightly lit	☐	☐
10. Signage for accessible bathrooms	☐	☐
11. Signage for accessible bathrooms located with signage for inaccessible bathroom	☐	☐
12. Signage for telephones	☐	☐
13. Signage for exits	☐	☐
14. Carpeted surface securely attached & not wrinkled	☐	☐
15. Surfaces stable, firm, & slip resistant	☐	☐
16. Available rest areas along a 50' or longer hallway	☐	☐
17. Accessible drinking fountain maximum of 27" high with knee space underneath; spout no higher than 36"	☐	☐

	YES	NO
18. Drinking fountain operable with closed fist	☐	☐
19. Vending machine controls maximum height of 48" & minimum of 15" for forward reach	☐	☐
20. Vending machine controls operable with closed fist	☐	☐
21. Vending machine selections involve number identification and/or matching & knowledge of coin combinations	☐	☐
22. Telephone area maximum height of 48" & minimum of 15" for forward reach	☐	☐
23. Amplification system identified & available for telephones	☐	☐

Comments _____
_____

I. MEETING SPACES

	YES	NO
1. Spaces are all on same floor	☐	☐
2. Spaces are on different floors	☐	☐
3. Spaces are accessible (e.g., doors, corridors)	☐	☐
4. Facility will modify space for accessibility if requested	☐	☐
5. Spaces clean & free of debris	☐	☐
6. Spaces brightly lit	☐	☐
7. High noise level while activity occurs	☐	☐
8. Variable noise level while activity occurs	☐	☐
9. Large open areas	☐	☐
10. Small defined areas	☐	☐
11. Spaces adjacent to accessible bathroom	☐	☐
12. Spaces not adjacent to accessible bathroom but route to bathroom no more than 3-minute walk for nondisabled person	☐	☐

J. BATHROOMS	YES	NO
1. Accessible men's room available	☐	☐
2. Accessible women's room available	☐	☐
3. Accessible unisex bathroom available	☐	☐
4. Signage on outside door & individual stalls is in words	☐	☐
5. Signage on outside door & individual stalls is in symbols	☐	☐
6. Signage on outside door & individual stalls is tactile	☐	☐
7. Signage on outside door & individual stalls is in high contrast	☐	☐
8. All doors minimum width of 32"	☐	☐
9. All doors operable with closed fist	☐	☐
10. Bathroom area free of obstruction & debris	☐	☐
11. Bathroom area has minimum turning space of 60" x 60" on the diagonal	☐	☐
12. Stall doors swing out	☐	☐
13. Stall doors open easily	☐	☐
14. Stall doors operable with closed fist	☐	☐
15. Accessible sink 34" high with knee space minimum of 30" wide, 29" high, & 19" deep	☐	☐
16. Accessible sink operable with closed fist	☐	☐
17. Bottom of mirror maximum height of 40" or tilted	☐	☐
18. All dispensers maximum height of 40"	☐	☐
19. All dispensers operable with closed fist	☐	☐
20. Accessible urinal rim maximum height 17"	☐	☐
21. Accessible toilet stall is a minimum width of 60" & minimum depth of 56" (wall of stall to door)	☐	☐
22. Top of toilet seat is 17" - 19" high	☐	☐

	YES	NO
23. Two grab bars mounted parallel to floor & 33" - 36" above floor	☐	☐
24. Vending machine controls are maximum height of 48" & minimum of 15" for forward reach	☐	☐
25. Vending machine controls operable with closed fist	☐	☐
26. Vending machine selections involve number identification, and/or matching	☐	☐
27. Vending machine involves knowledge of coin combinations	☐	☐
28. Light switch maximum height of 48" & minimum of 15" for forward reach	☐	☐
29. Light switch operable with closed fist	☐	☐

Comments _____
_____

K. LIBRARIES

	YES	NO
1. Minimum aisle width 36"	☐	☐
2. Check-out counter is maximum height of 36"	☐	☐
3. Card catalogs are maximum height of 54" & a minimum height of 18"	☐	☐
4. Computer system available for book availability/location system	☐	☐
5. Stacks of books/book shelves maximum height of 54"	☐	☐
6. Staff available for book retrieval/general assistance	☐	☐
7. Accessible quiet space available free of distractions	☐	☐
8. Sign language interpreters available	☐	☐

L. PLACES OF ASSEMBLY

	YES	NO
1. Ticket window maximum height of 36"	☐	☐
2. Concession stand maximum height of 36"	☐	☐

	YES	NO
3. Reserved seating for people who are blind/visually impaired & deaf/hard of hearing; number of reserved seats _____	☐	☐
4. Reserved seating available for nondisabled friends in these areas: number of reserved seats _____	☐	☐
5. Minimum aisle width of 32"	☐	☐
6. Turning radius at top & bottom of aisles 60" x 60"	☐	☐
7. Wheelchair accessible spectator seats available & distributed among different prices & areas of facility; number of reserved seats _____	☐	☐
8. Seating available for nondisabled friends in these areas	☐	☐
9. Listening system for people who are hard of hearing	☐	☐
10. Listening system can be used with a variety of hearing aids	☐	☐
11. Sign language interpreters available	☐	☐

Comments _____
_____

M. SWIMMING POOLS	YES	NO
1. Minimum 48" wide path of travel around pool	☐	☐
2. Slip resistant surface around pool	☐	☐
3. Access into pool is wide ramp with handrails	☐	☐
4. Access into pool is lifting device	☐	☐
5. Access into pool is steps only	☐	☐
6. Lifeguards on duty	☐	☐
7. Number of lifeguards on duty _____		
8. Signage for different water levels is made very clear	☐	☐
9. Shower stalls minimum 36" x 36" with curb maximum 1/2"	☐	☐
10. Shower stalls minimum 30" x 60", no curbs	☐	☐

	YES	NO
11. Shower has single lever control operable with closed fist	☐	☐
12. Shower head on slide bar with hose	☐	☐
13. Shower stall has two grab bars on wall 33"- 36" high	☐	☐
14. Shower has padded, hinged seat securely attached	☐	☐
15. Top of shower seat 18" high	☐	☐
16. Locker rooms minimum aisle width of 42"	☐	☐
17. Locker rooms have accessible bathrooms	☐	☐
18. Dressing cubicles 60" x 72" with an opening of 32"	☐	☐
19. Dressing cubicle opening is curtain or outswinging door	☐	☐
20. Sign language interpreters available	☐	☐

Comments _____
_____

N. SAFETY/EMERGENCY ACCOMMODATIONS

	YES	NO
1. Emergency/fire evacuation procedures exist	☐	☐
2. Facility security visible & adequate	☐	☐
3. Nurse on-site full time	☐	☐
4. Nurse on-site part time	☐	☐
5. Fire alarm maximum of 54" above floor	☐	☐
6. Fire alarm instructions are presented in words, symbols, tactile, & in high contrast	☐	☐
7. Fire alarm can be operated with closed fist	☐	☐
8. Audible warning signals	☐	☐
9. Visual warning signals	☐	☐

Comments _____
_____

REFERENCES

Adams, R., & McCubbin, J. (1991). *Games, sports, and exercise for the physically disabled.* Philadelphia: Lea & Febiger.

Americans with Disabilities Act of 1990 (ADA), P.L. 101-336. (July 26, 1990). 42, U.S.C. 12101 et seq: *U.S. Statutes at Large, 104,* 327–378.

Burkhart, L. (1980). *Homemade battery powered toys and educational devices for severely handicapped children.* College Park, MD: Author.

Burkhart, L. (1982). *More homemade battery devices for severely handicapped children with suggested activities.* College Park, MD: Author.

Dixon, J. (1988). *Adapting activities for therapeutic recreation service: Concepts and applications.* San Diego: State University Press.

Glennen, S., & Church, G. (1992). Adaptive toys and environmental controls. In G. Church & S. Glennen (Eds.), *The handbook of assistive technology* (pp. 173–205). San Diego: Singular Publishing Group, Inc.

Jansma, P., Decker, J., McCubbin, J., Combs, C., & Ersing, W. (1986). Adapted equipment for improving the fitness of severely retarded adults. *American Corrective Therapy Journal, 40*(6), 136–141.

Kennedy, D., Smith, R., & Austin, D. (1991). *Special recreation opportunities for persons with disabilities.* Dubuque, IA: William C. Brown Publishers.

Moon, M.S., & Bunker, L. (1987). Recreation and motor skills programming. In M. Snell (Ed.), *Systematic instruction of the moderately and severely handicapped* (pp. 214–244). Columbus, OH: Charles E. Merrill.

Musselwhite, C. (1986). *Adaptive play for special needs children.* San Diego: College-Hill Press.

Rynders, J., & Schleien, S. (1991). *Together successfully: Creating recreational and educational programs that integrate people with and without disabilities.* Arlington, TX: The Association for Retarded Citizens of the United States.

Technology-Related Assistance for Individuals with Disabilities Act of 1988, PL 100-407. (July 28, 1988). Title 29, U.S.C. 2201 et seq: *U.S. Statutes at Large, 102,* 1044–1065.

Wehman, P., & Schleien, S. (1981). *Leisure programs for handicapped persons: Adaptations, techniques, and curriculum.* Baltimore: University Park Press.

Winnick, J.P. (Ed.). (1990). *Adapted physical education and sport.* Champaign, IL: Human Kinetics Books

~SECTION THREE~

AGES AND SETTINGS
INCLUSION ACROSS THE LIFE SPAN

The third section of this book comprises three chapters devoted to specific activities that can be made inclusive for preschoolers, children, teenagers, and adults. Chapter Seven shows how families, child care providers, and infant and preschool educators can encourage inclusive play by introducing young children to age-appropriate commercially available toys. Chapter Eight targets the school-age youngster or teen and provides guidelines for making physical education classes inclusive, as this is the setting in which members of this age group most often participate in sports, dance, and individual fitness programs. Chapter Nine addresses the issue of getting adults with developmental disabilities involved in community-based leisure pursuits.

~seven~

Encouraging Play Among Children with Disabilities with Commercially Available Toys

Frances L. Kohl and Paula J. Beckman

"Play can provide a rich variety of experience and at the same time is immediately satisfying and enjoyable in itself—thus furnishing the child's immediate incentive for carrying out the exploration, experimentation, and skill learning involved in play" (Yawkey & Pellegrini, 1984, p. 274). For many years now, researchers have studied the value of play for young children. Others have referred to play as the work of all children. However, some young children with disabilities are at a distinct disadvantage when they are presented with toys and expected to play appropriately with them (Beckman & Kohl, 1984; Hendrickson, Tremblay, Strain, & Shores, 1981; Musselwhite, 1986; Quilitch, Christopherson, & Risley, 1973). Due to physical, intellectual, sensory, and/or emotional impairments, some children's play skills may be delayed. In such cases, assistance will most likely be necessary in order to facilitate the development of play and the ability to use toys functionally and creatively.

Appropriately selected toys can foster both the intellectual and physical growth of a child (Feeney & Magarick, 1984) and toy play can foster or strengthen a child's social development, especially in the area of interactions with peers and friends. This chapter will present information for parents, grandparents, siblings, care providers, and recreation professionals on selecting appropriate toys, facilitating toy play, and encouraging social interactions between young children with and without disabilities.

Specifically, the following information will be presented: 1) suggestions for selecting toys and encouraging the development of play skills; 2) suggestions for facilitating social interactions between peers with and without disabilities through the use of toys; 3) safety factors to be considered when selecting and purchasing toys; 4) a list of toys and activities that are appropriate for young children with and without disabilities; 5) a list of commercially available, age-appropriate, popular toys; and 6) a list of toy companies to contact for specific merchandise information, agencies and associations that focus on toy safety, and resources for acquiring or making adaptive toys.

SUGGESTIONS FOR SELECTING TOYS AND TEACHING PLAY SKILLS

The following suggestions for selecting appropriate toys and fostering play skills among children who have disabilities are presented as ideas to be considered for use with children between birth and about 8 years of age. The child's age and interests, as well as the type and degree of disability, must be considered when selecting appropriate play materials.

Consider the Purpose of the Toy

Each toy has one or more purposes that vary in their degrees of educational and social merit. When selecting toys, consider the type of activities that you wish to encourage your child, student, or camper to take part in and what you want him or her to learn from the experience. If color recognition is the theme, select toys or activities that involve color identification, such as art projects with multicolored crayons and yarns or a game of Candyland (in which players follow a color-coded road to reach the candy castle). If socialization with other children is the goal, select toys or activities that promote social interactions between two or more youngsters, such as puppets, T-ball (an adapted baseball game in which the ball is placed on a holder in front of the batter to eliminate pitching), play telephones, dress-up, or housekeeping. Chapter 4 provides many more suggestions for encouraging interpersonal interactions. The development of concepts such as one-to-one correspondence can be encouraged by providing such prompts as "Give everyone a cup" or "I think your baby needs a cookie too." For imaginative play, select figurines based on movie or television characters and encourage each child to develop his or her own story lines, to act out different roles, or to imitate parts of his or her favorite stories.

We recommend that you focus on more than one skill at a time when playing with any child. This is important for several reasons. First, children do not learn skills individually; they practice and learn different skills in combination with one another. Second, skill acquisition will be more efficient if you focus on more than one play skill at a time. For example, while playing with a Little People® Farm, a child could be learning the names of the animals (practicing verbal labels), moving the family members into and out of vehicles (refining pincer grasp), and also making a square-shaped pen with the pieces of fencing (constructing shapes). Children can also be encouraged to practice the same or similar skills across play with different toys in order to promote skill transfer. For example, toddlers learn about spatial relationship among objects by spending time putting objects in containers and taking them out again. Parents can encourage their child to move plastic containers into and out of their lower cabinets, to put clothes pins into and out of milk containers, or to move blocks into and out of bowls. These different activities provide the child with numerous opportunities to practice the same skill.

If one is unsure of what toys are appropriate for specific educational or social activities, various sources of assistance are available. For example, you can ask an experienced parent, neighbor, recreational specialist, or teacher for advice; these individuals are usually happy to be of help. One can also contact the consumer affairs office of the toy manufacturer; most large toy companies in the United States have employees who are eager to assist consumers in the safe use of their products. A list of popular toy manufacturers is provided at the end of this chapter.

Foster Longitudinal Toy Use

A toy can often be used for different kinds of activities to teach different skills across time. For example, for very young children, LEGOs®, Lincoln Logs, wooden blocks, or Wee Waffle® Blocks can first be introduced to help in the development of fine motor skills such as grasping and stacking, or of color recognition, or of understanding spatial concepts such as *in front of, behind,* or *next to.* As children grow, these same toys can be used to construct sophisticated structures; older children can build whole towns and learn about community living concepts such as community helpers and different types of transportation. Kitchen utensils can be used in similar longitudinal ways. Very young children may use silverware in a functional manner—stirring a spoon in a bowl, drinking from a toy tea cup, or feeding a doll with a spoon. As children grow older, these same materials can be used to encourage a variety of different imaginative play skills and functional domestic skills through play activities such as table setting, acting out a tea party, and cleaning up by washing and drying the dishes and putting items away in the appropriate places.

Parents in particular will want to encourage functional object use as their children grow. Functional object use means using an object in a practical way—drawing with a crayon, throwing a ball, or stacking blocks on top of each other. As your child grows older and learns to use objects or toys in meaningful ways, he or she will, perhaps with assistance, begin to use substitute objects to create play or pretend situations. Examples of this include using a fork as an imaginary drawing utensil, a block as a car, or a spoon and cup as a drum. These actions are referred to as object substitutions and should be encouraged, because they show that the child is being creative in toy selection and play.

Build in Choices

Frequently, children with disabilities are unintentionally denied the opportunity to make choices based on their own preferences (Guess, Benson, & Siegel-Causey, 1985). Adults are often eager for a particular child to learn a specific concept or to acquire a certain skill, causing them to unintentionally overlook a child's own likes and dislikes. Adults should allow children to make choices regarding the types of toys they would like to play with and the activities that they would like to participate in. The ability to make choices and have them respected is one of the keys to developing independence and self-awareness.

Display two to four toys on the floor or on a tabletop so that a selection can be made easily. If the child is nonverbal, encourage an alternative response such as a head nod, finger point, or directed eye gaze. Ask the child which toys he or she would like to play with now. You can also place the child's toys in open view on shelves or in large, clear plastic containers so he or she can visually scan the toy selections and make a choice. If the child is unable to reach for a desired toy, then before each play opportunity, present him or her with a choice such as "Do you want to play with the bristle blocks or the train set?" while showing the child each toy. The more items a child has to choose from, the more likely it is that he or she will find a preferred toy and have a more enjoyable and successful play experience.

Encourage Active Participation

For parents, teachers, care providers, and recreational facilitators for young children with and without disabilities, active participation in and supervision of children's play is mandatory. Select and oversee activities that encourage a child to manipulate (e.g., touch, turn, smell, hold, pound, and sometimes taste or throw) toys as actively and independently as possible. Young children learn more efficiently by actively manipulating toys in their environment than they do through passive observation (Abrams & Kauffman, 1990; Beckman, Robinson, Jackson, & Rosenberg, 1986).

Also, give children every opportunity to discover new ways to interact with a toy. Children initially spend time studying a new toy; after exploration, however, children become more imaginative and creative in the use of their toys. Another very helpful technique is to let another child, who is either older or has more experience with a particular toy, assist the child with disabilities in playing with the toy. Also, rather than choosing a complicated toy that another person will end up manipulating, select toys that children can use on their own or with assistance from friends, siblings, classmates, or parents. Another suggestion is to model the appropriate play skill with the toy and then have the child imitate the action. Once again, nondisabled peers without disabilities make terrific models. Remember to provide help only when it is necessary. Above all, never exclude a child from participating just because of a disability. Every child is capable of learning play skills that will allow him or her to participate to some degree in play activities (Baumgart et al., 1982).

Purchase Age-Appropriate and Interesting Toys

Choose toys that appeal to children, rather than those that appeal to adults. A parent may find an intricately hand-carved wooden train delightful, but if it doesn't appeal to the child, he or she won't be very likely to play with it. Ask your child's peers what the most popular and fun toys are. If your child is playing with a toy that other children also enjoy, it may encourage friends to join him or her in play, providing opportunities for learning, interaction, and friendship. Tie-ins with popular television shows and movies increase children's interest in particular toys, as well as influencing their social play and peer acceptance. Toy preferences will change with age, gender, sex, number of siblings, and life experiences. Chapter 3 presents a peer interest survey that identifies popular recreation possibilities across a variety of age groups.

Remember that you don't have to spend a lot of money on toys; there are many items around the home that your child will enjoy playing with. In fact, parents frequently comment that at birthdays or holidays, their young child enjoys playing with the paper wrappings more than the gifts inside. Recreational personnel may request that parents donate items that can be used for many different play activities. Old clothes, hats, shoes, boots, and other apparel are mandatory for playing dress-up. Old baby clothes can be used for dolls. Empty food cartons can be used to stock a toy kitchen. Paper, magazines, and cards can be recycled for art projects.

Expect Play Periods of Realistic Length

Young children's play sessions are usually brief; the younger the child, the shorter the play period. You shouldn't expect a child to play with one toy or participate in an activity for an extended period of time, or to engage in several consecutive activities for a total of more than 20 or 30 minutes. The length of any given play session will depend on the activity, the age of the child, and the other individuals involved.

Instill a Sense of Toy Responsibility

Selecting appropriate toys and supervising play are important, but they are not the only factors that adults need to consider for fun and safe play. Children need to be taught to take responsibility for their toys by taking care of them. Specifically, children should be taught to store their toys properly in designated areas when they are finished with them; they need to be taught that picking up their toys may prevent them from being broken, lost, or stolen, as well as preventing younger siblings or classmates from injuring themselves. Toy responsibility can be started at a very early age and increased as children grow older.

SUGGESTIONS FOR FACILITATING SOCIAL INTERACTIONS

Frequently, children with disabilities need to be taught how to interact with their peers in play situations (Gaylord-Ross, 1989; Kohl & Beckman, 1990; Kohl, Moses, & Stettner-Eaton, 1984; Stainback, Stainback, & Forest, 1989). The following strategies may facilitate interactions between a child with disabilities and his or her peers in order to increase toy play and help the child develop social skills and friendships.

Inform Peers about the Child's Disabilities

To encourage social interactions between a child with disabilities and his or her peers, spend some time discussing the child's disability with playmates. For example, explain why he or she uses a wheelchair, why he or she signs rather than talks, or even why he or she may have trouble putting a puzzle together. Children are naturally curious and will want to ask questions; encourage them to do so and answer them as simply and honestly as possible. You may even suggest some books about children with disabilities for peers to read. It is important to educate all children about disabilities, because it encourages tolerance and understanding of individual differences, as well as creating more opportunities for friendship. There are several excellent references that provide information on individual similarities and differences, integration strategies for school-age children, and social skill development; readers are referred to Gaylord-Ross (1989); Sailor et al. (1989); and Stainback et al. (1989).

Discuss Ways to Communicate with a Child Who Has a Speech-Language Disability

If a child has a speech-language disability, it is imperative to inform his or her peers about the way in which he or she communicates, whether it be through sign language, communication aids, head nods, or difficult-to-understand speech. Explain why the child has difficulty speaking or why a different method of communication must be used. Be sure that children can communicate with each other, or the play situation may falter. Parents or counselors may provide relevant books on communication, give directions on how to use an electric speaking device, teach some manual signs, and/or construct a manual-sign dictionary for each of the child's peers. Select signs, words, or symbols for things such as well-liked play activities, specific toys, requests (e.g., want more, let's do it again), and social amenities (e.g., please, thank you) that can serve as the basis for conversational exchanges.

Talk about Likes and Dislikes

Discuss the likes and dislikes of your child with his or her peers in order to assemble a mutually agreed-upon selection of toys and play activities. Select toys or activities that are preferred by all parties and that will contribute to more exciting and longer play experiences as well as promote friendships.

Size of the Group

One factor that seems to influence the social play of young children with disabilities is the size of the play group. In general, toddlers interact more with peers when they are in groups of two or three than they do in larger groups. If you find that a child is not interacting in large groups, try pairing the child with another and seeing how the two of them play together. In addition, give the child experience with peers whose play skills vary in sophistication. More-sophisticated partners provide role models for imitation, communication, and sharing; less sophisticated peers allow your child to lead and direct play, problem solve, and develop a sense of confidence.

Types of Toys

Evidence suggests that the type of toys made available to young children with disabilities will influence the way in which they interact with their peers (Beckman & Kohl, 1984; Quilitch et al. 1973). Certain toys, such as balls, puppets, and board games, encourage play with others, while others, such as books and crayons, promote solitary or parallel play. To facilitate socialization, counselors or teachers should generate goals once social toys or activities have been selected (e.g., while playing with blocks, the children could be asked to build a large tower; while playing with puppets, they could be encouraged to act out *The Three Little Pigs*). These goals help direct social play and provide opportunities for reciprocal interactions.

SAFETY FACTORS TO BE CONSIDERED IN SELECTING TOYS

Safety is the most important factor to consider when selecting and purchasing toys, and adults need to know all the facts when purchasing play items. Practically every toy manufacturer in the United States adheres to voluntary product safety standards developed by the Toy Manufacturers of America (TMA), a national trade organization. The TMA works very closely with the United States Consumer Product Safety Commission to develop safety testing procedures and to monitor toys that are currently on the market. Though the manufacturers' guidelines are carefully regulated, parents and adults who work with children, including children with disabilities, must be aware of additional safety factors to their well-being. Specifically, according to the Toy Manufacturers of America (1990), adults should adhere to the following suggestions:

Pay attention to recommended-age labeling; never give a child under 3 years of age toys recommended for older children. Moreover, this warning needs to be extended for children who continue to place objects into their mouth beyond 3 years of age.

Look for warnings and other safety messages on the toy's packaging and in the directions; read and adhere to them carefully.

Consider the possibility of younger siblings or classmates gaining access to a toy that could be potentially dangerous for a very young child.

When buying for children under the age of 3 (or who continue to put objects into their mouths beyond that age), avoid toys with small parts that could be swallowed, as well as those with sharp points or edges that could be dangerous.

Check for sturdy, well-sewn seams on stuffed animals and cloth dolls; be certain that eyes and noses on these items are securely fastened and cannot be pulled off or bitten apart. If necessary, remove small parts like buttons or eyes in order to eliminate risks.

Electric toys with heating elements are appropriate for children over 8 years of age, but only with adult supervision.

Look for the words "nontoxic" on painted toys, "flame retardant" or "flame resistant" on fabrics, "machine surface washable" on stuffed and cloth toys, and "UL (Underwriters Laboratories) Approved" on electrical playthings.

Select a toy chest that has a removable lid or a spring-loaded lid support, allowing the lid to remain securely open; check for smooth, finished edges, proper holes for ventilation, and adequate hinge-line clearances to prevent pinched fingers.

Always remove and immediately discard all packaging (particularly plastic wrap and staples) from a toy before giving it to a baby or young child.

Read instructions carefully to make sure that adults and children understand them.

Spot check toys routinely for minor damage and urge children to let you know when toys need repair; a toy damaged beyond repair should be promptly discarded or replaced.

Wash toys periodically, and sterilize them after they are used by a sick child.

AGE-APPROPRIATE ACTIVITIES AND COMMERCIALLY AVAILABLE TOYS

As discussed above, the particular toy or activity that you present to a child should be given careful consideration; specifically, your choice should be based on the purpose of the play activity and the age level and abilities of the child. A toy that requires manipulation that is beyond the child's abilities will only cause frustration and disenchantment. Table 1 provides some activity selections that are appropriate for children of different age ranges. Once again, if you are unsure about introducing a new toy or activity to a child, consult with the child's teacher or therapist, an experienced parent, or the toy manufacturer.

The toys listed in Table 2 are available in toy stores throughout the United States. These particular toys were chosen because they are popular, attractive, and interesting items that children under the age of 8 find appealing; they have multiple uses across different ages and ability levels, and they are easily obtained at toy and department stores across the United States. If a particular toy cannot be found, something similar made by a different manufacturer will probably be available.

Teachers and counselors, in particular, may wish to refer to Williams, Briggs, and Williams (1979) who have generated 11 considerations in selecting toys for children with disabilities. A comprehensive list of questions is provided with each consideration. This list can be helpful in purchasing toys for the classroom, school, or camp.

Table 1.   Age-appropriate toys and activities for young children

Toys	Activities

Birth to 18 Months

Toys	Activities
Rattles	Reaching/grasping for toys
Blocks	Stacking objects
Squeaky toys	Finger play
Tub toys	Peek-a-boo/pat-a-cake songs
Picture books	Imitating motor actions/sounds
Push–pull toys	Playing with musical instruments
Take-apart toys	Water play
Nesting squares/toys	Making mirror faces
Stacking toys	Dancing and singing
Musical toys	Playing lost and found
Teddy bears	Reading stories
Dolls	
Balls	
Play mirrors	
Busy boxes	

18 Months to 3 Years

Toys	Activities
Ride-on toys	Acting out stories
Tricycles	Playing tag
Push–pull toys	Throwing, kicking, catching ball
Wagons	Block building
Rocking horse	Playing follow-the-leader games
Blocks	Playing dress-up
Balls	Housecleaning
Sandbox/water table	Having a tea party
Play furniture	Reading stories
Play appliances, utensils	Having a parade with instruments
Dolls	Cutting and pasting paper items
Doll clothes	Matching items
Doll furniture	Sorting items
Tea sets	Counting items
Stuffed animals	Listening to music
Puzzles	Sand/water play
Games	Stringing beads
Take-apart toys	Practicing concepts (colors, size)
Clay/dough	Cooking
Crayons	Singing songs
Chalk/chalkboard	
Musical instruments	
Paints	
Trains/cars/other vehicles	
Books	
Toy phones	
Hammer/pounding board	
Bubbles	
Medical kit	
Camera	

(*continued*)

Table 1. (*continued*)

Toys	Activities
3 Years to 8 Years	
Dolls	Pretend-play situations
Puppets	Hide and seek
Toy clocks	Dancing
Play houses	Gymnastics
Housekeeping toys	Puppet shows
Storekeeping toys	Acting out favorite characters
Farm, zoo, town play sets	Counting/sorting items
Motor-vehicle toys: cars, farm equipment, trains	Asking "wh" questions
	Playing board games
Construction sets	Playing ball games
Bikes	Constructing buildings/towns/vehicles
Swing sets	Playing dress-up
Wagons	Arts/crafts projects based on themes
Records/tapes/CDs	Cooking
Coloring books	Singing/writing songs
Paints	
Markers	
Art supplies	
Board games	
Sports/hobbies	
Computers	
Electric trains	
Science/craft kits	
Magic sets	
Miniature figures	
Books	
Magnets/magnetic board	
Dominos	

Table 3 presents a list of popular toy manufacturers, their addresses, and phone numbers. Following this is a list of toy safety agencies and organizations and of toy companies and other resources for purchasing or constructing adaptive toys.

CONCLUDING COMMENTS

Given the suggestions above regarding play materials for children with disabilities, one should not overlook the most important aspect of play—having fun. We have discussed many aspects of play, including the types of toys to select, the various players involved, and the numerous possible learning strategies. However, the ultimate goal for any child is to enjoy the activity and feel good about him- or herself while engaging in play.

Table 2. Commercially available toys

Item	Age	Company	Cost	Description
Activity Center	0–2 years	Various	Varies	Activity toy
Activity Gym	0–2 years	Various	Varies	Activity toy
Big Semi Truck	3–10 years	Little Tykes	>$25.00	Multi-purpose vehicle
CANDYLAND®	3–6 years	Milton Bradley	>10.00	Game
Carry Along™ Tools	2–6 years	Little Tykes	>15.00	Manipulative
Cash Register	2–6 years	Fisher-Price	>15.00	Manipulative
Cassette Recorder	2+ years	Various	Varies	
Colorforms®	3+ years		>5.00	Plastic stick-ons
Crazy Combo™	3–7 years	Fisher-Price	>20.00	Musical instruments
Disney Talkin' Fun® Phone	2–5 years	Mattel	>25.00	Play telephone
Duplo®	2–5 years	Lego	>5.00	Building toy
Easy Hit™ Baseball Set	3–6 years	Little Tykes	>20.00	T-ball game
Etch-A-Sketch®	4+ years	Ohio Art	>10.00	Drawing toy
EXPRESS	3+ years	Playskool	>75.00	Train set
Family Van	3+ years	Little Tykes	>15.00	Toy vehicle
FLASHLIGHT	3+ years	Playskool	>15.00	
Flip-up Learning Center	3–6 years	Fisher-Price	>20.00	Alphabet/ number recognition
Happy Tune™	1–3 years	Playskool	>35.00	Walk/ride push vehicle
Jumbo Numbers	1+ years	CTW Sesame St.	>12.00	10 different numbers & colors
Lego®	3+ years	Lego	>5.00	Building toy
Letter Wood Blocks	2–5 years	Playskool	>10.00	Blocks
Little People® Farm, School, Main Street, Zoo, Garage, & Airport	2–5 years	Fisher-Price	>25.00	Creative play
Magna Doodle®	3+ years	Tyco	>15.00	Drawing toy
Marching Band	3–7 years	Fisher-Price	>25.00	Musical instruments
Mega Bloks®	1+ years	Ritvik	>5.00	Building toy
Mr./Mrs. Potato Head®	2–6 years	Playskool	>5.00	Manipulative
Party Kitchen	2–6 years	Little Tykes	>90.00	Creative play
Party Ware	2–6 years	Little Tykes	>20.00	Play dishes
Picture Lotto	2–8 years	Early Learning Center	>10.00	Game
PIZZA PARTY™	4–8 years	Parker Brothers	>12.00	Game
Play-Doh Fun Factory	3+ years	Kenner	>10.00	Modeling dough
Play 'N Pop™	9–36 months	Mattel	>15.00	Activity toy
Push 'n Ride™ Walker	1–3 years	Little Tykes	<25.00	Walker
Smile 'n Play™ Mirror	0–36 months	Fisher-Price	>20.00	Activity toy
Tap'n Turn Bench	1–3 years	Fisher-Price	>10.00	Pounding bench
Tottle Tots® School Bus	1–5 years	Little Tykes	>15.00	Manipulative
Wee Waffle® Blocks	2+ years	Little Tykes	>5.00	Manipulative
Xylophone	1–3 years	Little Tykes	>15.00	Musical instrument

This is not a complete list.
Prices are approximate.

Table 3.   List of popular toy manufacturers and toy safety agencies

Commercial toy manufacturers

Discovery Toys
2530 Arnold Toys
Suite 400
Martinez, CA 94553

Fisher-Price
636 Girard Avenue
East Aurora, NY 14052
1-800-432-5437

Hasbro/Playskool, Inc.
P.O. Box 1990
Pawtucket, RI 02862
1-800-752-9755

Johnson & Johnson Baby Products Co.
Child Development Division
Grandview Road
Skillman, NJ 08558

Kenner Products
1014 Vine Street
Cincinnati, OH 45202
1-800-347-4613

LEGO Systems, Inc.
555 Taylor Road
Enfield, CT 06082
1-800-422-LEGO

Little Tikes
2180 Barlow Road
Hudson, OH 44236
1-800-321-0183

Mattel
333 Continental Boulevard
El Segundo, CA 90245
1-800-524-TOYS

Playmates Toys, Inc.
16200 Trojan Way
La Mirada, CA 90638
1-714-739-1929

Texas Instruments, Inc.
P.O. Box 53
Lubbock, TX 79408

Tyco
6000 Midlantic Drive
Mount Laurel, NJ 08054
1-800-257-7728

Adaptive toy companies/resources

Linda J. Burkhart
8503 Rhode Island Avenue
College Park, MD 20740

Constructive Playthings
1227 E 119th Street
Grandview, MO 64030
(815) 761-5900

Crestwood Company
P.O. Box 04606
Milwaukee, WI 53204
1-414-352-5679

Discovery Toys
619 Atlantic Hill Drive
Eagan, MN 55123
(612) 454-7326

Jesana Ltd.
P.O. Box 17
Irvington, NY 10533
1-800-443-4728

Mayer-Johnson Co.
P.O. Box AD
Solana Beach, CA 92075-0838
1-619-481-2489

National Lekotek Center
2100 Ridge Avenue
Evanston, IL 60201
1-708-328-0001

Prentke Romich Co.
8769 Township Road 513
Shreve, OH 44676-9421

Salco Toys
RR 1, Box 59
Nerstrand, MN 55053
(507) 645-8720

Sportime
2905 E. Amwiler Road
Atlanta, GA 30360
(800) 241-9884

Theraplay Products
PCA Industries, Inc.
2924 40th Avenue
Long Island City, NY 11101
(718) 784-7070

Toys for Special Children
385 Warburton Avenue
Hastings-on-Hudson, NY 10706
(800) 832-8697

(continued)

Table 3.   (*continued*)

Toy safety agencies/organizations

Arts Hazards Information Center
Center for Safety in the Arts
5 Beekman Street, Suite 1030
New York, NY 10038
1-212-227-6220

National Safety Council
Public Relations Department
444 North Michigan Avenue
Chicago, IL 60611
1-312-527-4800

Toy Manufacturers of America
200 Fifth Avenue
New York, NY 10010
1-212-675-1141

U.S. Consumer Product Safety Commission
 (CPSC)
5401 Westbard Avenue
Bethesda, MD 20207
1-301-492-6550

REFERENCES

Abrams, B.W., & Kauffman, N.A. (1990). *Toys for early childhood development.* West Nyack, NY: The Center for Applied Research in Education.

Baumgart, D., Brown, L., Pumpian, I., Nisbet, J., Ford, A., Sweet, M., Messina, R., & Schroeder, J. (1982). Principle of partial participation and individualized adaptations in educational programs for severely handicapped students. *Journal of The Association for the Severely Handicapped, 7,* 17–27.

Beckman, P.J., & Kohl, F.L. (1984). The effects of social and isolate toys on the integrations and play of integrated and nonintegrated groups of preschoolers. *Education and Training of the Mentally Retarded, 19,* 169–174.

Beckman, P.J., Robinson, C.C., Jackson, B., & Rosenberg, S.A. (1986). Translating developmental findings into teaching strategies for young handicapped children. *Journal of the Division for Early Childhood, 10,* 45–52.

Feeney, S., & Magarick, M. (1984). Choosing good toys for young children. *Young Children, 40,* 21–25.

Gaylord-Ross, R. (Ed.). (1989). *Integration strategies for students with handicaps.* Baltimore: Paul H. Brookes Publishing Co.

Guess, D., Benson, H.A., & Siegel-Causey, E. (1985). Concepts and issues related to choice-making and autonomy among persons with severe disabilities. *Journal of The Association for Persons with Severe Handicaps, 10,* 79–86.

Hendrickson, J.M., Tremblay, A., Strain, P.S., & Shores, R.E. (1981). The relationship between toy and material use and the occurrence of social interactive behaviors by normally preschool children. *Psychology in the Schools, 18,* 500–504.

Kohl, F.L., & Beckman, P.J. (1990). The effects of directed play on the frequency and length of reciprocal interactions with developmentally delayed preschoolers. *Education and Training in Mental Retardation, 25,* 258– 266.

Kohl, F.L., Moses, L.G., & Stettner-Eaton, B.A. (1984). A systematic training program for teaching nonhandicapped students to be instructional trainers of severely handicapped schoolmates. In N. Certo, N. Haring, & R. York (Eds.), *Public school integration of severely handicapped students* (pp. 185–195). Baltimore: Paul H. Brookes Publishing Co.

Musselwhite, C.R. (1986). *Adaptive play for special needs children.* San Diego, CA: College Hill Press, Inc.

Quilitch, H.R., Christopherson, E.R., & Risley, T.R. (1973). The effects of play materials on social play. *Journal of Applied Behavior Analysis, 6,* 573–578.

Sailor, W., Anderson, J.L., Halvorsen, A.T., Doering, K., Filler, J., & Goetz, L. (1989). *The comprehensive local school.* Baltimore: Paul H. Brookes Publishing Co.

Stainback, S., Stainback, W., & Forest, M. (Eds.). (1989). *Educating all students in the mainstream of regular education.* Paul H. Brookes Publishing Co.

Toy Manufacturers of America. (1990). *The TMA guide to toys and play.* New York: Toy Manufacturers of America, Inc.

Williams, B., Briggs, N., & Williams, R. (1979). Selecting, adapting, and understanding toys and recreation materials. In P. Wehman (Ed.), *Recreation programming for developmentally disabled persons* (pp. 15–36). Baltimore: University Park Press.

Yawkey, T.D., & Pellegrini, A.D. (1984). *Child's play: Developmental and applied.* Hillsdale, NJ: Lawrence Erlbaum Associates.

~eight~

All Kids Can Participate
in General Physical Education

Martin E. Block

An ever-increasing number of students with disabilities are being placed in general physical education classes (Jansma & Decker, 1990), but, unfortunately, many instructors are ill prepared to provide individualized, appropriate physical education programs for these students. Many of these professionals have had very little preservice training in adapted physical education, and an even greater number have had little practical experience working with students with disabilities (DiRocco, 1978; Lavay & DePaepe, 1987). Often, the results are frustrated, resentful physical educators who have negative attitudes toward including students with disabilities in their programs (Aloia, Knutson, Minner, & Von Seggern, 1980). In addition, some physical educators may inadvertently provide inappropriate physical education for students with disabilities (DePaepe, 1984; Grosse, 1991). In some schools it has gotten so bad that students with disabilities are simply excused from physical education altogether (Morreau & Eichstaedt, 1983). These problems have led many professionals in the field of adapted physical education to argue that inclusive physical education for students with disabilities, particularly those students who need the most support, is inappropriate. These professionals argue that for the vast majority of students with disabilities, specially designed physical education activities should be provided in a segregated setting in which small groups of children are served by a certified adapted physical education specialist (Grosse, 1991).

Can students with disabilities receive appropriate physical education in a general physical education program? And if so, what factors must be in place for inclusion to be successful? The purpose of this chapter is to discuss a model in which students with disabilities can be safely, successfully, and appropriately included in general physical education programs. It begins with a brief review of the definition of physical education according to PL 94-142 (now PL 101-476, IDEA) and specific statements regarding the concept of least restrictive environment (LRE). This is followed by an outline of an organizational model for planning and implementing inclusive physical education programs. This outline also includes a variety of examples that illustrate various ways that students with disabilities can be successfully included in general physical education.

WHAT IS PHYSICAL EDUCATION?

According to PL 94-142, the Education for All Handicapped Children Act (EHA), and the 1991 Amendments, PL 101-476, the Individuals with Disabilities Education Act (IDEA), physical education is to be considered part of a general education program, rather than as a separate, related service like physical therapy or speech therapy. In fact, the law specifies that related services such as physical or occupational therapy *cannot* be considered a substitute for the physical education requirement. In essence, the inclusion of physical education within the definition of special education means that all students with disabilities *must* receive physical education. Physical education was defined in PL 94-142 as:

> . . . the development of physical and motor fitness, fundamental motor skills and patterns, and skills in aquatics, dance, and individual and group games and sports (including intramural and lifetime sports). The term includes special physical education, adapted physical education, movement education, and motor development. (*Federal Register,* August 23, 1977, p 42480)

This definition provides a framework for program planning and curriculum development. While units of instruction within each of these curricular areas should be based on several factors, such as a student's age, abilities, and interests, the law dictates that a comprehensive physical education program should include all of the components listed in the extract above.

Another important point covered in PL 94-142 is the requirement concerning "least restrictive environment" (LRE), which mandated that:

> . . . to the maximum extent appropriate, children with disabilities, including children in public and private institutions or other care facilities, [be] educated with children without disabilities, and that special classes, separate schooling, or other removal of children with disabilities from regular educational environments occur only when the nature or severity of the disability is such that education in regular classes with the use of supplementary aids and services cannot be achieved. (Federal Register, August 23, 1977, p. 42497)

This passage suggests that the LRE for students with disabilities should, whenever possible, be the same environment in which students without disabilities receive their education. Clearly, the lawmakers advocated placing students with disabilities in typical schools and general classes (including physical education classes) whenever possible (Aufsesser, 1991; Taylor, 1988; Turnbull, 1990). This passage also suggests that *appropriate* placement of students with disabilities in general settings may require the use of supplementary aids, support, and services. Thus, in cases in which inclusion is unsuccessful, it may not be the setting that is inappropriate, but rather the support that is given to a student with a disability within that setting (Block & Krebs, 1992).

In summary, physical education is a direct service comprising a diverse program of activities that all students, including students with disabilities, should have an opportunity to experience. Physical education can be provided in a variety of settings, including separate adapted physical education. However, the vast majority of students with disabilities can receive appropriate physical education in a general setting with their peers without disabilities if the proper supplementary support is provided. The following section provides an organization scheme for making physical education inclusive.

DESIGNING AN INDIVIDUALIZED EDUCATION PROGRAM

Students with disabilities can receive individualized, appropriate physical education within the general physical education setting. However, if we are to expect the program to be successful, several factors must be considered *prior to* placing the student. For example, it must be decided what activities will take place in the general program, what modifications will be needed so that the student with disabilities will be successful, and what types of inservice training should be provided to professionals and students without disabilities. Successful placement of students with disabilities in general physical education entails much more that simply placing the student in a class alongside his or her peers. The purpose of this section is to outline a model for successfully including students with disabilities in general physical education (see Table 1 for an outline of the model). Again, this model adheres to the philosophy that only with proper preparation will students with disabilities enjoy safe, successful, and beneficial experiences in general physical education.

Determining the Student's Specific Goals and Objectives

One of the complaints about serving students with disabilities in general physical education is that these students often do not receive an individualized physical education program designed to meet their particular motor needs (Grosse, 1991). The law clearly states that students with disabilities who, through evaluation, qualify for adapted physical education must be provided this service. Thus, the first step in this model is the development of individual goals and objectives for each student with disabilities. These goals should be developed through objective evaluation with the proper concern for each individual student's unique needs. In other words, goals should reflect the needs of each student, rather than the philosophy of the program or the availability of placement options and equipment. Individualized physical education goals should be developed collaboratively by the adapted physical education specialist, general physical educator, and special education teacher (with input from related-service personnel and parents as well). The adapted physical educator and general physical educator can evaluate the student and develop specific physical education goals. The special educator can assist the physical education specialists in incorporating global goals (e.g., those related to communication, behavior, or fine motor skills) into the physical education portion of the individualized education program (IEP). If an adapted physical education specialist is not available, then the general physical educator and special educator should collaborate to formulate the physical education portion of the IEP. Again, the physical educator will have expertise regarding motor, fitness, and sport-skill development, while the special educator will know how to write the IEP in behavioral terms, as well as how to incorporate the student's global goals.

Individualized physical education goals can and should be provided within the general physical education setting. Many general physical education activities are appropriate and beneficial for students with disabilities, while many other activities can be modified so that they focus on a particular student's unique needs. In addition, when general physical education activities seem inappropriate, the student with special needs can participate in alternate activities within the general physical education setting. Either the adapted physical education specialist or the general physical educator can provide an individualized physical education program

Table 1.   Model for including students with disabilities in regular physical education

1. **Determine what to teach**
   - Determine student's present level of performance.
   - Prioritize long-term goals and short-term instructional objectives.
2. **Analyze the general physical education curriculum**
   - What general physical education activities match the student's IEP?
   - What general physical education activities do not match the student's IEP but still seem important for the student?
   - What general physical education activities are inappropriate for a particular student?
   - What is the teaching style of the general physical educator?
3. **Determine modifications needed in general physical education**
   - How often will student receive instruction?
   - Where will student receive instruction?
   - How will student be prepared for instruction?
   - What instruction modifications are needed to elicit desired performance?
   - What curricular adaptations will be used to enhance performance?
   - How will performance be assessed?
4. **Determine how much support the student with disabilities will need**
   - Base on type of activities and abilities (cognitive, affective, and psychomotor) of student.
   - Utilize the "continuum of support" model (Block & Krebs, 1992).
5. **Prepare general physical educator**
   - Discuss the amount of support that will be provided.
   - Discuss the availability of consultation with the adapted physical education specialist and special education teacher.
   - Explain that he or she is responsible for the entire class, not just the student with disabilities.
   - Explain that his or her work load should not be increased.
6. **Prepare general education students**
   - Talk about students with disabilities in general.
   - Role-play various types of disabilities.
   - Invite guest speakers with disabilities to your class.
   - If the student attends special education class, allow other students to visit the special education classroom and meet student.
   - Talk specifically about the student who will be coming to the general physical education class (focus on abilities).
   - Discuss ways typical students can help student with disabilities and general educator.
7. **Prepare support personnel**
   - Discuss specific student with whom they will be working.
   - Discuss the student's physical education IEP.
   - Discuss their responsibilities in general physical education.
   - Discuss to whom they can go if they have questions.

Adapted from Block (1994).

within an inclusive setting. The adapted physical education specialist can provide direct and consultative support to the general physical educator as needed, particularly early on in the program, when the general educator might not yet feel comfortable with the student with disabilities. Later, as the general physical educator learns how to accommodate the needs of special students placed in the inclusive program, the adapted physical education specialist can become more of a consultant, meeting with the general physical educator every week or so. When an adapted physical education specialist is not available, special education staff (special education teachers, paraprofessionals, therapists) or peer tutors can assist the general physical educator in accommodating the student with disabilities. These professionals can provide one-to-one assistance to the student with disabilities, work on individual goals, develop adapted equipment, and provide suggestions for modifications to traditional physical education activities. Again, support can be weaned away as the general physical educator comes to feel more confident about his or her ability to serve students with disabilities in an inclusive setting.

Table 2 provides an example of a physical-education IEP developed for a 16-year-old student named John who has Down syndrome. John was collaboratively assessed by an adapted physical education specialist and general physical educator, and it was determined that he had weaknesses in several areas and required adapted physical education goals. The goals that were developed for John included improving physical fitness, developing age-appropriate sport skills, and improving lifetime leisure skills. Global goals such as communicating with peers and staff and following directions were suggested by John's special education teacher. At this point we are not concerned with *where* John will work on these goals, but only with their prioritization given John's age, abilities, and anticipated future placements.

As it turns out, John can work on the majority of these individual skills in a general physical education program. For example, he can work on his individual fitness skills at the same time other students do their warm-up activities. John has different ways of doing warm-up activities than his peers (e.g., standing jumping jacks, fewer sit-ups, modified push-ups). Also, he is required to practice running a little longer than the other students, since improving his cardiorespiratory endurance is one of John's major objectives. However, it is more motivating for John to work on these skills alongside his peers, who have been coached to assist him as needed and to encourage his efforts. Another of John's goals is to work on the development of age-appropriate individual and team sport skills. Again, John can work on these goals (in this case, soccer goals) alongside his peers without disabilities in a general physical education program. The difference between John and his peers is that John will use slightly different equipment and different criteria to evaluate his success and progress during the soccer unit. For example, John might practice dribbling a slightly deflated ball while moving straight ahead while other students are working on dribbling a regulation ball between cones. The important point is that John is working on individual goals designed specifically to meet his personal needs. By having John work on these skills in an inclusive environment, he is provided with role models and has the benefit of peers who can assist him and provide him with feedback. For example, John's tendency to act silly and talk too much is less acceptable to his peers without disabilities than to other students with disabilities, because these students are more familiar with the social and behavioral rules of the general physical education setting. Therefore, John's peers incidentally assist him in developing more appropriate social skills by modeling acceptable behavior and correcting him when he misbehaves or acts silly.

Analyzing the General Physical Education Curriculum

Once each student has been evaluated and his or her individual physical education goals have been determined, the next step in the model is to analyze the general physical education program. Table 3 lists common curricular elements of general

Table 2.   John's physical education IEP

Long-term goal:
John will improve his muscular strength and cardiorespiratory endurance.

Short-term instructional objectives:
1.   After a verbal cue, John will perform seven bent-knee sit-ups independently (with a peer holding his feet down) in 30 seconds or less, in four out of five tries.

2.   After a verbal cue, John will perform one push-up and nine modified knee push-ups independently in 45 seconds or less, in four out of five tries.

3.   With verbal cues, John will jog continuously for 15 minutes, walking no more than 1 minute during the entire timed period in three out of four tries.

Long-term goal:
John will develop the skills needed to participate in modified and regulation individual and team sports.

Short-term instructional objectives (specific to soccer):
1.   From 30 yards out, John will dribble the ball to within 10 yards of the goal, then shoot the ball into the goal mouth (in four out of five tries).

2.   John will play defense by staying within 5 yards of the person he is guarding when the person does not have the ball and within 2 yards when the person has the ball for 6 out of 10 minutes in a game situation (in two out of three tries).

3.   In a game situation, John will pass a ball to a teammate (who is 10 yards away) within 5 seconds of the teammate calling his name (in three out of four tries).

Long-term goal:
[a]John will develop the skills needed to participate in community-based leisure activities in integrated environments.

Short-term instructional objective:
1.   John will enter the YMCA, show his ID card, locate the locker room, put his clothes in a locker, lock the locker, then locate the weight room using only natural cues (including asking YMCA staff for assistance) with 100% accuracy on 4 out of 5 days.

2.   John will get on a stationary bike, set tension at level 2, set timer for 25 minutes, then ride the bike for 25 minutes independently (asking YMCA staff for assistance if necessary) with 100% accuracy on 4 out of 5 days.

3.   John will follow picture cards and complete a 6-station weight training circuit, performing the exercise for each machine correctly and completing one set of 10–12 repetitions per machine independently (or asking YMCA staff for assistance) with 100% accuracy on 4 out of 5 days.

4.   John will demonstrate appropriate behavior in the locker room and weight room by:
1) changing clothes quickly without acting silly, 2) saying only hi to strangers or responding appropriately when a stranger initiates a conversation in the locker room, and 3) not acting silly or talking to others while they are working out on the bikes or weight machines, unless others initiate conversation in the weight room, 100% of the time on 4 out of 5 days.

[a]John participates in community-based recreation training twice per week instead of going to regular physical education.

physical education at the lower elementary, upper elementary/middle, and high school levels. Yearly curricula are often part of a school district's general curriculum guides. These curricula will not specify when or how a particular activity is to be taught; rather, they describe what activities will be covered during the course of the year. Most general physical education teachers will be able to provide you with a more specific outline of the major activities he or she will be covering that year and his or her strategy for teaching them.

Table 3. Major content areas for general physical education by grade level

Lower elementary school (K–3rd grade)	Upper elementary/middle school (4th–7th grade)	High school (8th–12th grade)
Locomotor patterns • run • skip • jump • slide • gallop • leap • hop • climb	**Locomotor patterns for sports** • locomotor patterns used in sports • combine two or more locomotor patterns • locomotor patterns used in dance	**Locomotor sports** • track events • special sports applications of locomotor patterns • locomotor patterns used in dance • locomotor patterns used in leisure activities
Manipulative patterns • throw • catch • kick • strike	**Manipulative patterns for sports** • throw • volley • catch • dribble • kick • punt • strike	**Ball sports** • basketball, soccer, softball, volleyball, etc. • bowling, golf, tennis, racquetball, etc.
Body management • body awareness • body control • space awareness • effort concepts	**Body management for sports** • gymnastics • body management skills applied to sports	**Body management for sports** • body management skills applied to sports
Health and fitness • endurance, strength, and flexibility to perform locomotor and manipulative skills	**Health and fitness** • cardiorespiratory endurance • muscular strength and endurance • flexibility	**Health and fitness** • personal conditioning • lifetime leisure exercises • introduction to body composition concepts
Rhythm and dance • moving to a beat • expressing self through movement • singing games • applying effort concepts	**Dance** • folk • modern • interpretive • aerobic	**Dance** • folk • modern • interpretive • aerobic and social
Low organized games • relays and tag games • games with partners • games with a small group	**Lead-up games to sports** • lead-up games to team sports	**Modified and regulation sports** • modified sport activities • regulation sports

Adapted from Wessel, J.A., & Kelly, L. (1986). *Achievement-based curriculum development in physical education.* Philadelphia: Lea & Febiger; reprinted with permission.

In John's case, an examination of the 10th-grade curriculum revealed that all students participated in fitness-oriented warm-up activities prior to all classes and completed a unit on physical fitness, a unit on dance, and units on several different individual and team sports. With the exception of developing lifetime leisure skills, John's individual goals fit nicely into the general 10th-grade physical education program. Thus, John should be able to work on his individual goals with very few modifications to the general curriculum.

In addition to a global examination of the general physical education curriculum, a more in-depth examination of each unit plan should be conducted. Unit plans can be obtained from general physical education specialists a week prior to the introduction of that unit (more seasoned teachers may have their unit plans from previous years on file for your use). Table 4 is an example of a plan for a soccer unit.

Using John again as an example, an analysis of the soccer unit suggests that he will have to develop skills such as passing, shooting, dribbling, and defense, as well as learn concepts and strategies necessary for playing soccer games. By analyzing these skills ahead of time (even one week before the unit begins), you can begin to make decisions about what skills John (as well as other students with disabilities) can practice independently, what skills will require minor modifications, what skills will require alternative techniques, what special equipment you might need, and what extra support John might need in order to be successful.

Designing Specific Curricular Modifications

In John's case, the general program fits in quite nicely with his goals, and few adaptations are required. In other cases, a student's individual goals may appear to be slightly different from those emphasized in the activities offered in general physical education, which would require some minor modification to the general program. In still other cases, a student might have individual goals that seem to be completely incompatible with activities in the general program. Therefore, the focus at this point in the model is on critically analyzing the general physical education curriculum to determine what modifications or alternate activities might be necessary for a particular student.

One method for determining what modifications might be necessary for a particular student is to use the *ecological inventory with discrepancy analysis* (Brown et al., 1979). An ecological inventory provides a detailed analysis of what a student without disabilities typically does when participating in an activity. The analysis begins with identifying *sub-environments* and the *activities* that take place within each environment. This is followed by an analysis of how the student with disabilities currently performs these activities (discrepancy analysis). Finally, suggestions for modifications that will help the student become more independent and successful are developed. Figure 1 is a sample ecological inventory used to determine what modifications were needed for John.

Notice that John will perform his activities aimed at building strength slightly differently than his peers, and he will spend extra time working on improving his cardiorespiratory endurance. During soccer skills work, John will use a slightly deflated ball for dribbling to help with his control, and he will focus on shooting and passing the ball to peers who are stationary, rather than moving. During the game, John will play one of the wing defensive positions, since it requires less running and slightly less skill than others. In addition, the offensive person on his side

Table 4.   Sample 4-week softball unit plan

WEEK 1

Introduction to game
- equipment
- field dimensions
- basic rules
- basic concepts and positions

Warm-up activities
- stretching major muscles of upper and lower body
- strengthening abdominals, arms, and legs
- cardiovascular endurance activities (e.g., jogging around the base path)

Introduction to basic softball skills (emphasis on learning correct movements)
- striking
- throwing
- fielding
- base running

Lead-up games to work on skills
- base running relays, hot-box, 500
- pepper, 500
- home run derby, spot hitting

WEEK 2

Continue warm-up activities (have students lead warm-ups)

Team concepts and team strategies
- base running strategies; hitting ball to various places in field; hitting cut-off person
- view video of softball game that shows these techniques

Continue refinement of skills
- throwing from greater distances; throwing with varying force
- fielding balls hit to the side; fielding high flies in the outfield
- hitting faster-pitched balls; hitting balls in different parts of strike zone

WEEK 3

Continue warm-up activities (have students lead warm-ups)

Review of all softball skills

Introduce games:
- 10 v. 10 with outfield players practicing throwing balls back and forth during down time and batting team practicing hitting balls off a tee behind backstop while waiting
- modified game of softball for students who have less skill (including students without disabilities who have limited softball skills)

WEEK 4

Continue warm-up activities (have students lead warm-ups)

Continue to review softball skills

Continue games with less instruction (both regulation and modified)

Some anticipated accommodations for Sue:
1. have peer assist her during warm-ups (demonstration and occasional physical prompt)
2. have peer assist Sue as she moves from station to station and at station as needed
3. have adapted physical education specialist write activities for Sue to do at each station
4. use smaller ball (tennis ball) for throwing and catching with mitt
5. use lighter bat (whiffle ball bat) and have ball on tee for striking
6. have Sue play in outfield with a peer during games
7. allow Sue to run to a closer base when running to first and allow a peer to run with her around other bases until she understands'where to go
8. have Sue play in recreational, noncompetitive game

Ecological Inventory with Discrepancy Analysis

Student's name: John Schwartz Student's birthdate: 8–10–82 Teacher: M. Block (APE specialist)

Environment: Genl. Phys. Ed. —Soccer Initiation of program: 6–21–92 Suggested assistant: Steve Smith (peer tutor)

	What are the steps that a person without disabilities uses?	What assistance does the student with disabilities currently need?	What adaptations or levels of assistance might help this student?
Subenvironment: Locker room			
Activity 1:	Locate locker room.	V	Teach student to use natural cues on wall; add arrows on walls.
Activity 2:	Enter locker room.	I	None needed
Activity 3:	Locate empty locker.	V	Teach student to ID lockers without locks; color-code one locker.
Activity 4:	Take off clothes.	PP	Wear pull-on clothes; practice dressing at home; use Velcro instead of buttons.
Activity 5:	Place clothes in locker.	I	None needed
Activity 6:	Put on exercise clothes.	P	Use pull-on clothes; equip shoes with special ties; use Velcro instead of buttons.
Activity 7:	Lock locker.	P	Repeated practice; perhaps longer lock or key lock might be easier than combination lock.

(continued)

Figure 1. Sample ecological inventory with discrepancy analysis for 10th-grade physical education. APE = adapted physical education. (From Block, M.E. [1994]. *A teacher's guide to including students with disabilities in regular physical education*. Baltimore: Paul H. Brookes Publishing Co.; copyright © 1994 by Paul H. Brookes Publishing Co.; reprinted by permission.)

Figure 1. (*continued*)

	What are the steps that a person without disabilities uses?	What assistance does the student with disabilities currently need?	What adaptations or levels of assistance might help this student?
Subenvironment: Gym—Attendance			
Activity 1:	Locate gym.	V	Natural cues on walls; put extra cues on walls.
Activity 2:	Find squad and sit down.	V	Teach student to ID members of squad; have squad members cue student if he appears lost.
Activity 3:	Sit quietly with squad.	I	None needed
Subenvironment: Gym—Warm-up			
Activity 1:	Stand up with squad.	V	Have peers provide cues.
Activity 2:	Perform 10 jumping jacks.	VP	Have peers provide cues; do jumping jacks with arms only.
Activity 3:	Perform sitting-leg stretch.	VP	Have peers provide cues; have peer tutor provide physical assistance as needed.
Activity 4:	Perform 10 sit-ups.	VP	Pair up with peer tutor; perform 5 rather than 10.
Activity 5:	Perform 10 push-ups.	VP	Have peers provide cues; perform modified, knee push-ups.
Activity 6:	Run continuously for 3 minutes.	V	Have peers provide cues; alternate run/walk for 10 minutes.

(*continued*)

Figure 1. *(continued)*

	What are the steps that a person without disabilities uses?	What assistance does the student with disabilities currently need?	What adaptations or levels of assistance might help this student?
Subenvironment: Gym—Soccer stations			
Activity 1:	Locate squad and station.	V	Have peers provide cues.
Activity 2:	Practice shooting.	VP	Shoot from closer distance; shoot at wider goal; use lighter ball.
Activity 3:	Wait turn.	I	None needed
Activity 4:	Move to next station.	V	Have peers provide cues.
Activity 5:	Passing/trapping	VP	Stand closer to peer; use partially deflated ball; use tape markings on foot to cue correct contact point; pass to stationary partner.
Activity 6:	Wait turn.	I	None needed
Activity 7:	Move to next station.	V	Have peers provide cues.
Activity 8:	Dribbling	VP	Dribble with partially deflated ball or Nerf ball; work on dribbling straight ahead without obstacles; work on walking, then jogging, while dribbling.
Activity 9:	Wait turn.	I	None needed
Activity 10:	Go back to original squads.	V	Have peers provide cues.

(continued)

Figure 1. (*continued*)

	What are the steps that a person without disabilities uses?	What assistance does the student with disabilities currently need?	What adaptations or levels of assistance might help this student?
Subenvironment: Soccer game			
Activity 1:	Listen to instructions by teacher.	V	Have peer tutor reexplain rules in simpler terms.
Activity 2:	Put on assigned pinny.	PP	Have peer provide assistance.
Activity 3:	Go to assigned position.	V	Have peers provide cues.
Activity 4:	Play game.	VP	John will play a wing fullback, and a non-skilled peer will play opposite him.
Activity 5:	Watch flow of game.	V	Have peer tutor provide cues.
Activity 6:	Interact with teammates.	V	Have peer provide cues.
Activity 7:	Shake hands with other team.	V	Have peers provide cues.
Activity 8:	Take off pinny.	PP	Have peer assist student.
Activity 9:	Put pinny away.	V	Have peers provide cues.
Activity 10:	Walk to locker room.	V	Have peers provide cues.
Subenvironment: Locker room			
Activity 1:	Locate locker room.	V	Use natural cues on wall; use additional wall cues.
Activity 2:	Enter locker room.	I	None needed
Activity 3:	Locate locker.	V	Tape colored sign on locker; have peer provide cues as needed.

(*continued*)

Figure 1. (*continued*)

	What are the steps that a person without disabilities uses?	What assistance does the student with disabilities currently need?	What adaptations or levels of assistance might help this student?
Activity 4:	Take off gym clothes.	PP	Have peer provide assistance as needed.
Activity 5:	Place exercise clothes in gym bag.	I	None needed
Activity 6:	Get towel, soap, and shampoo.	V	Have peer tutor provide cues as needed.
Activity 7:	Locate shower.	V	Place extra sign on wall, have peer provide cues.
Activity 8:	Turn on water and modulate water temperature.	PP	Practice starting with cold and gradually add hot; have peer tutor assist.
Activity 9:	Shampoo hair and wash self.	PP	Start from top and work down; practice at home; have peer provide assistance.
Activity 10:	Turn off shower and collect personal items.	PP	Step away from water, turn off hot, then cold; have peer assist as needed.
Activity 11:	Dry self.	V	Start from top and work down; practice; peer can give verbal cues as needed.
Activity 12:	Locate and use deodorant.	V	Have peer provide cues as needed.

(*continued*)

Figure 1.   (*continued*)

	What are the steps that a person without disabilities uses?	What assistance does the student with disabilities currently need?	What adaptations or levels of assistance might help this student?
Activity 13:	Put on street clothes.	P	Use pull-on clothes; use special ties for shoes; have peer assist as needed.
Activity 14:	Go to mirror and comb hair/check appearance.	V	Start from top and work down; cue in on hair combed and shirt tucked in; shoes on correct feet; peer gives cues as needed.
Activity 15:	Place all personal belongings in gym bag.	V	Teach student to check area and locker; use picture cue card; peer gives cues.
Activity 16:	Leave locker room and go to class.	V	Use natural cues on wall; use additional wall cues; have peer tutor assist as needed.

Key: I   = independent
    V   = verbal cues or reminder
    PP = partial physical assistance
    P+ = physical assistance (student tries to help)
    P   = physical assistance (student is passive)
    P− = physical assistance (student fights assistance)

of the field is a less skilled general education student who does not mind "taking it easy" on John. For John, these very minimal modifications are all that are necessary for him to be successful in the soccer unit.

Students with more complex needs may require more modifications to successfully participate in general physical education. For example, a student named Sue (a 17-year-old girl in the 11th grade who has moderate spastic diplegic cerebral palsy and mental retardation) has individual goals that include: 1) improving walking balance in a variety of school and community environments, and 2) improving her ability to hold and manipulate objects that are age-appropriate and facilitate leisure-skill development. She also has goals reflecting her need to improve her physical fitness and develop lifetime leisure skills. Sue works on some of the same warm-up activities as the other students (e.g., stretching, doing sit-ups with the assistance of a partner), and also performs some specialized activities (with more emphasis on stretching the muscles in her legs) while her peers complete the rest of their own warm-up. When the other students run their laps, Sue walks around the field while carrying a soccer ball (working on walking balance and holding onto objects). During skill work, Sue works on her walking skills during dribbling (Sue tosses a soccer ball forward then walks to retrieve it). During passing practice, a peer traps the ball and gives it to Sue, who must then hold onto the ball while walking to another peer, then toss the ball to the peer. During shooting practice, Sue works on tossing the ball a short distance toward the goal. During game play, Sue has a special zone where she stands with a peer who helps retrieve balls for her and protects her if an errant ball comes near. The peer can also move out of the zone in an attempt to retrieve the ball for Sue (this allows the peer to be active in the game). When the peer does successfully retrieve the ball, she hands it to Sue, who must then walk to the edge of the zone and toss the ball towards a teammate. Thus, with a certain amount of adaptation, Sue can work on her own individual goals while being an active participant in general physical education.

Finally, some other students might have individual goals that seem incompatible with the activities comprising the general program. In these cases, alternative activities can be performed by the student with disabilities while students without disabilities work on their own goals. Block (1992) suggests several alternate ways in which traditional elementary and secondary school physical education activities can be performed by students with significant disabilities. These suggestions include adapting equipment, using switches, and making slight rule modifications (see Table 5 for a list of these suggestions).

For example, Jason is a 14-year-old boy who has spastic quadriplegic cerebral palsy that drastically limits his range of motion, strength, and fine motor skills. Jason has very limited head control, and he cannot push his wheelchair independently. Jason also has mental retardation and is legally blind. Jason's goals are to improve his head control in a variety of lifetime leisure activities, to maintain his range of motion so that he can independently activate switches during leisure activities, and to use his residual vision during lifetime leisure activities. These goals would seem to be completely different from those usually associated with 9th-grade general physical education. However, Jason can work on these goals during general physical education class alongside his peers. While the other students are doing their warm-up activities, Jason is working on improving his range of motion with the assistance of a paraprofessional. The warm-up activities Jason completes have been developed by his physical therapist. Jason does not have to go to a physical therapy room or even to a corner of the gym to do these special exercises. Rather, he is mixed in with his peers. The only difference is that Jason is performing specialized warm-up activities. While the other students do their laps, Jason is pushed around the field in his wheelchair by a peer, who has been told that Jason is only to be pushed when he keeps his head up (working on head control). Jason does well keeping his head up because he gets a lot of positive feedback from his peers as they jog by him.

Table 5. Chronological age–appropriate activities and sample modifications for elementary-age students with significant disabilities[a]

Age-appropriate activities	Modifications
Manipulative patterns	
Throwing	Pushing a ball down a ramp, grasp and release
Catching	Tracking suspended balls, reaching for balloons
Kicking	Touching balloon taped to floor, pushing ball down ramp with foot
Striking	Hitting ball off tee, hitting suspended ball
Locomotor patterns	
Running	Being pushed quickly in wheelchair while keeping head up
Jumping/hopping	Lifting head up and down while being pushed in wheelchair
Galloping/skipping	Moving arms up and down while being pushed in wheelchair; also, student can use adapted mobility aids such as scooterboards and walkers
Perceptual-motor skills	
Balance skills	Propping up on elbows, prone balance over wedge
Body awareness	Accept tactile input, imitate simple movements
Spatial awareness	Moving arms in when going in between, ducking head under objects
Visual-motor coordination	Track suspended objects, touch switches
Physical fitness skills	
Endurance	Tolerate continuous activity, move body parts repeatedly
Strength	Use stretch bands, use isometric exercises
Flexibility	Perform ROM activities as suggested by PT
Team sports	
Soccer skills	Passing/kicking/shooting—push ball down ramp using foot
Soccer game	Set up special zones, use ramps for kicking
Volleyball skills	Track suspended balls, reach and touch balls
Volleyball game	"Buddy" catches ball, student has 3 seconds to touch the ball
Basketball skills	Using switch that shoots ball into small basket, keeping head up and arms out on defense; pushing ball off tray for passing
Basketball game	Buddy pushes student into offensive or defensive zone, ball passed to buddy, student has 5 seconds to activate switch that shoots his ball into small basket
Individual sports	
Bowling	Use a ramp (play at community facility when possible)
Bocce (lawn bowling)	Same as above
Miniature golf	Push ball down ramp using mini-putter
Golf (driving range)	Activate switch that causes ball to be hit
Physical fitness skills	
Endurance	Move body parts during aerobic dance program
Strength	Use stretch bands, isometrics, free weights
Flexibility	Perform ROM activities as suggested by PT during aerobics or during warm-up activities prior to team sports

From "What is Appropriate Physical Education for Students With Profound Disabilities?" by M.E. Block, *Adapted Physical Activity Quarterly,* (Vol. 9, No. 3), pp. 201-202. Copyright 1992 by Human Kinetics Publishers. Reprinted by permission.
[a]In all activities, utilize the principle of partial participation to ensure that the student is successful.

After warm-ups, students begin to work on their soccer skills. Since Jason really cannot play soccer in the traditional sense, he works on the following skills, which are more relevant to his individual goals: 1) keeping his head up during defense drills (head control), 2) pushing a ball down a ramp during passing drills (maintaining range of motion in his upper body), and 3) activating a switch on a tabletop soccer game during shooting drills (activating switches). Jason practices these skills with his peers at the various skill stations set up by the teacher. A paraprofessional assists Jason at each station, and his peers provide extra encouragement. In fact, peers enjoy taking turns assisting Jason in his skill work, particularly when he is practicing at the tabletop soccer game.

When it is time to play the game, Jason participates for part of the period and works on his tabletop soccer game for the rest. During the game, Jason stays in a special zone (similar to the one developed for Sue). Another student is also in the zone so that Jason will have some opportunities to play while still being protected from errant balls. When the ball comes into Jason's zone, the peer tutor places the ball on Jason's ramp, and Jason must push the ball down the ramp toward a teammate. Jason stays in the game for about 10 minutes so that he gets 2–3 turns in the game. Jason also enjoys listening to his peers running and talking to each other during the game. For the last 10 minutes of the period, Jason continues to work on his ability to participate in leisure activities by practicing his tabletop soccer game. Jason has limited vision, but the game has lots of sound that he seems to enjoy. Jason's peers also enjoy the game, and they take turns rotating off the soccer field to play it with Jason. Jason enjoys being around his peers, and he has become quite popular with them because of all of his neat games. Even though Jason does not play soccer the way his peers do, he is working on soccer-type skills that are also designed to help him achieve his individual goals of improving his head control, maintaining his functional range of motion, and using switches in leisure activities. In addition, his placement in general physical education gives him the opportunity to interact with his peers without disabilities, and vice versa.

There are a variety of resources that can be used in modifying physical education activities. Adapted physical education specialists are perhaps the best resource for developing appropriate modifications to general physical education activities for students with disabilities. Sports organizations that deal exclusively with individuals who have disabilities can also provide expert advice on special equipment and rules that have been designed to accommodate persons with specific limitations. For example, the United States Association for Blind Athletes (USABA) has developed special equipment and rules for such activities as beep baseball, goal ball, and track and field. In addition to these human resources, there are several other good sources of information on modifying physical education activities. Three works in particular that provide very practical information are Arbogast and Lavay (1986), Block (1992), and Winnick (1978). Many adapted physical education textbooks and program guides also contain suggestions for modifying individual and group games to allow students with disabilities to participate; see, for example, Adams and McCubbin (1991), Block (1988), Dunn and Fait (1989), Florida Department of Education (1982), and Marsallo and Vacante (1983). Table 6 provides the addresses and phone numbers of national sports organizations that serve persons with disabilities.

Determining How Much Support a Student with Disabilities Will Need

Examples presented in step 3 of this model have demonstrated how students like John, Sue, and Jason can enjoy successful, individualized, physical education

Table 6.   Selected sports associations affiliated with individuals with disabilities

American Athletic Association of the Deaf (AAAD) 3607 Washington Blvd., Suite 4 Ogden, UT 84403-1737 801/393-8710	Special Olympics International (SOI) 1350 New York Ave., N.W., Suite 500 Washington, D.C. 20005 202/628-3630
Dwarf Athletic Association of American (DAAA) 418 Willow Way Lewisville, TX 75607 214/317-8299	United States Association for Blind Athletes (USABA) 33 N. Institute St. Brown Hall, Suite 015 Colorado Springs, CO 80903 719/630-0422
National Handicapped Sports (NHS) 451 Hungerford Dr., Suite 100 Rockville, MD 20850 301/217-0960	United States Cerebral Palsy Athletic Association (USCPAA) 500 S. Ervay, Suite 452B Dallas, TX 75201 214/761-0033
National Wheelchair Athletic Association (NWAA) 3595 East Fountain Blvd., Suite L-1 Colorado Springs, CO 80910 719/574-1150	United States Les Autres Sports Association (USLASA) 1101 Post Oak Blvd., Suite 9-486 Houston, TX 77056 713/521-3737

alongside their peers. However, none of these students would have successful experiences without the support of peer assistants, paraprofessionals, and/or an adapted physical education specialist.

Once you have determined what modifications or alternate activities you will need to employ for particular students, the next step in the model is to determine who will implement these strategies. How much support a student will need, as well as who will provide that support, will depend on the type of activities being presented and on the physical and cognitive abilities and behavior of the student. For example, a kindergarten student with Down syndrome in a physical education class on movement exploration could probably participate with no support other than an occasional consultation by an adapted physical education specialist. However, when this child reaches high school and has to participate in team sports, chances are, he or she might need some extra support in the form of peer tutors and rule modifications. In cases in which the health and safety of a particular student are a major concern (e.g., those involving a student with osteogenesis imperfecta or muscular dystrophy), a trained teacher, therapist, or paraprofessional should assist the student rather than a peer tutor. Similarly, if a student with a significant behavior disorder is prone to outbursts and poses a threat to him- or herself or to peers, then a trained teacher, therapist or paraprofessional should assist the student. Block and Krebs (1992) describe a "Model of Support to Regular Physical Education" that delineates a systematic approach to providing support to students with disabilities in general physical education programs (see Table 7). The important point is that the decision on *who* provides support to a student with disabilities should be a thoughtful process, rather than an attempt to simply foist responsibility onto whichever peer tutor or paraprofessional happens to be free during a particular period.

Regardless of their background, individuals who provide support should participate in some type of training program that provides information on the following subjects: 1) what is expected of them, 2) what the purpose of physical education is

Table 7. A continuum of support to regular physical education

LEVEL 1: NO SUPPORT NEEDED
        1.1   Student makes necessary modifications on his or her own.
        1.2   RPE teacher makes necessary modifications for student.

LEVEL 2: APE CONSULTATION
        2.1 No extra assistance is needed.
        2.2 Peer tutor "watches out" for student.
        2.3 Peer tutor assists student.
        2.4 Paraprofessional assists student.

LEVEL 3: APE DIRECT SERVICE IN RPE 1x/WEEK
        3.1 Peer tutor "watches out" for student.
        3.2 Peer tutor assists student.
        3.3 Paraprofessional assists student.

LEVEL 4: PART-TIME APE AND PART-TIME RPE
        4.1 Flexible schedule with reverse mainstreaming.
        4.2 Fixed schedule with reverse mainstreaming.

LEVEL 5: REVERSE MAINSTREAM IN SPECIAL SCHOOL
        5.1 Students from special school go to regular physical education at regular school 1–2x per week.
        5.2 Nondisabled students come to special school 2–3x per week for reverse mainstreaming.
        5.3 Students with and without disabilities meet at community-based recreation facility and work out together.

From "An Alternative to Least Restrictive Environments: A Continuum of Support to Regular Physical Activity" by M.E. Block and P.L. Krebs, *Adapted Physical Activity Quarterly* (Vol. 9, No. 2), p. 104. Copyright 1992 by Human Kinetics Publishers. Reprinted by permission.
APE = adapted physical education; RPE = regular (general) physical education.

and what activities are involved, 3) what general modifications are appropriate for certain students in order to ensure their success, 4) what contraindications (and safety precautions) are important to note for certain students, 5) what methods can be used for encouraging peers to interact with students who have disabilities, and 6) to whom support personnel should talk if they have questions. This training (which should be both preservice and ongoing) can be conducted by a general physical education specialist who has had success in including students with disabilities in general physical education and/or an adapted physical education specialist. In addition, during every physical education class, the general physical educator and/or adapted physical education specialist should provide information to support personnel regarding that day's specific activities and suggested modifications. Too often, untrained (i.e., untrained for physical education) special education teachers, paraprofessionals, and peer tutors are asked to provide support to a student with disabilities who is placed in general physical education. This inevitably results in confusion on the part of the support person, on-the-spot decision making, and unorganized, and perhaps even unsafe, physical education.

Preparing the General Physical Educator

Steps 1–4 in this model allow you to develop goals for a child and to determine how these goals can be met in general physical education programs. At this point, you are just about ready to include the student in general physical education, but first you must make sure that the instructor and the other students feel comfortable having a person with disabilities in their class (Morreau & Eichstaedt, 1983). While some general physical educators will feel comfortable with this situation, others will feel very threatened (Minner & Knutson, 1982; Santomier, 1985). Those who feel uncomfortable argue that they have not had the necessary training, that the student will take too much of their time, that it will be dangerous, or that the other students will not accept the child with a disability.

For inclusion to be truly successful, the physical education teacher must learn to feel comfortable with the notion of having students with disabilities included in the general program. This can be accomplished in several ways. First and foremost, those physical educators who feel most threatened should be assured that they will receive both direct and consultative support from an adapted physical education specialist or a special educator with training in adapted physical education. This specialist will be responsible for developing the individual program for the student with a disability, obtaining and setting up adapted equipment, and developing appropriate modifications to the general program. Assurances should be given that including a student with disabilities will not result in more work for the general physical educator. In addition, general physical educators should be assured that students with disabilities, especially those with the most significant disabilities, will receive support from peer tutors, paraprofessionals, a special educator, or an adapted physical educator. The general physical educator should not be left alone with the student until he or she feels comfortable with the situation.

It is also important that the general physical educator understand his or her responsibilities when including a student with disabilities in a program. As always, the instructor's responsibilities are to the entire class, not just to one or two students. The general physical educator should not spend any more time with the student who has disabilities than he or she does with other students and should feel comfortable talking with, correcting, and reinforcing the student with a disability, just as he or she would with any other child. In addition, activities should continue to be challenging for all students; the general program should never be compromised. For example, skill hierarchies should be extended to accommodate students with disabilities while still providing challenging activities for more skilled students (see Figure 2). Similarly, modifications to group activities and team sports should be made so that students with disabilities can be included without detracting from the program for the other participants. For example, it would be inappropriate to play sit-down volleyball (in which all students sit in chairs) to make the game more equitable for a student who uses a wheelchair. This would change the game for the students without disabilities and potentially cause them to resent having a student with disabilities in their class. A better modification would be to allow the team that includes a student who uses a wheelchair to have an extra hit before they have to hit the ball over the net (the reason for this modification being that the student who uses a wheelchair will have difficulty hitting the ball directly over the net, but will be able to pass it to teammates well). The student who uses a wheelchair could also be allowed to move closer to the net when serving. Such modifications would not effect students without disabilities, yet would allow the student with disabilities to successfully play volleyball with his or her peers (see Table 6 for organizations that can provide information on modifications of group games and team sports). It is important that general physical educators understand how certain modifications to games affect the entire class, and they should strive to implement only those modifications that allow a student with disabilities to participate without drastically effecting the other students in the class.

_____ will:

1. _____ touch ball with hand/head stick when ball is placed on lap tray.
2. _____ hold ball on lap tray.
3. _____ hold ball on lap tray while he or she is pushed in wheelchair around gym.
4. _____ push ball off lap tray.
5. _____ drop ball to floor.
6. _____ drop ball to floor, then reach down to touch ball before it bounces three times.
7. _____ drop ball to floor, then reach down to touch ball before it bounces two times.
8. _____ drop ball to floor, then reach down to touch ball before it bounces one time.
9. _____ push ball to floor with two hands so that ball bounces up to approximately waist height.
10. _____ push ball to floor with two hands two times in succession.
11. _____ push ball to floor with two hands three times in succession.
12. _____ push ball to floor with one hand two times in succession.
13. _____ push ball to floor with one hand three times in succession.
14. _____ push ball to floor with one hand five times in succession.
15. _____ push ball up and down repeatedly with one hand.
16. _____ dribble ball while standing still for 10 seconds.
17. _____ dribble ball while standing still for 20 seconds.
18. _____ dribble ball while walking forward slowly.
19. _____ dribble ball while walking forward at normal walking speed.
20. _____ dribble ball while walking forward quickly.
21. _____ dribble ball with dominant hand while jogging forward.
22. _____ dribble ball with dominant hand while running forward.
23. _____ dribble ball with nondominant hand while walking forward.
24. _____ dribble ball with nondominant hand while jogging forward.
25. _____ dribble ball with nondominant hand while running forward.
26. _____ dribble ball with either hand while weaving through cones.
27. _____ dribble ball using a cross-over dribble while weaving through cones.
28. _____ dribble ball with either hand while moving in a variety of directions.
29. _____ dribble and protect ball while guarded by opponent going at full speed.

Cue Key (prompts can be given by physical educator, teacher assistant, or peer tutor):

I   = independent
IN   = indirect cue
V   = verbal cue
G   = gestural cue
M   = model
T   = touch prompt
PP   = partial physical assistance
P+   = physical assistance (student tries to help)
P   = physical assistance (student passively participates)
P−   = physical assistance (student fights assistance)

Performance Key:

+   = student performs skill 4 out of 5 tries
+/− = student performs skill, but not 4 out of 5 tries
−   = student does not perform skill

Figure 2. Extension of traditional skill station for dribbling a basketball. (From Block, M.E., Provis, S., & Nelson, E. [1994]. Accommodating students with special needs in regular physical education: Extending traditional skill stations. *Palaestra, 10*[1], 32–38; reprinted by permission.)

Preparing Class Members without Disabilities

A final consideration in inclusion is the attitude of students toward having a person with disabilities in their physical education class. It is often assumed that the initial response of many students to inclusive physical education will be negative because of fear, prejudice, or lack of awareness. Surprisingly, early results from a study conducted by Block and Zeman (1992) suggested that children in middle school actually had positive attitudes towards including students with disabilities in the general physical education program. Female students tended to be more positive than males, and students who had already had a peer with disabilities in their physical education class tended to be more positive than those who had not.

While attitudes toward integration may be positive, too often students are overly sympathetic toward their peer with disabilities; they tend to "baby" them, or are not sure how to approach or assist them. Thus, peers will need some training to effectively support students with disabilities. There are several ways in which you can help peers develop a more positive attitude toward inclusive physical education. First, students should be taught about persons with disabilities in a positive manner. One method for changing attitudes is to bring in guest speakers who participate in sports such as wheelchair racing or basketball, sit-skiing or skiing for the blind, or Special Olympics inclusive sports such as Unified soccer or softball. These people can dispel stereotypes that hold that persons with disabilities cannot play sports. Local organizations affiliated with national sports associations (e.g., the United States Association for Blind Athletes, National Wheelchair Sports Association, Special Olympics) are excellent resources for recruiting speakers.

A second method for changing attitudes is role playing in which students are given a disability. This technique has been used for years in Red Cross adapted aquatics classes, as well as in physical education programs in which students with disabilities are to be included (Mizen & Linton, 1983). Students can be asked to move through an obstacle course while wearing a blindfold, to sit in chairs and play volleyball or basketball, or to try to hit a softball with one arm tied up. The teacher should facilitate discussions regarding how a peer with a disability might feel when he or she is trying to participate in these activities. Discussions should also include how, in some situations, a person with a disability may actually be at an advantage over the typical student. For example, a person who is blind can move around his or her home when the lights are out much better than a sighted person can.

A final method for changing attitudes is to discuss the purpose of sports rules and how they can be modified to successfully include all students. Discussion should include the concept of "handicapping" (e.g., in sports such as golfing and horse racing) in order to equalize competition and how this method can be applied to physical education. For example, a student who is blind might have difficulty hitting a pitched ball and running to first base. A fair modification for this student might be allowing him to hit a ball off of a tee. When he or she must run to first base, a peer can guide the student. Since it takes longer for the student to run to first base, the bag could also be moved closer to home plate. This would also make it more challenging for the students' peers to tag him or her out. Ideally, several distances to first base should be established so that very skilled students must run farther than average students, who in turn must run farther than students with physical disabilities.

In addition to general methods designed to change attitudes, the instructor should discuss with students the specific disabilities (and abilities) of the student who will be integrated into the class, focusing on how similar this student is to them. For example, it could be pointed out that this student is the same age they are, likes to wear similar clothes, enjoys playing and watching sports, hates the food in the cafeteria, and argues with his parents about bedtime or curfew. The students should discuss positive ways in which peers can assist a student with disabilities during physical education by helping him or her with retrieving balls, locating stations, and moving from one part of the gym to another. Also, peers should be allowed to visit the student in a special class, or in other integrated classes such as art, history, industrial arts, or music. Similarly, the student with disabilities should be encouraged to visit the general physical education class, and his or her peers should be encouraged to introduce themselves and chat. By preparing the students ahead of time, many common fears, misconceptions, and stereotypes can be shattered before they can affect the class itself.

Preparing students is important for successful inclusion, but encouragement should not stop once a student with a disability enters a program. Too often, students with disabilities are ignored in physical education because their peers do not know how to interact with or assist them. The teacher should provide ongoing encouragement to peers (both through modeling and direct suggestion) to talk to the student with disabilities, to provide feedback and positive reinforcement, to gently correct or redirect the student when he or she misbehaves, and to periodically ask the student if he or she needs assistance. Rather than having a single peer assigned to a student with a disability, every member of the class should be encouraged to do his or her part. For example, if a student who has mental retardation does not know which station to go to, any one of his peers who happens to be nearby can assist him or her. Similarly, if a student who is blind has lost the ball he or she was dribbling, any peer can help retrieve it. Peers should be continuously prompted and reinforced for interacting with the student with disabilities. As the year progresses the students will begin to feel more comfortable, and interactions are likely to become more spontaneous.

CONCLUDING COMMENTS

The purpose of this chapter is to outline a model for including students with disabilities in general physical education. The model begins with establishing individual goals for students with disabilities—goals that are beneficial to the student regardless of his or her placement. This is followed by a detailed analysis of the general physical education curriculum and suggestions for modifications and support. Modifications are designed to help a student achieve his or her individual goals, as well as to facilitate inclusion in general physical education. The model concludes with the subject of training for support personnel, general physical educators, and students without disabilities. Proper training of all persons who are directly involved in inclusion will ensure its success.

Included in the discussion of this model are numerous suggestions on how students with disabilities can be successfully included in general physical education. The model takes a proactive approach to integration in which planning and training prior to inclusion are the keys to success. Too often, students with disabilities are hastily placed in a general physical education class with little or no support, or are assisted only by peers or paraprofessionals without any specialized knowledge about physical education. Such attempts at inclusion are rarely successful. It is no wonder that so many adapted physical education professionals argue against the inclusion of most students with disabilities in general physical education. However, general physical education can be an appropriate placement for students with disabilities, including those who need the most support. When inclusion is implemented properly, students with disabilities can work on their individual goals in general physical education settings while also experiencing positive interactions with their peers without disabilities. With the proper guidance, typical students are given an opportunity to learn about and appreciate students with different abilities. When conducted properly, inclusive general physical education is the best environment for *all* students to improve physical fitness, fundamental motor skills and patterns, individual- and team-sport skills, and lifetime leisure skills.

REFERENCES

Adams, R., & McCubbin, J. (1991). *Games, sports and exercises for the physically handicapped* (4th ed.) Philadelphia: Lea & Febiger.

Aloia, G., Knutson, R., Minner, S.J., & Von Seggern, M. (1980). Physical education teachers' initial perception of handicapped children. *Mental Retardation, 18*, 85–87.

Arbogast, G., & Lavay, B. (1986). Combining students with different ability levels in games and sports. *Physical Educator, 44*, 255–259.

Aufsesser, P.M. (1991). Mainstreaming and the least restrictive environment. How do they differ? *Palaestra, 7*(2), 31–34.

Block. M.E. (1988). *Motor Activities Training Program Guidebook*. Washington, DC: Special Olympics International.

Block, M.E. (1992). What is appropriate physical education for students with profound disabilities? *Adapted Physical Activity Quarterly, 9*, 197–213.

Block, M.E. (1994). *A teacher's guide to including students with disabilities in regular physical education*. Baltimore: Paul H. Brookes Publishing Co.

Block, M.E., & Krebs, P.L. (1992). An alternative to the least restrictive environment. A continuum of support to regular physical education. *Adapted Physical Activity Quarterly, 9*, 95–113.

Block, M.E., Provis, S., & Nelson, E. (1994). Accommodating students with severe disabilities in regular physical education: Extending traditional skill stations. *Palaestra, 10*(1), 32–38.

Block, M.E., & Zeman, R. (1992). [Development and validation of "Children's Attitudes Towards Integrated Physical Education (CAIPE) Scale]. Unpublished raw data.

Brown, L., Branston, M.B., Hamre-Nietupski, S., Pumpian, I., Certo, N., & Gruenewald, L. (1979). A strategy for developing chronological-age appropriate and functional curricular content for severely handicapped adolescents and young adults. *The Journal of Special Education, 13*, 81–90.

DePaepe, J.L. (1984). Mainstreaming malpractice. *Physical Educator, 41*, 51–56.

DiRocco, P. (1978). Preparing for the mainstreamed environment: A necessary addition to preservice curriculums. *JOHPERD, 49*(1), 24–25.

Dunn, J., & Fait, H. (1989). *Special physical education*. Dubuque, Iowa: Wm. C. Brown.

Education for All Handicapped Children Act of 1975, PL 94–142. (August 23, 1977). Title 20, U.S.C. 1401 et seq: *U.S. Statutes at Large, 89*, 773–796.

Education of Handicapped Children: Implementation of Part B of the Education of the Handicapped Act. (1977, August 23). *Federal Register, 42*, 42474–42518.

Florida Department of Education (1982). *Comprehensive Physical Activity Curriculum* (Project COMPAC). Miami: Dade County Public Schools.

Grosse, S. (1991). Is the mainstream always a better place to be? *Palaestra, 7*(2), 40–49.

Individuals with Disabilities Education Act of 1990 (IDEA), PL 101–476. (October 30, 1990). Title 20, U.S.C. 1400 et seq: *U.S. Statutes at Large, 104*, 1103–1151.

Jansma, P., & Decker, J. (1990). *Project LRE/PE: Least restrictive environment usage in physical education*. Washington DC: Department of Education, Office of Special Education.

Lavay, B., & DePaepe, J. (1987). The harbinger helper: Why mainstreaming in physical education doesn't always work. *JOHPERD*, *58*(7), 98–103.

Marsallo, M., & Vacante, D. (1983). *Adapted games and developmental motor activities for children*. Annandale, VA: Marsallo/Vacante.

Minner, S.H., & Knutson, R. (1982). Mainstreaming handicapped students into physical education: Initial considerations and needs. *Physical Educator*, *39*, 13–15.

Mizen, D.W., & Linton, N. (1983). Guess who's coming to P.E.: Six Steps to more effective mainstreaming. *JOHPERD*, *54*(8), 63–65.

Morreau, L.E., & Eichstaedt, C.B. (1983). Least restrictive programming and placement in physical education. *American Corrective Therapy Journal*, *37*(1), 7–17.

Santomier, J. (1985). Physical educators, attitudes and the mainstream: Suggestions for teacher trainers. *Adapted Physical Activity Quarterly*, *2*, 328–337.

Taylor, S.J. (1988). Caught in the continuum: A critical analysis of the principle of the least restrictive environment. *Journal of The Association for Persons with Severe Handicaps*, *13*, 41–53.

Turnbull, H.R. (1990). *Free appropriate public education: The law and children with disabilities* (3rd ed.). Denver: Love Publishing Co.

Wessel, J.A., & Kelly, L. (1986). *Achievement-based curriculum development in physical education*. Philadelphia: Lea & Febiger.

Winnick, J.P. (1978). Techniques for integration. *JOHPERD*, *49*(6), 22.

~nine~

Promoting Inclusive Recreation and Leisure Opportunities for Adults

Pam Walker

Much has been learned in the early 1990s about assisting children with developmental disabilities to participate in inclusive recreation and leisure experiences at camps, neighborhood centers, schools, and other settings within the community (Heyne, 1987; Walker & Edinger, 1988; Walker, Edinger, Willis, & Kenney, 1988). But considerably less has been written about adults with disabilities, even though research indicates that recreation opportunities are lacking even for those who live in the community (Reiter & Levi, 1986; Sparrow & Mayne, 1990). Further effort needs to be directed toward increasing the leisure options available to adults by supporting their participation in a wide variety of community activities and settings. This chapter focuses on strategies for promoting inclusion in recreation and leisure activities and for creating opportunities for social relationships and valued community roles and membership to develop.

The chapter begins with some general principles of inclusive recreation and leisure. Next, three broad steps for promoting inclusion are highlighted. The final section presents examples of four disability-service agencies and community organizations that are making efforts to facilitate and support integrated recreation opportunities for adults.

PRINCIPLES FOR INCLUSIVE RECREATION AND LEISURE

There are a number of principles that should guide thinking about inclusive leisure opportunities for adults:

Recreation and leisure should be defined broadly to include participation in formal and informal programs and activities with groups of people, with one or a few friends, and by oneself (G. Allan Roeher Institute, 1988)

Preparation of this chapter was supported in part by the U.S. Department of Education, Office of Special Education and Rehabilitative Services, National Institute on Disability and Rehabilitation Research (NIDRR) through Cooperative Agreement No. H133B00003-90 awarded to the Center on Human Policy, Division of Special Education and Rehabilitation, School of Education, Syracuse University. The opinions expressed herein are those solely of the author and no official endorsement by the U.S. Department of Education should be inferred.

The author would like to acknowledge the assistance of Michelle Brown, Chris Liuzzo, Deborah Reidy, and Betsy Edinger for their comments on earlier drafts of this chapter.

People with even the most significant disabilities have the right to participate in and enjoy a wide variety of age-appropriate leisure experiences together with people without disabilities across their life span (Schleien & Ray, 1988)

The role of agencies and programs should be to facilitate and support the inclusion of people with disabilities in general recreation and leisure programs, settings, and experiences (Center on Human Policy, 1991)

People with disabilities should have maximum choice among recreation and leisure activities, and when assistance in the selection of activities is necessary, family members, friends, and others who know the person with a disability well should be involved (Rynders & Schleien, 1991; Voeltz, Wuerch, & Wilcox, 1982)

Recreation and leisure settings, programs, and activities should be physically accessible to people with disabilities (Schleien & Ray, 1988)

People with disabilities should be provided with whatever types and levels of support they need in order to participate in integrated leisure activities (Center on Human Policy, 1991)

Supports should create opportunities for social interaction and the development of friendships (Johnson, 1985; McGill, 1987; Rynders & Schleien, 1991; Walker, 1990).

STEPS TO PROMOTE INCLUSIVE RECREATION AND LEISURE

Promoting inclusive recreation and leisure opportunities for adults takes the combined efforts of people such as family members, residential service staff, educators, specialized recreation personnel, community recreation personnel, and other community members (Schleien, Light, McAvoy, & Baldwin, 1989). There are three keys to promoting inclusive recreation for adults: getting to know the person; knowing the community; and supporting participants in their relationships, settings, and activities.

Getting to Know the Person

In planning ways to involve an adult in leisure activities, one of the best places to begin is getting to know the person him- or herself. This entails spending time with the person and with those who know him or her well in order to learn about the person's family, background, experiences, racial/cultural/ethnic identifications, strengths, and likes or dislikes.

In this way, one can begin to discover a person's interests so that they can be further developed or pursued. O'Brien and Lyle (1987) speak to the importance of interests:

> Interests link the personal and the social. They express individual gifts, concerns, and fascinations and call for activities, information, and tools. Shared interest founds associations. People point to interests when they describe what gives their lives meaning. (p. 35)

Table 1 illustrates some specific steps that can be taken to learn about a person and his or her interests. Over time, a person can establish a "leisure identity" (McGill, 1987) by developing an interest to the extent that it becomes one of his or her primary defining characteristics. This can help take the focus off of a disability as a primary defining characteristic.

Table 1.   Menu for discovering a person's interests

Listen carefully and respond actively to the person, to family and friends, and to direct service workers. Show people that what they say makes a difference. The longer a person's own ideas and wishes have been ignored the longer this can take.

Decrease social distance between staff and the people who rely on them. Do away with practices and language that separate "us" from "them."

Increase personal knowledge through shared experiences and conversations.

Increase the person's control of the immediate environment, of the schedule and choice of activities, and of the people who assist.

Negotiate conflicts rather than overpowering a person. Look for ways that each party to a conflict can win. When safety is not at risk, be willing to "lose" in order to build a more equal relationship.

Use objections as the basis of plans instead of as a reason not to act.

Catch yourself making self-fulfilling prophecies. Instead of saying, "It's impossible," ask, "What would it take for the person to do it and what would the benefits and risks be?"

Discover what you can of the person's history. Think about what the person's experiences have been like. Look for clues to past interests or connections.

From O'Brien, J., & Lyle, C. (1987). *Framework for accomplishment.* Lithonia, GA: Responsive Systems Associates; reprinted by permission.

Some people will have had very limited opportunities to try a variety of activities in different settings with a diversity of people. They may also have difficulty communicating ideas about potential interests. Thus, there may be a need to spend significant amounts of time with a person with a disability who is trying out different activities and settings. An assistant or supporter may have to make some initial "best guesses" as to what types of things to try, and may also want to gather family, friends, and others together with the person him- or herself to brainstorm ideas.

For one middle-age woman who had lived most of her life in an institution and was moving to a small group home, the only interest indicated in her records was that she liked chocolate. Based on only this, several minutes of brainstorming generated a number of ideas for potential activities (see Table 2). These included activities that she could do alone and with others, in her home and in a variety of community settings, and activities through which she could make a valuable contribution to her community. With this as a starting point, one interest might lead to others, to the development of friendships, and to involvement in community organizations and associations. It could also contribute to the establishment of a positive and valued identity for the woman within the community.

In other instances, people's expressed interests may seem to be either totally unreasonable or inappropriate for their age. In such cases, the typical response is to dismiss the interests entirely. This is a serious mistake that can result in choice being taken out of the person's hands, and to future reluctance on his or her part to express interests.

As an alternative, staff, family members, and others can help explore possible pursuits related to the expressed interest that may satisfy, at least in part, the person's desires. When a person's interests are not age-appropriate—if, for example, an adult collects stuffed animals—it is probably best not to deny the person that interest, but to also begin encouraging the development of related, more age-appropriate interests.

Table 2. Examples of preferences and corresponding potential activities

Preference:	Likes chocolate
Activities:	1. Sample different recipes at restaurants
	2. Obtain cookbooks at the library or bookstore
	3. Bake a cake and invite others to a gathering, take it to a gathering, share it with a neighbor or friend, or donate it for a bake sale or community event
Preference:	Wants to be an airplane pilot
Activities:	1. Take a plane trip
	2. Build/collect model airplanes, join a club
	3. Go to air shows, aeronautical museums
	4. Obtain magazines and books on airplanes and related topics at the library or bookstore
Preference:	Collects stuffed animals
Activities:	1. Maintain collection with valued, attractive items
	2. Pursue other interests related to animals—own one, work in a pet shop
	3. Start collections of other valued, age-appropriate items

Knowing the Community

A second step in helping people become involved in recreation and leisure activities is to become aware of opportunities within the community (Center on Human Policy, 1990; Center for Urban Affairs and Policy Research, 1988). This involves: 1) investigating usage of various neighborhood and community settings (finding out who uses them, when, and for what purposes); and 2) investigating various neighborhood and community organizations and associations (finding out what groups are active in the community, and what it takes and means to be a member of each of them). This type of information can be gathered by observing and talking to a variety of people in different community settings and by reading community newspapers, bulletin boards, and directories. Table 3 provides a sample of the range of different types of groups and organizations that might be found within a typical community. Chapters 3 and 4 provide advice on gathering information on recreational opportunities in your own community.

Supporting People in Relationships, Settings, and Activities

A third key to implementing inclusive recreation is assisting people to participate in activities and interactions in various settings. This often entails some level of facilitation or "bridgebuilding" to achieve not only physical, but also social inclusion in a setting or group (Mount, Beeman, & Ducharme, 1988). It can involve such things as accompanying a person with a disability to a setting for the short or long term; assisting the person with eating, drinking, and so forth during the activity; assisting in communication and social interaction; and identifying and nurturing other people as potential allies and sources of support.

Lutfiyya (1991, pp. 10–11) discusses these roles as falling under the three broad headings of facilitation, interpretation, and accommodation. *Facilitation* refers to activities that help bring people together; *interpretation* to those occasions when a person is presented in a positive and enhancing way to others; and *accommodation*

Table 3. An associational map

Artistic organizations: choral, theatrical, writing

Business organizations: Chamber of Commerce, neighborhood business associations, trade groups

Charitable groups and drives: Red Cross, Cancer Society, United Way

Church groups: service, prayer, maintenance, stewardship, acolytes, men's, women's, youth, seniors

Civic events: July 4th, art fair, Halloween

Collectors groups: stamps, antiques

Community support groups: friends of the library, nursing home and hospital volunteers

Ethnic associations: Sons of Norway, Black Heritage Club, Hibernians

Health and fitness groups: bicycling, jogging, exercise

Interest clubs: poodle owners, antique car owners

Men's groups: cultural, political, social, educational, vocational

Mutual support (self-help) groups: Alcoholics Anonymous, Epilepsy Self-Help, La Leche League

Neighborhood and block clubs: crime watch, neighborhood beautification, holiday decorating

Outdoor groups: gardening, Audubon Society, conservation

Political organizations: Democrats, Republicans, caucuses

School groups: printing club, PTA, child care

Service clubs: Zonta, Kiwanis, Rotary, American Association of University Women

Social cause groups: peace, rights, advocacy, service

Sports leagues: bowling, swimming, baseball, fishing, volleyball

Study groups: literary, bible study

Veterans' groups: American Legion, Amvets, Veterans of Foreign Wars and Auxiliaries

Women's groups: cultural, political, social, educational, vocational

Youth groups: 4H, Future Farmers, Scouts, YWCA

Prepared by John McKnight, Northwestern University, Center for Urban Affairs and Policy Research, 2040 Sheridan Road, Evanston, IL 60208.

to the actual changes in the physical or social environment that make it easier to include an individual in some way.

In the context of the relationship that developed between Melvin, a man with significant disabilities, and Lori, a paid support worker, Traustadottir (1991) provides some examples of facilitation and of interpretation or "translation":

> Melvin's inability to participate in group conversations is mostly due to how slow his speech is, how long it takes him to prepare himself to say something, and how long it takes him to say one sentence. Thus, it is impossible for him to "jump in" or keep up with the flow of the conversation in a group. Lori is very skilled at facilitating Mel's participation . . . To a large extent Lori participates in the conversation on Melvin's behalf by referring to him constantly. She tells stories about what he has done, what he said, how he acted in certain situations, what his opinion is about certain things, and so on. She also draws Melvin into the conversation by opening up a "space" for him to add a sentence. . . . Another important function Lori fulfills as Melvin's support person is to "translate" for him. The translating Lori does goes two ways; she translates from Mel to other people, and to Mel what other people say (due to his hearing loss). Melvin is very hard to understand and when people do not understand what he says Lori will repeat it. In addition, because it is such an effort for Melvin to speak, Lori often adds explanations or information about what he is talking about. Lori also translates on a different level . . . Lori conveys to other people what Mel wants to do, what he can and cannot do . . . and so on. (pp. 24–27)

This kind of connecting or bridgebuilding support may be provided by either professionals or volunteers. Most important is the relationship between the two people—that there is a close personal bond characterized by mutuality and trust (Traustadottir, 1991). When paid employees are involved in this type of effort, it is important to recognize that the human services system does not inherently promote the development of this type of relationship, and in fact creates barriers to it (O'Brien & Lyle O'Brien, 1991; Traustadottir, 1991). As more has been written about the development of natural supports (Nisbet & Hagner, 1988) and about interweaving formal and informal supports (Bulmer, 1987), attention has been drawn to related service system issues, including: 1) the fact that the efforts of unpaid people (e.g., family members, and mothers in particular) often go unrecognized by the service system; 2) ways that the efforts of unpaid people are thwarted or hindered by the service system (e.g., having to sign up as an agency volunteer in order to be a friend); and 3) the difficulties and challenges of service system recruitment and securing the assistance of unpaid community members to support people with disabilities (in order to guard against "dumping" people into the community without adequate assistance).

A number of lessons have been learned by people who make such bridgebuilding efforts on behalf of those with disabilities (Mount et al., 1988):

1. ***These efforts are best made on a small scale*** It can take a lot of time and effort, sometimes much longer than anticipated, to help a person with disabilities form community ties. Therefore, it is best that the facilitator be involved in trying to generate community support and connections for only a few people at any one time.

2. ***The personal, local connections of the bridgebuilders are critical to their efforts*** It is often through knowledge of the community and personal connections that the bridgebuilder can best assist the person with a disability to develop relationships. These personal resources are generally more valuable than any type of professional training.

3. ***There are no set rules or models to follow*** Bridgebuilding calls for creative decisions and judgments. Also, there is no set time that a bridgebuilder or facilitator should remain in a setting with a person; this can vary from several days or a few weeks to as long as the participant him- or herself is involved. The field of developmental disabilities has traditionally been oriented toward an assumption of progression along a continuum of support from dependence to independence (Taylor, 1988). Part of bridgebuilding is to refute this assumption—to decrease people's dependence on paid human services workers while at the same time maintaining a commitment to providing paid support as long as it is needed or desired. Ending paid support too soon may result in negative experiences for the person with disabilities and/or for other community members. Even when paid support workers are no longer actively providing direct support in a situation, it may be important for them to maintain contact in case a problem arises or the situation changes somehow (e.g., if a committed ally leaves the setting or organization). In addition, there may be certain persons who will always require or desire that a paid individual be present to assist them (some people, for example, do not want their friends or associates to have to provide certain kinds of support).

The next section focuses on agencies that utilize components of the steps above in order to promote inclusion and participation. It also describes in detail the philosophical basis and efforts of one community organization that strives to be inclusive of a wide diversity of people.

AGENCIES AND ORGANIZATIONS THAT PROMOTE INCLUSIVE RECREATION AND LEISURE OPPORTUNITIES FOR ADULTS

This section describes four diverse agencies or organizations that provide support to facilitate the inclusion of adults with disabilities in recreation or leisure pursuits. They include: a residential service agency, the recreation/leisure initiative of a community education and training organization, a county-level ARC, and a community organization.

Wildwood: A Residential Service Agency[1]

One private, nonprofit residential service agency created a "community bridge-builder" staff position focused on assisting people with disabilities in community residences to become members of community clubs or associations and, in some cases, to establish one-on-one personal relationships with peers without disabilities. Over $1^1/_2$ years, 12 people were assisted to become members and participants in groups and settings such as a Civil War Roundtable, a history club, a church group, and an environmental center.

Some of the strategies used by Michelle, the bridgebuilder, include: 1) getting to know people well; 2) doing research on groups, clubs, and settings in the community; 3) doing research on the nature of these settings—the characteristics of people who attend and the routines and activities that take place; and 4) when a potential match is found, going, either alone or with the person whom she is assisting, to visit the site and meet with group members. Michelle matches people with groups and activities based primarily on her instinctual judgment on a situation-by-situation basis.

Once the person has begun participating in the club or setting, Michelle thinks of possible ways to encourage friendships between the person whom she is assisting and others in the setting and to decrease her presence while maintaining her availability and support. Some of her strategies include:

Looking for people in the setting who seem to have or be interested in establishing a connection with the person and thinking of ways to encourage this, if necessary (e.g., inviting the person for coffee after a meeting; asking the person to provide occasional transportation)

Getting to know others in the setting and, on this basis, encouraging relationships between them and the person whom she is assisting

Staying in touch with and available to group members (to answer any questions or provide necessary assistance) if and when she is no longer coming to the setting regularly

Recruiting a "staff advocate" within the person's residential setting to play a primary role in assisting the person to maintain his or her connections and participation in the group or setting.

Connections, for some people, may develop quickly, whereas for others this may take longer. For example, one man whom Michelle assists who joined the history club has been going for $1^1/_2$ years, and, according to Michelle, is "just now getting to know some people there." In order to determine if the setting and/or group is work-

---

[1]This section is based on an interview with Michelle Brown and Chris Liuzzo, of Wildwood Programs, on June 25, 1991.

ing well, Michelle tries to take the person's perspective to evaluate the situation and tries to determine whether he or she seems to enjoy the activities and the other participants.

It is not possible for Michelle, by herself, to both establish and maintain connections for everyone served by the agency, so she conducts annual training for the other staff, enabling and encouraging them to incorporate some of the bridgebuilding strategies into their every day work. She uses information gained from her training in areas such as Citizen Advocacy, Social Role Valorization, and Personal Futures Planning,[2] as well as from her contacts with others making bridgebuilding efforts elsewhere around the country. This gives all the staff members the basic skills and strategies necessary to help maintain some of the connections that Michelle has initiated, as well as to initiate some on their own. One of her frustrations is the rate of staff turnover at the agency, which can cause disruption or discontinuity of people's connections and relationships.

The agency created Michelle's position with funds allocated for a "community residence counselor." Such changes require flexibility and creativity as agencies seek to redefine staff roles and responsibilities to better match agency values and priorities. They are sometimes possible through use of existing funds, as was done at Wildwood, but sometimes require that additional funds (internal or external), such as grants (e.g., from a state developmental disabilities council or a foundation), be sought.

The Association Integration Project[3]

The Association Integration Project (AIP) was also designed to help foster people's sense of belonging in the community through membership in community organizations and associations. It is part of a larger, ongoing project, Education for Community Initiatives (ECI), the purpose of which is to encourage, support, and educate citizens to allow them to take constructive actions with and on behalf of people with disabilities. Throughout the 3-year course of the AIP, which was funded through a grant from a state developmental disabilities council, 19 adults with developmental disabilities were assisted in joining community groups or associations consistent with their interests and desires. There were two staff people—a project coordinator (full-time) and a project supervisor (quarter-time). The responsibilities of the project coordinator included:

> identifying community organizations; matching individuals with organizations; and giving advice, encouragement, and practical help to the person with a disability and to other members of the community groups; and gradually phasing out her involvement while ensuring that the member with a disability was able to continue participating as long as he or she chose. (Reidy, 1990, p. 1)

The intent of the project was to encourage those with disabilities to go beyond mere attendance or participation in a community organization by filling valued roles, such as officeholder or member of a working committee.

---

[2]Citizen Advocacy involves efforts to match "advocates" without disabilities in one-to-one relationships with "protégés" with disabilities. Social Role Valorization was formerly known as the normalization principle. Personal Futures Planning is an alternative to traditional human services planning; it involves more control and choice being exercised by the person with a disability and less by professionals.

[3]This section is based on an interview with Deborah Reidy, Director, Education for Community Initiatives, on March 14, 1991. It draws heavily on Reidy, D. (1990). *Executive summary: The Association Integration Project.* Holyoke, MA: Education for Community Initiatives.

During the course of this project, adults with disabilities have become involved with groups such as a Bible Study, a walking club, the NAACP, the Junior League, a Puerto Rican–American Club, the Holyoke League of Arts and Crafts, the Knights of Columbus, and the American Association of Retired Persons (AARP). Based on individual desires and needs, some adults have been paired with peers in a one-on-one relationship rather than with a community association or organization.

Those who designed the AIP intentionally adhered to the following guidelines:

1. The project was carried out using traditions and practices familiar to community members (e.g., relying on informal discussions rather than training as a means of education; employing local residents).
2. There was a major emphasis on the personal qualities of the individual assisting directly in the process of inclusion (e.g., maturity, credibility, good judgment, sensitivity, common sense, local "connections," natural instinct for hospitality).
3. Since the relationships between the project, community groups, and participants with disabilities were strictly voluntary, the process of enlisting support and participation necessitated great delicacy.
4. The project was deliberately kept small scale and focused on a limited geographic area in order to ensure the greatest possible impact and depth.
5. Each situation was carefully pursued in order to emphasize valued roles for the person with a disability and to build on common interests.
6. Those conducting the project were careful to avoid introducing more than one person with a disability into any single community group.
7. Project staff encouraged voluntary support from within the group rather than offering extra assistance or additional funds.
8. Constancy and quality of leadership were considered important qualities; staff members were required to have a deep commitment to personal inclusion and significant theoretical and practical experience in this area, and to place emphasis on systematic and intentional support in order to avoid "dumping."
9. The emphasis of the project was educational, and staff members were committed to carefully recording and evaluating their efforts.

The staff of the AIP learned a number of lessons from their experiences. One thing they noted was that community members will usually welcome a person with a disability into their group or activity. This does not happen automatically, nor, in some situations, easily, but much of what has been characterized as resistance is actually just a reflection of the long history of separation between people with disabilities and other community members.

Those involved in AIP also learned that the most effective approach is an individualized one. This applies to the people with disabilities as well as facilitators. There are many dangers in over-formalizing this kind of effort.

A third lesson was related to the acceptance of people by community organizations. It was found that the match between the person and the group was a much more significant factor than the type or degree of disability.

Finally, in terms of generating support, it proved to be more effective to recruit a member from within the group to take on a sponsorship role than it was to leave it up to the group to do something on their own; group members were hesitant to take on such roles without outside encouragement. This seemed to reflect not unwillingness, but initial uncertainty and discomfort concerning how best to relate to the person with a disability.

In summary, there are two limitations of the AIP approach: 1) the project was of limited duration—3 years is a relatively short period, especially with regard to helping community groups move toward including persons with disabilities on their own; and 2) not all people's needs are best met through membership in a group—some may benefit more from the establishment of a one-on-one relationship.

The majority of those involved in the AIP continued to participate in their groups even after the project ended. The AIP demonstrated that membership in community organizations is possible and realistic for persons with disabilities. Membership in these groups has had significant impact on these person's lives, as well as on the groups and their members. It has resulted in, at minimum, increased social activity and interactions for those involved within the context of group activities, and for some people, it has also led to close personal relationships that extend beyond the group's activities.

ARC Suburban[4]

ARC Suburban is an example of an agency that changed its direction from providing segregated leisure services to encouraging integrated leisure supports. In the mid-1980s, staff at this ARC came to the conclusion that, based on the values of inclusion, segregation was not acceptable, and they should commence a process of change. This 3-year process entailed the development of a new mission statement, new goals, and strategies to achieve these goals (see Table 4). The mission statement read: "The ARC Suburban exists to lead the community toward an improved quality of life for citizens with mental retardation and related conditions."

The agency's new goals included: providing individuals and families with information and education in order to allow them more opportunities within their communities and increasing the linkages between the agency and community in order to further promote inclusive recreation. The strategies included: 1) the use of materials and resources that focused on effective inclusion to educate consumers, professionals, and the general public; and 2) the provision of training and technical assistance to public and private leisure services personnel and other community members involved in the development of inclusive leisure services. According to the agency's director, these changes were not easily accepted, and there was an "enormous public outcry" at the loss of segregated programs. In particular, there was heated controversy over the decision not to support the Special Olympics.

In order to implement some of the strategies designed to promote integrated recreation, this ARC hired an "integration facilitator," whose role was threefold: 1) to provide assistance to individuals and families in gaining access to community leisure opportunities and obtaining supports and adaptations as needed; 2) to provide training and support to community leisure service providers (direct-service staff and administrators) in the inclusion of people with developmental disabilities; and 3) to provide information and referrals regarding community leisure options. This effort contributed to the inclusion of children and adults in leisure activities within settings and organizations such as schools, Parks and Recreation Departments, YMCAs, Community Education Departments, the Girl Scouts, camps, and neighborhood centers. In addition to the focus on leisure organizations, the facilita-

---

[4]This section is based on a site visit to ARC Suburban, then located in Burnsville, Minnesota, in July, 1989. It reflects the agency as it was at that time, and not any changes that have occurred since then.

Table 4.   ARC Suburban 3-year plan 1988–1990

This plan reflects new initiatives and those initiatives requiring increased attention for the next few years. ARC Suburban will maintain its efforts in such areas as family education and support, public information, advocacy, and demonstration project development.

Program initiatives	Desired outcomes	Key strategies
Strengthen individuals and their families to gain opportunities within their communities.	Individuals and families will access information/education in new multi-media ways as well as traditional ARC approaches.	Obtain state-of-the-art audio, video, and written resources geared toward families and the professionals working with them. Focus resources on effective integration.
		Market these resources to the professionals who have direct contact with families and adults with mental retardation.
		Develop and support contacts in informal parent networks, initiate co-sponsorship of informational programming for families, professionals, and community leaders.
	Individuals and their legal representatives will have an adequate level of individual advocacy service.	Increase staff support for individual advocacy services.
Build bridges to the community.	Direct linkages exist between ARC volunteer leadership and policy makers.	Provide training and technical assistance to volunteers focusing on effective integration.
		Develop and implement an adequate information flow system.
		Increase staff support for public policy development.
	Community acceptance of ARC mission and philosophy.	Focus public information on integration and target the general public.
	Public and private community operated, leisure services are used by children and adults with mental retardation and related conditions.	Promote the development of integrated leisure alternatives.
		Provide technical assistance to local public and private leisure services.
		Educate consumers and professionals regarding the value of integrated options.

(continued)

Table 4. (continued)

Management initiatives	Desired outcomes	Management
Increase independent funding sources for Community Integration Services and for Community Leisure Services.	Any ongoing service or program will have multiple funding sources.	Design and implement a strategic plan which emphasizes agency flexibility in meeting community needs and is volunteer driven.

From ARC Suburban. (1988). *ARC Suburban three year plan 1988–1990.* Unpublished document, Burnsville, MN; reprinted by permission.

tor worked to assist some people in developing or increasing their personal social network and provided support for advocacy and self-advocacy.

The process of change within this ARC took some time and did not proceed without conflict. In addition, funds for the facilitator position were eventually eliminated. Yet, it is important to note the many positive outcomes of such an effort. Through their working together to resolve conflict, members of the organization developed an increased sense of ownership of the agency and a deeper commitment to the mission and values behind the process of change. In addition, many more community agencies and organizations are now willing and able to include some children and/or adults with disabilities. Furthermore, involvement in recreation and leisure activities in inclusive settings led to increased opportunities for many children and adults to get to know a wide diversity of people and to increase their sense of participation and membership in the neighborhoods and communities in which they live.

The Syracuse Community Choir[5]

The Syracuse Community Choir is a community organization built on a philosophy of inclusion. The choir's mission statement appears in Table 5. As a result of this philosophy, and of the conscious and intentional efforts of the director and members of the choir, the choir includes a wide diversity of people of different ages, racial and ethnic backgrounds, musical talents, and physical and intellectual abilities.

Among the 50–60 members of the choir is Ann, who is blind and has significant developmental disabilities. Ann lives in a group home with five other residents. A staff member from the home heard about the choir and initially assisted Ann and two other residents in joining. Within a short time, it became clear that Ann liked to sing and enjoyed the choir, while her two housemates did not get as much enjoyment out of the group. The choir director brought this to the attention of the group home staff, who agreed that only Ann should remain a member of the choir.

Ann's participation in the choir is supported by both group home staff and choir members; staff transport her to and from rehearsals and concerts, while choir members assist her during these activities. Over time, two problems arose that illustrate ways in which residential service providers can inadvertently create barriers to a person's social integration into a community organization. One was that, at least for a time, the group home staff had as a goal for Ann that she would independently ride a "call-a-bus" service to choir events. However, there were some choir events to

[5]This section is based on discussions with Karen Mihalyi, Director, Syracuse Community Choir, Syracuse, NY.

Table 5.   Syracuse community choir mission statement

The Mission of the Syracuse Community Choir is to:

Create a musical community which is open to everyone. To that end, the only requirement
   is a desire to sing and a willingness to learn new music. (There will be no auditions.)

Sing music that is progressive and alternative, such as:
   Songs that address issues of oppression.
   Songs of peace, freedom, justice, and liberation movements.
   Songs of people's stories, struggles, resistance, and victories.
   Songs that reflect our reverence for the earth.
   Songs that give a vision of what a better world will be and open up possibilities for change.
   Songs and music that reflect a variety of cultures and countries.
   Songs and music of many diverse styles including (but not limited to) musicals, classical,
   jazz, and popular.
   Songs by musicians not heard in the mainstream culture.

Perform and promote this music in the greater community.

Build community within the Choir
   We seek to provide a safe, open, inclusive community which is accessible to *all*. For
   example, we attempt to accommodate people who would like to improve their singing
   ability, people who need childcare, we practice and perform in facilities that are accessible
   to people who use wheelchairs, we provide music in Braille, our concerts are interpreted
   for people with hearing impairments, and we attempt to assist people who need
   transportation to rehearsals and performances.
      We also seek to promote community by providing opportunities for education,
   information and discussion with members about oppressions such as racism, sexism, and
   homophobia.

Build community outside the Choir through our concerts and events

Provide lessons, workshops, and collaboration with other artists such as writers,
   composers, poets, dancers, musicians, and graphic artists. We do this 1) for concerts,
   events, productions; 2) to improve the quality of choir musicianship; and 3) in conjunction
   with events in the greater community.

Sound good and have fun

From Syracuse Community Choir. (1991). *Syracuse Community Choir Mission Statement.* Unpublished document, Syracuse, NY; reprinted by permission.

which all the other members carpooled. Thus, when staff rigidly stuck to this goal,
Ann missed out on opportunities to ride with other choir members and on the
socializing that took place during the drive. Second, Ann often arrived either late or
just in time for choir and left immediately afterward. Because choir members do
most of their informal socializing just before and after rehearsal, Ann missed out on
many opportunities to mingle with members of the group. Communication initiated
by choir members has helped alleviate this problem to some extent, but staff
turnover at the group home results in a lack of continuity in these areas if new staff
members are not properly informed about the situation.

   Ann spends a good portion of her life surrounded by people with disabilities—
in her home and at her day treatment program. Although she makes a lot of trips in
the community with group home staff, the choir is one of the only places where she
goes regularly and where she has the opportunity to develop and maintain relationships over time with nonprofessional persons without disabilities. Her communication is difficult to understand, and her needs include assistance with any movement

(e.g., before and after rehearsal, during breaks, to the restroom) necessary to perform a choir activity or socialize. Over the 5 years that Ann has been in the choir, the number of other members who know her (understand her communication, know some things about her personal life and her interests) and who are comfortable providing assistance to her has increased significantly.

This example illustrates how critically important it is that residential services staff maintain communication with members of community organizations. They must be willing to listen to and learn from representatives of community organizations in order to increase their understanding of how such groups work and to best support people's fullest possible membership and participation.

FUTURE DIRECTIONS AND ISSUES

Many more adults with disabilities live, work, and enjoy recreation in the community today than in the past. However, as Bogdan and Taylor (1987, p. 210) point out, "Being in the community is not the same as being part of the community." Further effort must be made to help people gain access to integrated leisure experiences that also provide opportunities to develop social relationships and to assume valued roles in the community. The strategies described above represent efforts toward this objective. Based on the experience of these agencies and organizations, some critical issues surrounding the inclusion of adults with disabilities are:

Ensuring that adequate supports are provided   Agencies must have a commitment to ensure, as much as possible, that supports are provided—through either volunteers or professionals—to help generate a positive experience for people with disabilities and other community members. This will be a step toward helping community members learn to initiate inclusion on their own.

Directing more resources toward the development of integrated options, and not using choice as a rationale to promote segregated activities   In the past, segregated recreation and leisure programs were the only option for many adults with developmental disabilities. However, if we believe in and value inclusion, our efforts should be focused on expanding inclusive options, and our vision should be one that includes eliminating the need to choose segregated options.

Learning about, and from, community settings and organizations   There is an ongoing need to learn about the nature and culture of community settings and, based on this information, to develop strategies to assist and support people with disabilities to become active participants in them (O'Connell, 1990). It is also important for human services agencies to listen to and learn from those involved in community organizations that already include people with disabilities, such as the community choir described earlier.

Collaboration among diverse human and community services providers and community members   In order to provide the best opportunity for recreation and leisure, representatives of diverse human- and community services agencies will need to collaborate with one another and with others in the community (Schleien et al., 1989). This includes people such as family support workers, service coordinators, residential service providers, and specialized and generic recreation personnel. For adults in particular, residential service providers can have a strong effect on integrated recreation—either by creating significant barriers or significant opportunities. Recently, some residential service agencies, such as Options in Community Living and Centennial Developmental Services, Inc., have made it a priority to help people become involved in their communities and develop social relationships (Johnson, 1985; Walker & Salon, 1991). These agencies devote staff-meeting time to problem solving and formulating strategies for providing whatever types and level of support will be necessary to assist people with disabilities—including the ongoing, active involvement of staff members with those whom they support—in community activities.

Building community coalitions People with disabilities will benefit from the recognition that the recreational needs of adults with disabilities may not be very different from those of other community members. For example, the need for activities for older adults with disabilities may simply reflect a broader, community-wide need of older adults in general. Or, the need for transportation for people with disabilities may indicate a lack of transportation for others in the community who have mobility problems (such as older adults and those with small children) and/or those with limited incomes. It is important that people in disability-related fields increase their efforts to work collaboratively with other community members, as this will help community members recognize all that people with disabilities have in common with others, and will benefit the lives of many, not just those with disabilities.

The examples provided throughout this chapter illustrate a variety of strategies used by diverse organizations to support adults participating in inclusive recreation activities and programs. These supports are based on common values—on the right of all people to be part of the community, with the supports they need, and to experience social relationships and valued social roles. Providing such support takes time and hard work, and there is no single best way to approach the task. Inclusive recreation can lead to interaction and social relationships, just as friendships can provide a vehicle for increased leisure activity. Also, there is no single person or group of people who are best qualified to make these efforts, or who should be responsible for doing so; these efforts can, and should, involve the person with a disability, family members, educators, recreationists, residential service providers, and other community members. As integrated recreation becomes a priority for a wider range of people, adults with disabilities will have increased opportunities to enjoy the same activities and experiences as other community members, and the quality of their lives will be enhanced.

REFERENCES

ARC Suburban. (1988). *ARC Suburban three year plan 1988–1990.* Unpublished document, Burnsville, MN.

Bogdan, R., & Taylor, S.J. (1987). Conclusion: The next wave. In S.J. Taylor, D. Biklen, & J. Knoll (Eds.), *Community integration for people with severe disabilities* (pp. 209–213). New York: Teachers College Press.

Bulmer, M. (1987). *The social basis of community care.* London: Allen & Unwin.

Center for Urban Affairs and Policy Research, Northwestern University and Department of Rehabilitation Services, State of Illinois. (1988). *Getting connected: How to find out about groups and organizations in your neighborhood.* Springfield, IL: Author.

Center on Human Policy. (1990). A guide to knowing your community. *CTAT Field Report,* 1(1), pp. 8–9.

Center on Human Policy. (1991). *Principles for integrated recreation/leisure.* Syracuse, NY: Author.

G. Allan Roeher Institute. (1988). *Leisure connections: Enabling people with a disability to lead richer lives in the community.* Richmond Hill, Ontario, Canada: Author.

Heyne, L. (1987). *Integrating children and youth with disabilities into community recreation agencies: One agency's experience and recommendation.* St. Paul, MN: The Jewish Community Center of the Greater St. Paul Area.

Johnson, T.Z. (1985). *Belonging to the community.* Madison, WI: Options in Community Living and Wisconsin Council on Developmental Disabilities.

Lutfiyya, Z.M. (1991). *Tony Santi and the bakery: The roles of facilitation, accommodation, and interpretation.* Syracuse, NY: Center on Human Policy.

McGill, J. (1987). Our leisure identity. *Entourage, 2*(3), 23–25.

Mount, B., Beeman, P., & Ducharme, G. (1988). *What are we learning about bridge-building?* Manchester, CT: Communitas, Inc.

Nisbet, J., & Hagner, D. (1988). Natural supports in the workplace: A reexamination of supported employment. *Journal of The Association for Persons with Severe Handicaps, 13*(4), 260–267.

O'Brien, J., & Lyle, C. (1987). *Framework for accomplishment.* Lithonia, GA: Responsive Systems Associates.

O'Brien, J., & Lyle O'Brien, C. (1991). *Members of each other: Perspectives on social support for people with severe disabilities.* Lithonia, GA: Responsive Systems Associates.

O'Connell, M. (1990). *Getting connected: How to find out about groups and organizations in your neighborhood.* Evanston, IL: Center for Urban Affairs and Policy Research, Northwestern University, and Department of Rehabilitation Services, State of Illinois.

Reidy, D.E. (1990). *Executive summary—Association Integration Project.* Holyoke, MA: Education for Community Initiatives.

Reiter, S., & Levi, A. (1986). Leisure activities of mentally retarded adults. *American Journal of Mental Deficiency, 86*(2), 201–203.

Rynders, J.E., & Schleien, S.J. (1991). *Together successfully: Creating recreational and educational programs that integrate people with and without disabilities.* Arlington, TX: Association for Retarded Citizens of the United States.

Schleien, S., Light, C., McAvoy, L., & Baldwin, C. (1989). Best professional practices: Serving persons with severe multiple disabilities. *Therapeutic Recreation Journal, 23*(3), 27–40.

Schleien, S.J., & Ray, M.T. (1988). *Community recreation and persons with disabilities: Strategies for integration.* Baltimore: Paul H. Brookes Publishing Co.

Sparrow, W.A., & Mayne, S.C. (1990). Recreation patterns of adults with intellectual disabilities. *Therapeutic Recreation Journal, 24*(3), 45–49.

Syracuse Community Choir. (1991). *Syracuse Community Choir Mission statement.* Unpublished document, Syracuse, NY.

Taylor, S.J. (1988). Caught in the continuum: A critical analysis of the principle of the least restrictive environment. *Journal of The Association for Persons with Severe Handicaps, 13*(1), 41–53.

Traustadottir, R. (1991). *Supports for community living: A case study.* Syracuse, NY: Center on Human Policy.

Voeltz, L.M., Wuerch, B.B., & Wilcox, B. (1982). Leisure and recreation: Preparation for independence, integration, and self-fulfillment. In B. Wilcox & G.T. Bellamy (Eds.), *Design of high school programs for severely handicapped students* (pp. 175–209). Baltimore: Paul H. Brookes Publishing Co.

Walker, P. (1990). *Resources on integrated recreation/leisure opportunities for children and teens with developmental disabilities.* Syracuse, NY: Center on Human Policy.

Walker, P., & Edinger, B. (1988). The kid from cabin 17. *Camping Magazine,* May, 18–21.

Walker, P., Edinger, B., Willis, C., & Kenney, M.E. (1988). *Beyond the classroom: Involving students with disabilities in extracurricular activities at Levy Middle School.* Syracuse, NY: Center on Human Policy.

Walker, P., & Salon, R. (1991). Integrating philosophy and practice. In S.J. Taylor, R. Bogdan, & J.A. Racino (Eds.), *Life in the community: Case studies of organizations supporting people with disabilities* (pp. 139–152). Baltimore: Paul H. Brookes Publishing Co.

~SECTION FOUR~

INCLUSION IN ACTION

The final section of this volume brings it all together by showing how the right philosophy, facilitators, strategies, and knowledge about age-group preferences can be used to change systems, whether community organizations, school programs, or entire municipalities. Chapter Ten provides a model for making municipal recreation and parks departments programs inclusive, as these organizations are the traditional providers of most community leisure activities. Chapter Eleven shows how day camps, where most school-age children spend at least some part of their summer, can be made inclusive. Finally, Chapter Twelve presents ideas for providing disability awareness training to adolescents without disabilities in school programs. Helping this group accept their peers with disabilities and learn to facilitate inclusive leisure participation will be the key to future efforts in this arena.

~ten~

A Model for Making County and Municipal Recreation Department Programs Inclusive

Gina Wagner, Laura Wetherald, and Billie Wilson

Montgomery County, Maryland, is made up of a diverse population of over 750,000 citizens with a wide variety of income levels, educational backgrounds, and cultural influences. The Montgomery County Department of Recreation is located in the heart of the county, surrounded by Washington, D.C., suburbs, rural farmlands, and waterways. As a department, we strive to provide quality recreational and leisure opportunities to all citizens of the county, including the approximately 75,000 residents with disabilities. In 1980, at the urging of parents and advocates, the Montgomery County Department of Recreation established the Therapeutic Recreation Section, a division whose major goal is to enhance the quality of life of individuals with disabilities through recreation and leisure activities.

As the department grew in its commitment to meeting the needs of individuals with disabilities, it became clear that inclusion was the only sensible policy to follow. In 1984, after much research, planning, and study, a very challenging inclusion initiative was instituted. The department director and staff adopted a philosophy based on the assumption that people with disabilities had been traditionally but wrongly denied their right to participation in community recreational programs. What follows is a description of Montgomery County's plan to include citizens with disabilities in general recreation and leisure activities.

THE PROCESS OF INCLUSION

The implementation process employed by the department is characterized by a level of flexibility necessary to meet the individual needs of each participant. It is also nonintrusive in nature, because only essential accommodations that do not draw undue attention to the participant's disability are provided. The goal is simply to allow each individual with a disability to make a comfortable transition into general recreation programs. Table 1 is an outline of the implementation process; elements of this process and the roles of the key participants are described below.

The integration supervisor is responsible for assisting individuals with disabilities of all ages in gaining access to programs, camps, and classes that are offered by the department of recreation to residents of Montgomery County. The supervisor oversees the training and education of the entire recreation department, including program supervisors and the classroom instructors, who must be informed about the individual's specific strengths and needs. This is typically handled by making phone calls and mailing a disability-awareness sheet, which gives details on a child's particular condition, before a class begins to meet. When additional accommodations, such as an integration companion or interpreter, are necessary, the instructor is also informed that someone will be attending the class, program, or camp to assist the individual with a disability to successfully participate. The supervisor manages a team of integration facilitators and a paid volunteer coordinator who assists in the provision of support and accommodations necessary for success. Chapter 2 provides more detailed information on the roles of professionals serving as integration supervisors and volunteer coordinators.

Step 1: Initial Contact/Registration

Requests to participate in activities are made in a variety of ways. Although the majority of contacts are either self-initiated or initiated by a family member or advocate, outside-agency referrals also often occur. Such referrals are encouraged by the integration supervisor through regular outreach to such organizations as schools, churches, group homes, day activity centers, and other human services agencies. Supervisors of therapeutic recreation programs may also encourage and assist an individual with a disability to initiate an inclusive endeavor.

The initial contact is made either with the integration supervisor or directly with the targeted program or class. To facilitate the direct registration process, an integration plan has been developed (see Figure 1) so that a recreation supervisor or others can guide an individual with a disability in the right direction.

Table 1. Implementation process for inclusive recreation

Step 1: *Initial contact and registration process*   The individual's interests are assessed, a suitable program is identified, the application is reviewed, and the individual is registered.

Step 2: *Data gathering*   The individual with a disability or his or her parents are contacted to discuss questions, concerns, and requests for specific accommodations.

Step 3: *Accommodations*   The need for assistive equipment, interpreters, transportation, financial assistance, and/or companions is determined and filled.

Step 4: *Training*   Staff, companions, and other participants are given information and training on inclusion and disabilities in general, as well as any relevant information on the future participant's specific disability.

Step 5: *Participation*   After the individual with a disability, program staff, and companion have received a copy of the Integration Plan, the individual begins to join in the activity or program.

Step 6: *Follow-up*   The Integration Supervisor or companion appraises the degree of success of the accommodations.

Step 7: *Evaluation*   Participants and companions assess their experience.

Step 8: *Documentation*   The Integration Supervisor documents progress and logs statistics.

Step 9: *Process continuation*   Staff and companions stay in touch with the individual and encourage him or her to become involved in other inclusive programs.

INTEGRATION PLAN

Date _____

Season _____
(S)ummer, s(P)ring, (W)inter, (F)all

INTEGRATION PLAN Returning __ yes __ no

* Participant's Name: _____ Age: __ DOB: __ / __ / __

 Address: _____ H. Phone: (___) _____

 _____ W. Phone: (___) _____

 Parent/Guardian _____

 Race: (C)aucasian   (B)lack   (H)ispanic   (A)sian   American (I)ndian _____

 School: _____ Teacher: _____ Phone: (___) _____

 ACCOMMODATIONS Please Check: ☐ Companion   ☐ Scholarship   ☐ Transportation

 ☐ Interpreter   ☐ Notify Instructor   ☐ Equipment   ☐ Facility

 Other _____

 Primary Disability: _____   (P)hysical (L)earning (R)etardation (E)motional
                                  (H)earing (V)isual sei(Z)ure (M)ultiple (O)ther

 Secondary Disability: _____

 Special Instructions: _____

 _____

AGREEMENT

 Camp/Class/Other _____ Session _____ Class # _____

 Location _____ Address _____

 Supervisor _____ Area __ CODE: (E)astern, (N)orthern, (W)estern, (G)aithersburg, (R)ockville

 Phone (___) _____ Section _____ CODE: s(P)ecial services, (S)enior,   (T)herapeutics,
                                                        a(Q)uatics,   (A)rts,   (O)ther

 Name of Instructor/Director _____ Phone (___) _____

 Address _____ City _____ State __ Zip _____

 Date Begins ___ / ___ / ___ Day(s) _____ Week(s) _____ Total Comp/Partic. Hours _____

 Date Ending ___ / ___ / ___ Time commitment from _____ to _____ Total Daily Hours _____

* Companion's Name: (☐ V ☐ P) _____ Total Hours Participated ___

 Address _____ City _____ State _____ Zip _____

 Phone (H) (___) _____ (W) (___) _____ Driver's Lic. # _____

 Signature _____ Date ___ / ___ / ___

 Interpreter's Name _____ M.C. # _____ Total # Hours _____

IMPORTANT   ### INFORMATION CHECKLIST

* It is the responsibility of the Participant/Guardian to contact the   ☐ Companion   ☐ Supervisor
 Companion and Integration Facilitator if you are unable to attend   ☐ Instructor   ☐ Vol. Coordinator
 as planned.   ☐ Interpreter   Follow-Up ☐ P ☐ C ☐ I
                                                                        ☐ Participant   Evaluation ☐ P ☐ C ☐ I
 INTEGRATION FACILITATOR   ☐ Scholarship   Thank Yous ☐ P ☐ C ☐ I

 _____

 W. PHONE: 217-6890   H. PHONE:

_____

(*continued*)

Figure 1.   Montgomery County Department of Recreation integration plan form.

Figure 1.   *(continued)*

NOTES TO COMPANION

_____

_____

_____

_____

_____

COMPANION'S STATEMENT OF COMMITMENT

- I understand I am committing myself to this relationship for one session.

- I understand I am expected to work cooperatively in the program to provide a high quality recreation program for this individual.

- I understand it is important for me to attend staff meetings and participate in training sessions (camp staff only).

- I understand I will be supervised by the Integration Supervisor and will be evaluated at the conclusion of the session.

- I understand this is a *serious commitment*, and *dependability is essential*. Therefore, I will make every effort to arrive at my work site on time and, in the event of illness or family emergency, to call my assigned participant and Integration Supervisor as much in advance as possible.

- I further understand that Montgomery County Department of Recreation has the right to terminate my position at any time if my conduct is not compatible with the goals and objectives of my assigned position.

Step 2: Gathering Data

The inclusion planning sheet (Figure 1) serves as a data-gathering tool to help facilitate an individual's entry into a department activity. If the individual who desires to be included registers directly with a program or class, the supervisor of the activity is expected to complete the first two sections of the form before forwarding it to the integration supervisor. The integration supervisor then continues to use the form as a follow-up sheet to chart progress in the coordination of the inclusion effort. In some cases, the integration supervisor may need to contact the individual requesting inclusion to discuss accommodations or possible program alternatives, and this information would also be recorded in the plan. The plan is also used to record information on companions, whose role is described in the next section.

Step 3: Planning Accommodations and Determining Challenge Level

Although not always necessary, the step of planning accommodations is usually the most important and time-consuming part of the process of inclusion. Accommodations may include, among other things, financial assistance, transportation arrangements, an interpreter, additional staff training, adaptive equipment or techniques, or an inclusion companion. Because of the importance of the support provided by an inclusion companion, this role is described in greater detail below.

Challenge Levels Because including individuals with disabilities in recreation programs does not follow the same pattern of support and accommodations each time the process is implemented, challenge levels were developed and have become an integral part of the process of inclusion. As depicted in Table 2, the concept of varying challenge levels has been developed to describe the many possibilities for inclusion, depending on the participant's needs. This concept does not represent a progression through which an individual must achieve increasing independence but, instead, each challenge level is viewed as a separate entity. Thus, a participant might move back and forth between levels to suit his or her particular level of independence for a specific recreation activity. For instance, someone might be comfortable in a Challenge Level I ceramics class, but might need more support for an aerobics class, and so be in Challenge Level III for this activity. Table 2 shows the type of support provided at each level with examples.

The Inclusion Companion as an Accommodation Perhaps the most significant accommodation that can be made to ensure the success of an inclusive placement is the provision of an inclusion companion who can accompany an individual with a disability to programs or classes. This person provides support by acting as

Table 2. Accommodations and challenge levels

Challenge level 1: *No accommodations* (participation is self-initiated by the person with a disability with, at most, a single telephone consultation by a support person.)

Examples: A man who uses a wheelchair begins to attend a photography class in his community after a telephone call to check on whether the building is accessible; a 7-year-old boy with learning disabilities is registered for an afterschool T-ball program after the coach is notified and given adaptation suggestions.

Challenge level 2: *Limited accommodations*

Examples: A woman with a visual impairment is provided transportation and financial assistance in order to allow her to attend a ceramics class in the community; a 9-year-old girl attends a gymnastics class with the help of a cued speech interpreter.

Challenge level 3: *Substantial accommodations*

Examples: A child with Down syndrome needs one-to-one assistance to attend an area summer camp, so an inclusion companion is assigned; a man with cerebral palsy has poor coordination and balance problems, but is able to join a local weaving class after the loom is adapted with extenders and other participants are given advice on how to assist him if necessary.

Challenge level 4: *Separate programs* (structured to focus on the skills necessary to ensure success in the community: socialization, appropriate behavior, communication, money management)

Examples: An Adult Social Club is attended by persons 18 and older who participate in weekend activities, community trips, and so forth; children attend a special camp for 2- to 5-year-olds with speech and language delays.

an advocate—by highlighting the individual's abilities, underscoring his or her similarities to peers, diffusing subtle attitudinal barriers, and developing a climate of acceptance. The companion also has the opportunity to allay any barriers or insecurities within the individual with a disability and to help him or her develop healthier, more open attitudes. The companion should also provide one-to-one assistance so that the time of the members of the general recreation staff is not unfairly monopolized by the student with a disability.

Because the role of the integration companion seems so vital to the success of many programs, the Montgomery County Department of Recreation has placed a great deal of emphasis on matching companions to individuals wishing to be included. Although 85% of the companions are volunteers, when a volunteer with the appropriate expertise for a particular situation is not available, a qualified companion is hired to work on an hourly basis. We have found this to be a particularly attractive job for teenagers and college students, who regularly participate in our programs.

The volunteer coordinator—a paid staff member who works 20 hours each week—recruits, selects, trains, and provides follow-up for the inclusion companions.

Step 4: Training

Training professional staff, companions, and participants without disabilities is an essential part of the process of inclusion. A variety of formats and tools have been developed for use in such training, including manuals, information and awareness sheets, bi-monthly newsletters, and inservice workshops.

The integration supervisor is responsible for providing workshops for recreation staff and integration companions throughout the year. Workshop topics have included: 1) the benefits of inclusive leisure service, 2) methods for accommodating participants with disabilities, 3) characteristics of different types of disabilities, 4) the function of the integration companion, and 5) enhancing sensitivity of and communications with participants without disabilities. Inservice formats are not only intended to enhance the skills and confidence of professional staff and companions but also to provide individual orientation and hands-on experience prior to the inclusion of particular individuals.

Step 5: Participation

As participation begins, the Integration Plan (see Figure 1) is used as a communication tool concerning the accommodations being provided. Copies are distributed to the participant, the general recreation staff, and the companion (when applicable) to ensure that all arrangements are clearly understood by the individuals involved.

Step 6: Follow-Up

When an integration companion is not required, the integration supervisor contacts the participant and the instructor of the program or activity after the first session to appraise the success of the accommodations. Unless a change is needed, the integration supervisor then assumes the role of consultant. When an integration companion is involved, follow-up is primarily carried out through him or her and is ongoing in nature. The volunteer coordinator acts as liaison between the integration supervisor and companions and monitors the progress of the companions during most activities.

Step 7: Evaluation

Evaluation is very important to the inclusion process because it provides the means for continual improvement. Every participant (or his or her guardian) and every integration companion evaluates each activity (see Figures 2 and 3) once the activity has ended. These data allow program staff to change activities or instructors, to provide different types of training to companions, or to work more closely with families to develop new activities or program accommodations.

Step 8: Documentation

Keeping a quantitative record of the department's efforts at inclusion has become an important part of the integration supervisor's job. This yearly and seasonal data helps justify both staff positions, such as that of the integration supervisor and volunteer coordinator, and predicts when and where accommodations and companions are likely to be necessary. As Table 3 indicates, the growth in the numbers of people with disabilities served in the integrated activities as well as increases in companions and accommodations over the past 4 years is significant.

Step 9: Process Continuation

The final step in the process of inclusion depends on communication with each participant to encourage continued involvement in parks and recreation programs. Personal letters and phone calls to guardians and participants regarding upcoming activities is one way to facilitate ongoing participation. A call or visit from a former companion can also be effective. The main point here is to simply stay in touch with participants so that they know what is available and feel welcome.

The success of the integration efforts of the Montgomery County Department of Recreation is rooted in the commitment of the citizens of the county and their government to equal access to recreation for people of all ages and ability levels. Years of planning, a willingness to continually try new programs, and the provision of funds and professionals devoted solely to making activities inclusive have allowed us to open all of our programs to all citizens of the county.

REFERENCE

Schleien, J., & Ray, M.T. (1986). *Integrating persons with disabilities into community leisure services.* Minneapolis: University of Minnesota.

MONTGOMERY COUNTY DEPARTMENT OF RECREATION
THERAPEUTIC RECREATION SECTION

Name _____   Instructor/Director _____

Date _____   Program _____

Code _____   Companion _____

EVALUATION FORM: PARTICIPANT/GUARDIAN

We would appreciate your thoughtful evaluation of the program attended. Please answer the
questions that are appropriate and return promptly to:
  Integration Facilitator
  Montgomery County Department of Recreation
  Therapeutics Section
  12210 Bushey Drive
  Silver Spring, MD 20902-1099

Thank you for your help as we work toward improving future programs.

PART I.   Program Evaluation

1.   How did you hear about the program? _____
_____

2.   Please rate the program *(Excellent, Good, Fair, Poor or Not Observed)* and comment:

Punctuality of the program   _____
Organization of the program   _____
Communication of program information   _____
Staff and volunteer sensitivity   _____
Your/your child's integration socially   _____
Level of enjoyment   _____
Cost of the program   _____

Comments: _____
_____

3.   What were the observed strengths of the program/class? _____
_____

4.   What were the observed weaknesses of the program/class? _____
_____

(continued)

Figure 2.   Participant/guardian program evaluation form.

Figure 2. (*continued*)

For Office Use Only:

   Name of Companion _____ Program _____

   Name of Participant _____ Date _____

PART II   **Integration Facilitator Evaluation**

    Integration Facilitator's Name _____

1.   Please rate the Integration Facilitator's service *(Excellent, Good, Fair, Poor, Not Observed)* and comment:

    Accommodations provided   _____
    Communication of information   _____
    Providing helpful information   _____
    Sensitivity and Understanding   _____
    Timely response   _____
    Overall satisfaction of the service   _____

    Comments _____

    _____

PART III   **Integration Companion Evaluation** (If a companion was provided)

1.   Please rate the Integration Companion *(Excellent, Good, Fair, Poor, Not Observed)* and comment:

    Friendly attitude   _____
    Personal Appearance   _____
    Enthusiasm   _____
    Prompt/Dependable   _____
    Encouraged Independence   _____
    Overall satisfaction of their service _____

    Comments _____

    _____

2.   Did the Companion contact you before the program started?   ☐ Yes   ☐ No

3.   Did you think the pre-contact was helpful? _____

    _____

4.   What were the Integration Companions' strengths? _____

    _____

5.   What were the Integration Companions' weaknesses? _____

    _____

6.   Would you request an Integration Companion again?   ☐ Yes   ☐ No

MONTGOMERY COUNTY DEPARTMENT OF RECREATION
THERAPEUTIC RECREATION SECTION

Companion Name_____
Program/Class_____
Participant's Name_____
Date _____

EVALUATION FORM: INTEGRATION COMPANION

Dear Integration Companion;

　　We would appreciate your thoughtful evaluation of the program in which you were assigned as a companion. Please answer the following questions and return it promptly to:

Montgomery County Department of Recreation
Therapeutics Section
Integration Staff
12210 Bushey Drive
Silver Spring, MD 20902-1099

1.　Do you feel you received adequate orientation regarding your integration assignment? If not, what do you suggest?

_____

_____

_____

2.　How useful did you find the Integration Companion Handbook? Please circle:
　　　　Excellent　　Very Helpful　　　Helpful　　Fair　　　　Poor

Comments:

_____

_____

_____

3.　Was the program leader or the individual who supervised the program supportive? Please explain.

_____

_____

_____

Figure 3.　Integration companion program evaluation form. (Adapted from Schleien & Ray, 1986.)

Figure 3.   (*continued*)

4.   In what ways was the experience beneficial to you personally and professionally?

_____

_____

_____

5.   Did you feel the experience was worthwhile?   Explain:

_____

_____

_____

6.   Did you feel overworked during the program?   If so, in what ways?

_____

_____

_____

7.   Would you volunteer for another assignment as an integration companion?

_____

_____

8.   Additional Comments:_____

_____

_____

_____

9.   What level of disability do you feel comfortable with? _____

_____

_____

Table 3. Overview of the Montgomery County Department of Recreation inclusion initiative

	Disabilities								Companions			Accommodations			Sections					
	M R	Physical	Emotional	Visual	Hearing	Learning	Multiple	Total	Volunteer	Paid	Hours	Interpreter	Financial	Transportation	Special Services	Senior	Therapeutics	Aquatics	Arts	Other
1989																				
Summer	18	12	13	0	6	15	5	69	18	22	2,812.0	4	4	5						
Fall	12	5	5	4	3	0	4	33	24	1	280.0	3	6	–						
Winter	8	5	4	2	7	2	0	23	12	2	103.0	6	2	10						
Spring	8	5	4	2	7	2	0	28	18	0	2,546.5	7	3	15						
Total	42	26	25	11	22	17	10	153	72	25	3,449.5	20	15	30						
1990																				
Summer	17	23	20	4	21	52	2	139	27	53	4,191.0	15	2	5	13	10	0	18	0	18
Fall	9	5	6	1	5	0	11	37	10	10	146.0	4	6	4						
Winter	10	14	5	18	11	0	18	76	14	10	224.0	11	1	22						
Spring	18	14	8	18	8	0	0	66	18	10	193.5	8	5	26						
Total	54	56	39	41	45	52	31	318	69	83	4,754.5	28	14	57	13	10	0	18	0	18
1991																				
Summer	20	24	16	4	34	29	3	130	29	32	5,566.0	18	3	6	28	9	1	8		
Fall	6	5	11	15	10	0	36	83	16	1	118.0	10	9	16	33	7	–	8		
Winter	8	6	17	18	6	5	46	106	20	0	260.5	11	6	15	12	8	–	20		
Spring	18	14	8	18	8	0	0	66	18	10	193.5	8	5	26						
Total	52	49	52	55	58	34	85	385	83	43	6,138.0	47	23	63	73	24	1	36		
1992																				
Summer	53	14	18	32	41	51	34	243	108	22	7,933.0	22	–	7	6	2	–	4	–	3
Fall	23	11	6	14	15	0	2	71	18	6	313.0	13	7	25	13	9	–	20	–	12
Winter	11	9	8	18	19	4	17	85	21	12	337.5	18	6	36	17	1	–	4	–	33
Spring	12	18	20	14	14	4	9	84	22	12	439.5	12	16	29	65	–	–	14	–	23

~eleven~

Including Children with Disabilities at Summer Day Camps
A Process for City-Wide Change

M. Sherril Moon,
Paula Rogerson, and Cheska Komissar

One of the most popular community recreation settings for children and adolescents in this country is summer camp, both local day camp and sleep-over camp (Mitchell, Robberson, & Obley, 1977). In fact, aside from school, camp is usually the primary place where children and adolescents learn popular sports, hobbies, and games such as those described throughout this book. It is also where children make many of their friends. Summer day camps have become especially popular in the last 2 decades as more and more families find themselves in need of a substitute for schools to care for children while parents are at work during the day.

Children and adults with disabilities in many communities have, in the past, benefited from segregated camps and camping experiences (Rynders, Schleien, & Mustonen, 1990), but separate camps for children with and without disabilities are no longer needed or justifiable. In fact, the Americans with Disabilities Act (ADA) mandates that segregated programs such as special camps be eliminated as the primary settings for this kind of experience. However, the literature is virtually void of suggestions on how a community or group can make a summer camp program inclusive (Edwards & Smith, 1989).

This chapter illustrates how one community closed down a segregated camp for children and teens with disabilities and reorganized other existing summer programs to be inclusive. This example will be helpful to families, advocates, and program providers for several reasons. First, it demonstrates how one of the most age-appropriate types of recreation programs can be made accessible to a large number of people within a short period of time. Second, it shows how families and agen-

Development of this chapter was supported through a grant from the Office of Special Education and Rehabilitative Services of the United States Department of Education (#H086U00030) to the Training and Research Institute for People with Disabilities at Children's Hospital, Boston, Massachusetts.

cies can work together to plan a new program. Third, it documents the cost effectiveness of an integrated summer program.

THE PLAN FOR THE FIRST YEAR

During the 1980s the Greater Waltham (Massachusetts) Association for Retarded Citizens (GWARC) along with the city school system and parks and recreation department, developed a summer camp, Camp Discovery, specifically for children and adolescents with disabilities. This "special" camp, strongly supported by the GWARC board of directors, parents, and the city, was an important part of the agency's operations, serving approximately 30–50 campers during the summer months. In early 1990 several of the GWARC members (primarily parents of elementary-age children with disabilities) and the recreation director decided that children with disabilities from Waltham should be able to attend inclusive day camps in the city. This group anticipated that some families (primarily parents of older adolescents with disabilities) and GWARC staff would object to a sudden and complete elimination of Camp Discovery. Therefore, the goal for the first half of 1990 was to determine how best to provide the kinds of camp experiences that all families desired for the upcoming summer. Full inclusion across camps and the elimination of Camp Discovery was the plan for 1991.

The general director and recreation director of GWARC and a community leisure facilitator (CLF) from Boston Children's Hospital Project REC met several times and decided to try to offer families several options during this first summer of change. These options included enrolling their sons or daughters with developmental disabilities in one of four city camps, where GWARC camp counselors and other GWARC personnel would provide extra support to each camp's staff. Parents could also enroll their child in the "Camp within a Camp" at the YMCA. In this program, GWARC counselors would accompany campers with disabilities to and from the YMCA each day and provide some separate activities specifically designed for their benefit. GWARC had its own meeting space at the camp, provided some equipment, and applied to the city for a separate operating license. The intent at this camp was to include the participants with disabilities in as many of the YMCA camp activities as possible. This was relatively easy to implement—GWARC personnel simply scheduled activities for campers with disabilities to occur simultaneously with those of the other programs at the YMCA camp.

The City Camps

The GWARC recreation director approached each city camp director during the months of January and February to discuss including campers with disabilities and GWARC staff in their programs. Although a couple of directors were hesitant at first, they were ultimately convinced that having a ratio of one new (GWARC) counselor to every two to four new campers (children with disabilities) was a good idea. They were also assured that the recreation director, the CLF from Boston Children's Hospital, and the GWARC nurse would be on call to assist during any emergency. The other fear expressed was that fees would have to be increased or enrollment would need to be dropped in order to accommodate campers with disabilities. But this was not the case, because GWARC was providing extra staff who would be working with all campers and because children with disabilities would be paying fees equivalent to those of other campers. Actually, enrollment, as well as supervision, would increase.

The GWARC recreation director stressed the importance of the city camps serving all families and the potential benefits of sharing resources. She was quick to point out that families would be very disappointed if the camps were not open to including their children and that they would do everything possible to make this a successful effort. All of the camp directors agreed that their camps should be open to every citizen of the city, and all were willing to try the new approach. A description of the camps in Waltham is provided in Table 1.

Meeting with Parents

The GWARC executive director, the GWARC recreation director, and the consulting CLF held a special meeting for families during late March, immediately after all city camp directors agreed to the plan. The various options and staffing plans were described and families were given the opportunity to sign their kids up for any of the camps for 2-week sessions. Parents could even choose several different camps over the 6-week period: for example, a family could choose the YMCA Camp within a Camp for the first 2 weeks, Girl Scouts for the second 2, and either Boy's or Girl's Club for the final 2 weeks. The only real deterrent to participation was the cost of the camps, which ranged from $90 to $200 for a 2-week period. GWARC did offer scholarships to some families who could not afford all the costs. Families were asked to make their decisions by the first week in May so that 6 weeks would be left to make final plans for making the camps inclusive.

Staffing Plans

Decisions concerning staffing patterns, transportation plans, and final budgets for the camps depended heavily on where families decided to enroll their sons or daughters with disabilities during each 2-week period. The original plan was to hire the same number of counselors (a total of seven) as in previous years, but to assign them to various camps as needed. Of course, the training program would be altered so that counselors would learn to work with *all* campers and would be able to facilitate inclusion. As it turned out, the original hiring pattern was sufficient. Table 2 shows where campers with disabilities were enrolled and how counselors who formerly worked at Camp Discovery were assigned over the entire summer.

One of the factors that facilitated the process of inclusion at various camps was the accessibility of the GWARC recreation director, the CLF, the nurse, and a part-time behavior specialist, all of whom were on call to go to any camp when necessary. The recreation director kept a beeper and could have been at any of the camps within a half-hour, although, incidentally, this never proved to be necessary. The CLF, particularly during the first 2 weeks, visited all the camps to meet with counselors, directors, and parents and alleviate any anxieties about the "new kids" at camp. The CLF and behavior specialist only worked about 10 hours each week, and the nurse was in attendance during weeks when children with physical disabilities or complex medical needs were attending camps.

Training Counselors

Camp counselors hired by GWARC had always received 2½ days of training prior to the beginning of camp each summer. The length of this training period was not changed during the reorganization, but the content was altered to accommodate the new functions of the counselors. Most importantly, they were provided training on how to get the kids with and without disabilities to participate together in activities

Table 1. Description of city camps

	Boys/Girls Club Camp	Girl Scout Camp	City Camp	YMCA Camp
Age of campers	4–13 years	6–14 years (15–16 for Counselors in Training)	4–13 years	3–12 years (13–15 for Counselors in Training)
Age of counselors	16–25 years+	17–40 years+	17–21 years	16–22 years (raised to 18–25+ in 1991)
Duration	From one week to all summer	Two-week sessions (waiting list for more than one session)	One to two weeks (waiting list for additional weeks)	From one week to all summer
Cost to attend	Ages 4–6: $11/day Ages 7–12: $50/week $5 discount per each additional child	$200/2 weeks	$45/week	$80/week, plus $16/week for transportation
Environment	Nature reserve, several other camps of comparable size, several roofed structures, large lake, children grouped by age in mixed-gender groups	Large wooded estate (67 acres), several buildings as well as other roofed structures, international counselors, outdoor pool, girls grouped by age	City-owned, municipal recreation area, outdoor temporary pool, hiking trails, one building, children grouped by age and gender	Located at YMCA, indoor/outdoor pools, large field, gym, and daycare center, inner-city Hispanic camp plus a preschool camp add 110 children to the site), children grouped by age and gender
Typical schedule	8–9 meet at Boys Club/load buses 9:30–10 arrival at camp 10–10:30 group meeting 10:30–4 boating, swimming, crafts, games, occasional team sports, hiking 4:30 return to Boys Club	8:30 arrival 8:30–9:00 opening ceremonies 9–3 swimming, crafts, adventure course, educational lectures, games, singing, long walks between activities 3–3:30 closing ceremony/departure	9 arrival 9–9:15 open play 9:15–3 in increments of 45 minutes: swimming, sports/games, hikes, crafts, singing, talent shows, contests 3–3:15 departure	9–9:30 singing 9:30–4 outdoors: archery, sports and games, swimming, crafts; indoors: drama, gym, first aid. First year: lots of time where children had free play. For a more detailed description of the second year schedule see Table 6.

Table 2.   Enrollment of campers with disabilities and counselor assignments

	Boys/Girls Club Camp		Girl Scout Camp		City Camp		YMCA Camp	
Week 1–2	campers:	1.00	campers:	1.00	campers:	0.00	campers:	18.00
	counselors:	1.00	counselors:	0.50	counselors:	0.00	counselors:	4.50
Week 3–4	campers:	5.00	campers:	2.00	campers:	0.00	campers:	18.00
	counselors:	1.00	counselors:	0.75	counselors:	0.00	counselors:	4.25
Week 5–6	campers:	3.00	campers:	2.00	campers:	1.00	campers:	18.00
	counselors:	1.00	counselors:	0.50	counselors:	0.50	counselors:	5.00

Decimal figures denote a counselor splitting his or her time between camps as needed.

and specifically on how to interact with the kids without disabilities. The counselors also received new training in positive behavior management techniques and communication alternatives. All counselors visited the new camps to which they were assigned to meet each other and to become familiar with the schedules.

During one session, counselors from the general YMCA camp and those from the Camp within a Camp were jointly trained on inclusion strategies by the GWARC recreation director and the CLF. It was realized, in retrospect, that more of this kind of joint training would have been helpful, and in future years the plan was changed to provide for the training of *all* counselors together. This is important for several reasons. First, counselors who have not worked with kids with disabilities need to know how to interact with these campers. They also need training in facilitating interactions between campers with and without disabilities. Second, counselors who have only worked with campers with disabilities are not used to the unstructured nature and high level of activity in typical camps. Third, most counselors are outgoing, older teenagers in high school or college who may tend to view people with disabilities as being "special" or "different." Any type of training in inclusion that they receive is likely to be a first, and therefore very powerful. The personnel who carried out this plan were in a unique position that allowed them to change the attitudes of many young people, in this case over 100, in a single summer.

Transportation

Prior to the initiation of inclusion, a van or bus provided by GWARC had carried campers with disabilities from their homes to Camp Discovery, and this practice was continued for the YMCA Camp within a Camp. Transportation was also provided to the other camps, but campers and counselors had to meet the buses at designated central sites around the city. Parents were responsible for getting their children to these sites or directly to the camps. Bus drivers and all counselors were given instructions on what to do in certain situations involving campers with disabilities (e.g., if parents were late to meet a camper or if a camper refused to get on or off the bus).

THE PLAN FOR THE SECOND YEAR

Beginning in January after the first successful summer of inclusion, the GWARC recreation director began meeting with the CLF from Boston Children's Hospital Project REC in order to discuss what options might be most appropriate for the second summer. Although a few parents were initially hesitant about inclusion, feeling that it would result in their children losing services, the success of the first summer as demonstrated by the enthusiasm of the children put these parents' fears to rest. It was therefore decided that in order to achieve the full inclusion of all children in summer camp, no Camp within a Camp option needed to be made available the second year; instead, all children would be enrolled in the four city camps. GWARC would continue to hire counselors to provide extra support to the camps' staffs, but a separate operating license would not be necessary. Licensing is an important issue when integrating camps because in many states (e.g., Massachusetts) camps that children with disabilities attend must have one or more registered nurses on staff. GWARC personnel circumvented this requirement by writing the state board of health to assure them that a registered nurse from GWARC would be on call at all times during camp hours.

Meeting with the Camp Directors

During the months of February and March, the GWARC recreation director met with the directors of the other camps. Although the responses of the directors varied, all were excited to continue what had been started the previous year. One director felt that he would need no assistance if a child with a disability attended his camp. He stated that he had learned enough the previous year to include any child in his camp, but was thankful that he could call on GWARC for assistance if the need arose. Two of the camp directors asked the recreation director to assist them in training their counselors and to provide support to campers only if a problem arose. Both of these directors assured GWARC that they would accept any child who applied to their camps, regardless of the type or significance of disability, as long as camp directors could call on GWARC for assistance as necessary.

Finally, because most of the parents expressed an interest in the YMCA camp the second year, GWARC personnel concentrated their efforts there. From early March through the beginning of camp in June, the GWARC recreation director had numerous meetings with the new director of the YMCA camp in order to address all of his questions. Once again, his main concern was that he might have to decrease enrollment in order to accommodate campers with special needs. However, after several meetings he understood that all campers would be registering directly with his camp and that enrollment would actually increase. Throughout these preparatory meetings, both directors agreed that the personnel from the YMCA and from GWARC should be treated as a single unified staff in order to build a more cohesive group, hence benefiting all of the campers.

Meeting with Parents

In March, the GWARC recreation director sent letters to all parents who had children with disabilities enrolled in GWARC programs. In the letter, the different camps were described, and assurances were given that GWARC personnel would continue to be available to provide support to those campers who needed it. The parents were asked to fill out a form stating which camp(s) they would like their children to attend and during what times. It was explained that this was not a final registration and that in order to register their children, the parents would need to contact the camp directly and request an application. This preliminary form provided a means of discerning what types and amounts of support GWARC would need to provide. The fees for the camps were still a deterrent for some parents, but

GWARC was able to provide some assistance, as well as help parents apply for scholarships for their children directly from the camps that they wished them to attend. Families were told that each camp had its own deadline for applications and that it was up to them to meet these deadlines, but the recreation director did assist some families with the application process.

In April, follow-up calls were made to those parents who did not reply to the preliminary letter, and one meeting was held in early May for any parents needing further assistance (only two parents attended).

Staffing Plans

Because staff at most of the camps felt comfortable with the idea of having children with disabilities attend programs with only minimal support, it was decided to concentrate support at the YMCA camp, which most of the campers with disabilities would be attending. Furthermore, as was discovered in the first year of inclusion, staff at most of the camps did not need much more than an initial meeting to discuss the child's strengths and needs. For those reasons, staffing patterns were changed during the second year. An assistant director, who had previously been a counselor at Camp Discovery, was hired to be at the YMCA camp every day, carry a beeper at all times, and be available in case of an emergency or to cover for any counselors who were absent. This freed the recreation director to work more closely with the director of each camp and to troubleshoot when problems arose. It also allowed her to devote more time to programs other than the summer camps. Four additional counselors were also hired, one of whom stayed for only half the summer (it was not necessary to replace him).

In order to facilitate inclusion a behavioral consultant and the CLF from Children's Hospital were again made available on a part-time basis. A nurse was no longer needed, since the children applied directly to the camps, each of which hired a nurse. In addition, although the recreation director was not at camp every day, she was available if the need arose. The behavioral consultant worked with certain counselors upon request, regardless of whether the camper in question had a disability. She worked an average of 8 hours per week, and as it turned out, worked much more often with the children without disabilities. The CLF was primarily involved during the first week, meeting with counselors, directors, and parents. For the remainder of the summer, she was only needed to troubleshoot through brief telephone conversations. Finally, a volunteer was available 1–3 days a week and was able to provide some extra training for those in the Counselor-in-Training (CIT) programs.

Training Counselors

The training program for the counselors hired by GWARC was the same as that for the YMCA counselors, since that was where they would be spending most of their time. The director of the YMCA camp and the GWARC recreation director planned the training sessions together. Although there was a specific time scheduled for disability issues to be introduced and questions and concerns addressed, "disability awareness" was incorporated into all of the activities. For example, each specialist gave a talk about his or her area of specialty, such as sports or arts and crafts, and at that time the group would discuss how all children could be included in the activity and what steps counselors could take to facilitate full participation. Finally, all counselors were made aware of which personnel had experience with children with disabilities in the past and were assured that it was acceptable, even expected, for them to ask questions of these counselors at any time. Training included an overview of the camp (rules, regulations, paperwork, etc.) and instruction in first aid, positive behavior management techniques, role-modeling, and communication and skill enhancement. Each counselor attended one 4-hour evening session and one full-day session. Appendix A provides a schedule for these sessions and samples of some of the joint training activities, while Appendix B comprises some of the sample scenarios presented to the counselors-in-training. In addition, staff members went on an overnight camping trip to further refine their camping skills and build a more cohesive team. Despite the fact that counselors were hired in two different manners and for different reasons, they were all incorporated into one staff. Everyone received training on how to work with children with and without disabilities, and it was constantly emphasized that everyone was there to serve *all* the children. In this way, each counselor was encouraged to be responsible for each child and the YMCA felt full ownership of the program. Table 3 shows the camper and staff ratios in each of the camps over the entire summer.

Transportation

In the second year parents were encouraged to take advantage of transportation offered by the camp their child attended or to provide their own transportation. Since there was always a parent or a counselor at one end of the bus ride, it was not necessary for GWARC staff to ride on the vans or buses with the campers. GWARC was also able to help arrange carpools in a few instances. However, there were two children who would not be able to attend camp without door-to-door transportation. In order to ensure that all children would be included, GWARC arranged for transportation for these children by a private cab company. To avoid the expense of private transportation, GWARC planned to only utilize carpools in the future, as there were many parents willing to drop off and pick up children.

BUDGET COMPARISONS

Making summer camps inclusive does not have to be an expensive proposition. As indicated in Table 4, the amounts spent during each of the 3 years while GWARC made the transition from a totally segregated camp (1989) to full inclusion (1991) are very close. In fact, the 1991 budget was slightly lower than that in 1990.

Of course, some individual items in the budget were quite different because of the different staffing patterns and fee arrangements that inclusion involves. For example, there was no behavioral consultant at Camp Discovery in 1989, but during that year and 1990, GWARC had to provide nursing staff because of licensing requirements. In 1991, there was no need for activity fees and less need for supplies and materials, since campers with disabilities registered directly with the city camps. Direct registration also eliminated the need for payment of camper fees directly to GWARC. Expenses related to hiring counselors were very steady across the years. The differences were in the training provided and the roles that counselors filled, rather than in the numbers hired. It is important to remember that although GWARC continued to hire counselors who had experience in the disability field, they were trained with other counselors in 1991 to be regular members of the city camp staff and to work with all campers. Everyone agreed that it was most beneficial for GWARC to hire some specialized staff and provide funding to help

Table 3. Camper-to-counselor ratios at selected camps

	YMCA Camp Cabot		YMCA Pooh's Camp		City Camp Prospect		City Kinder Camp		Girl Scout Camp Cedar Hill	
	Campers with disabilities: counselors hired by GWARC	Total campers: total counselors	Campers with disabilities: counselors hired by GWARC	Total campers: total counselors	Campers with disabilities: counselors hired by GWARC	Total campers: total counselors	Campers with disabilities: counselors hired by GWARC	Total campers: total counselors	Campers with disabilities: counselors hired by GWARC	Total campers: total counselors
Week 1	4:1.75	107:11.75	1:1	13:3	0:0	38:6	0:0	15:3	1:0.25	350:35.25
Week 2	4:2	111:14	1:1	39:5	0:0	75:10	0:0	15:3	1:0	350:35
Week 3	9:1.5	125:14.5	1:1	41:6	1:0.25	75:10.25	2:0.25	15:3.25	0:0	350:35
Week 4	8:1.5	122:14.5	1:1	48:6	1:0.25	75:10.25	2:0.25	15:3.25	0:0	350:35
Week 5	6:2	128:15	2:1	37:5	0:0	75:10	0:0	15:3	0:0	350:35
Week 6	4:2	130:185	4:1	36:5	0:0	75:10	1:0.5	15:3	0:0	350:35
Week 7	5:2	115:14	4:1	37:5	0:0	75:10	0:0	15:3	1:0.75	350:35.75
Week 8	8:2.5	113:14.5	1:1	37:5	camp not in session		camp not in session		1:0.25	350:35.25

Decimal figures denote counselors who split their time between different groups and different camps.

Figures for totals include campers with disabilities and counselors hired by GWARC.

Figures for campers with disabilities do not reflect totals—at least 40 additional youth with disabilities attended the camps without any direct support.

Table 4. GWARC camp budgets for 1989–1991

	1989	1990	1991
Revenues			
Funding from City of Waltham	$25,000	$30,000	$20,000
Camper Fees	3,000	3,750	0
Donations	2,850	1,500	12,000
Total Funding	30,850	35,250	32,000
Expenses			
Salaries and Related Expenses			
Camp Director	3,600	3,500	3,810
Counselors (1991–5, 1990–7, 1989–6)	10,515	12,700	12,715
Counselors In-Training (1991–2)	0	0	1,260
Medical Staff	2,945	3,550	0
Consultant - Behaviorist	0	2,195	1,460
FICA	1,060	1,510	1,545
Workmen's Compensation	110	180	220
Unemployment Insurance	310	540	625
Total Salaries and Related Expenses	18,540	24,175	21,635
Transportation	4,200	3,000	3,000
Supplies and Materials	1,450	1,050	250
Activity and Event Fees	1,000	850	0
Insurance	310	250	250
Administrative Expenses (GWARC Management, Secretarial, Public Relations, Employment Ads, Office Supplies, Postage and Rental Fees, Scholarships)	5,350	5,925	6,865
Total Expenses	$30,850	$35,250	$32,000

defray some of the cost of transportation and camper scholarships, rather than having the city camps assume full responsibility for these areas. Finally, administrative costs remained fairly consistent: there was the same need for advertising, meetings with various groups (administrative time), and office expenses regardless of whether campers attended segregated or inclusive camps.

CONCLUDING COMMENTS

The process of changing the summer camp experience in Waltham took less than 2 years, from January 1990 through August 1991. Through careful planning and commitment, costs were held constant and the basic roles of paid staff did not change. And everyone involved in making the city camps inclusive has been pleased with the results.

Campers and their families experienced the greatest benefits of inclusion. Now "camp buddies" have become school friends, and parents of campers with disabilities are becoming interested in other school and community programs. Facilities such as the YMCA have begun to invite people with disabilities to join inclusive classes and activities, rather than always initiating a separate program for those participants.

The experience of integrating summer camps over two summers resulted in some consistent feedback on practices that work and pitfalls to avoid; many of these lessons are listed in Table 5. Other simple things that parents can do, and that staff can assist with, are listed in Table 6. These small reminders can really have an impact on an inexperienced or very young camper.

Giving children and teenagers with disabilities the chance to have fun with other kids from their local neighborhoods through an integrated summer camp experience can be rewarding for everyone involved, but it takes planning, communication, commitment, and a willingness to take risks. However, with the right leadership, inclusion can be achieved in a short period of time and within the constraints of an existing budget.

Table 5.   Tips for enhancing inclusion

1. Train all staff together on all topics.

2. If using the "camp within a camp" approach, make sure that schedules are the same and that there are not separate areas for some activities. If you can avoid this intermediate step, try to do so, but it does provide an alternative for families who insist on special programs.

3. Provide direct training to older campers on how they can include campers with disabilities in various activities. Talk with them about what disabilities are and allow them opportunities to ask questions.

4. Provide immediate and consistent feedback to parents so that they won't worry. Photographs of kids having fun are great "success proofs."

5. Assign someone such as the recreation director or a very experienced, mature counselor to float between campers and to be available in crisis situations. A beeper can be a very useful tool!

6. Be prepared for much less structure in summer camps. The campers probably won't have any problems with this, but parents and counselors need to understand that this is a normal situation.

7. Don't force kids with disabilities to socialize or to participate in every activity. They will need a little time to adjust to the new situation. In many instances, if kids with and without disabilities are in the same area, doing the same things, they will eventually initiate interactions themselves; staff should be ready to reinforce this when it occurs.

8. Camp directors (if there are more than one) should share supervision of all staff and jointly plan all activities and training.

9. The roles of counselors should be meshed as much as possible, so that all counselors are responsible for assisting all children. In other words, move away from the concept of "special" counselors for "special" campers.

10. Give children with disabilities the space and freedom to be kids like everyone else. Fade into the background as much as possible and give others the chance to interact. Don't hover unnecessarily! When you can totally fade from a site because other counselors are providing enough assistance, do so. Just make sure that parents are aware of your plan.

11. Give parents of campers with disabilities plenty of time to adjust to the idea of integration, especially if their son or daughter previously attended a separate camp. Have them visit camps, meet directors, and become familiar with daily schedules. Make sure they understand that there is plenty of support and expertise available at all times.

Table 6. Daily guide for sending children to camp

1. Camp is a fun but messy place: don't send your child in new or fancy clothing.

2. Camp is very physical. If most of the other children wear shorts and t-shirts to a particular camp, your child should too.

3. Don't forget to put your child's name (first and last) on every piece of his or her clothing (shoes and socks included). Make sure to mark clothing discreetly so that your child will suffer no embarrassment. Keep in mind that, as a rule, children at camp lose things. No matter how well you mark their clothing, something will get lost.

4. Good sneakers are a must! Children spend a lot of time at camp running from activity to activity, as well as during activities.

5. Water fights, mud, and drink spills all make for messy clothing—an extra set is a real help. Inquire at the camp office because often they have a special area to leave extra clothing so your child will not have to carry it all day.

6. Children may be expected to change back and forth from swimsuits to clothes several times a day. Buttons, hooks, and ties make this slow going for many children. Shorts with elastic waists are easier than those with zippers and snaps. Pullover shirts with a design on one side make it easy to see which way the shirt goes on. Shoes with Velcro are much easier than pull-ons (which are difficult to get onto wet feet) or those with laces.

7. Let counselors know about your child's abilities and preferences, not just what he or she dislikes or can't do (they will learn of these things soon enough!). This could be a growing experience for both of you.

8. Even though it may be frightening, give your child permission to participate in special events and go on field trips. If you are too nervous to allow your child to participate independently for the first time, ask if you can come along. Volunteers are usually welcome.

9. Perspiration from the amount of activity at camp easily causes glasses to slip; a strap can be used to secure them.

10. Do not send more than is necessary with your child. An overstuffed backpack can become quite a burden when a child has to carry it all over camp. And a backpack is better than a carrier with just shoulder straps or handles.

11. Put sunscreen on your child in the morning instead of sending the entire bottle for your child to carry all day. If your child is extremely sensitive to the sun and will need applications throughout the day, contact a counselor and ask him or her to be responsible for the bottle. A strong screen of SPF 15 is a must.

12. An extra juice box is wonderful for snack time.

13. Extra food that will not crush easily can be put in small bags for snack time. Do not put the bags in with a child's lunch—children tend to eat whatever is in front of them at snack time, and lunch needs to be saved until lunchtime.

~Appendix A ~

Schedule for Joint Training Sessions for Counselors

Evening session

5:00–5:15	**Icebreaker** Might include a New Game or some type of name game. Emphasize that many things, like this activity, used throughout the training may also be used with the campers.
5:15–5:30	**Welcome** Philosophy of the camp/organization: what is camp to kids? To counselors?
5:30–6:00	**Tour of camp/introduction to adult supervisors** Different specialty areas (e.g., pool, lunch, arts and crafts); areas to avoid (e.g., woods, child care area for tots).
6:00–6:15	**Safety** Emergency procedures: What to do if a child is injured/sick, choking, not breathing; assisting a child who uses a wheelchair.
6:15–6:30	**Obstacle course (icebreaker)** Another team-building game.
6:30–7:00	**Explanation of groups/units/schedules** How are kids organized in groups? Who is in charge? Who do counselors report to? What should each day be like?
7:00–7:30	**Group/problem management** Kids who never want to participate, bullies, shy kids, kids who don't talk, kids who hit.
7:30–7:45	**Overnights/family nights** Discussion on overnights (one per camp session) and family nights, when parents are invited to see children's work (e.g., plays, art).
7:45–8:00	**Planning session for overnight retreat for counselors/questions**

Day session

9:00–9:30	**Trust walk or other team-building activity** Another New Game to foster team cohesiveness
9:30–10:00	**Child development** Introduction to how to treat and communicate with kids of different ages. What happens when kids are having problems, and how counselors can help.
10:00–11:30	**Aquatics** Water safety rules, intro to basic swimming strokes (or, if no pool is available, ideas for sprinkler or water-play games [e.g. balloon tosses]). Specific strategies and safety considerations in working with children with physical disabilities or complex medical needs.

11:30–12:30	**Lunch**
12:30–2:00	**Dealing with campers with disabilities or problem behaviors (scenarios)** Counselors who have the most experience with disabilities are identified (so that others will know where to come with questions). Although the entire evening and day of training includes information about disability and inclusion (e.g., when the aquatics people talk, various methods of how to support people with disabilities in the water to enhance inclusion are included in their discussion), this time focuses specifically on disability and on improving counselors' knowledge of how to react in certain situations. Next, counselors are given scenarios and broken up into small groups to come up with ideas/solutions. Then they come back to the group, read their scenario, and share solutions with the other counselors. Finally, all counselors are given disabilities (with an emphasis that this as an exercise in problem solving, not an exercise in how it feels to be disabled) and introduced to a few simple New Games, as well as a few well-known activities (e.g., kickball) and have to include everyone in the games.
2:00–3:15	**Specialists discuss different areas** (e.g., art, field games) *or* counselors can be given ideas about different activities that they should be trying with kids throughout the day.
3:15–3:45	**Rainy day do's and don'ts** Alternate plans and games for indoor days, emphasizing accountability for all campers (e.g., don't let a kid go to an activity in which he or she shouldn't participate).
3:45–4:00	**Leave for overnight retreat**

~ Appendix B ~

Sample Scenarios Presented during Joint Training

Billy is a 12-year-old in your group of 13 kids. He is a real leader, but unfortunately does not seem to be able to follow. You frequently find yourself in a power struggle with Billy when you tell your group what the next activity will be and he says that he wants to do something else. Not only does he often decide on another activity, but he always manages to convince a couple of other kids to follow him. He then proceeds to lead his small group of followers in beginning the activity that he has decided on. You either have to give in and follow along with the rest of the kids (which of course causes them to complain because they were looking forward to the activity that you suggested) or leave the rest of the group waiting while you are discussing the matter with him. This happens several times each day. In general, Billy always disagrees and seems to need to get his own way to be a part of the group. You are exhausted at the end of each day and are growing tired of the struggle. What could you do to alleviate this situation?

You are a counselor for a very energetic group of children who run from one activity to another without ever tiring. Katie, one of the campers in your group, uses a wheelchair, and you find yourself having to slow the group down several times a day to wait for her. There have also been a few times when the kids wanted to play a game or take a hike that you thought would be too strenuous for Katie, so you suggested alternative activities, even though Katie was just as eager to try as were the other children. Although Katie fits into the group and has made a few good friends, you have recently heard some grumbling and snatches of conversation that indicate that the kids often feel that they are moving too slowly and don't get to do the things they like to do. What do you do in this situation?

You have just finished your first day of camp and you are exhausted. You are counselor for a group of 10 children who have all been vying for your attention all day, yet a good deal of your energy was spent preventing one child from bullying the others. Fred is huge for an 8-year-old, and every time your back was turned (and sometimes when it wasn't) he was either doing something dangerous (e.g., climbing a fence) or was teasing, taunting, pushing, or hitting one of the other children. You tried telling him to stop, but this seemed to only increase his bad behavior. You are not sure whether you will be able to work this way the entire summer. Furthermore, you are neglecting the nine other children in your group. What could you do to alleviate the stress you are feeling about having Fred in your group?

You are a counselor for a group of 14 campers. Halfway through the summer, a new child, Elisia, is placed in your tight-knit, very cliquish group of children. The director tells you that Elisia has mental retardation, but should be able to participate as a full member of the group. You have gotten quite used to this group of children, and they have become relatively easy to manage. Elisia, however, rarely follows your directions during activities and therefore often gets left out, and when she does participate, the other kids generally tend to ignore her. Elisia also tends to wander away from the group, and there have been several instances when it took some effort to locate her. In short, Elisia isn't participating: she isn't making friends, never gets the ball, and frequently eats lunch alone. Thinking that maybe she is just shy, you try to draw her into the group, but she never really initiates or maintains conversation, even though you can tell by her laughter and expressions that she wants to be included. How can you assist Elisia to become a member of the group?

You are a counselor for a group of 14 campers. Most of them are rambunctious 10- or 11-year-olds who drag you around camp all day and get away with anything they can. One day Johnny's mother asks you how he is doing in the group. She is concerned that he is too shy and doesn't participate enough with the other children. You wrack your brain and finally remember that Johnny is that wonderful boy who always follows the group and does as he is told—a counselor's dream come true. You rave about him to his mother, but for the next few days, you keep an eye on Johnny and, thinking about what his mother said, realize that although he never causes problems and doesn't ever complain, he is also just as his mother describes him—a loner. How can you assist Johnny in making friends?

REFERENCES

Americans with Disabilities Act of 1990 (ADA), PL 101-336. (July 26, 1990). Title 42, U.S.C. 12101 et seq: *U.S. Statutes at Large, 104,* 327–328.

Edwards, D., & Smith, R. (1989). Social interaction in an integrated day camp setting. *Therapeutic Recreation, 23*(3), 71–78.

Mitchell, A., Robberson, J., & Obley, J. (1977). *Camp counseling.* Philadelphia: W.B. Saunders.

Rynders, J., Schleien, S., & Mustonen, T. (1990). Integrating children with severe disabilities for intensified outdoor education: Focus on feasibility. *Mental Retardation, 28*(1), 7–14.

~twelve~

Disability Awareness Training
and Social Networking

Laura Zygmunt,
Melanie Sloniker Larson, and George P. Tilson, Jr.

Recently, models of service delivery to persons with disabilities have tended to focus on the importance of social interactions with peers without disabilities. Most experts agree that social bonds shared with peers and friends are not luxuries, but necessities (Chadsey-Rusch, 1990; Stainback & Stainback, 1987; Stainback, Stainback, & Wilkinson, 1992); in order to be an integral part of the community, a person must develop relationships and social support systems with neighbors.

In some districts, students with disabilities are returning to their neighborhood schools, where they can be included not only in general academic classes, but also in extracurricular programs. It is in these schools, especially during leisure and recreation activities, that students with disabilities are given their best opportunities to practice social skills in natural settings. Many schools have experimented with social inclusion by using peer tutors to assist students with disabilities in the general education classroom, by including students with disabilities in school clubs and organizations, and by pairing students with disabilities and their peers without disabilities for orientation. These methods encourage *all* children and teens to learn and to play together, and they help cultivate bonds of friendship that will develop into long-term acceptance and interdependence (Strully & Strully, 1985).

Interactions between students with significant disabilities and their peers without disabilities can result in a number of positive outcomes for both groups (Boone, Fabian, Sloniker-Larson, & Zygmunt, 1992). Some benefits to those without disabilities include: learning about the needs of others, developing a deeper understanding and appreciation of one's own personal characteristics and social cognition, increasing one's awareness of similarities and differences among people, reducing anxiety and fear of people who look or behave differently, and increasing confidence in one's own ability to respond appropriately and effectively to other individuals (Peck, Donaldson, & Pezzoli, 1990). Some of the more notable benefits of inclusion to students with disabilities are more-active participation in the classroom, improved self-worth and a sense of belonging, and opportunities for communication and social inclusion (see Figure 1) (Cole, Meyer, Vandercook, & McQuarter, 1986; Stainback & Stainback, 1987). Advantages to members of the larger community include a heightened awareness of individual differences and of the benefits that result from these differences.

A MODEL PEER-NETWORK PROJECT

The peer-network project described below is part of a larger 5-year demonstration project at TransCen, Inc., funded by the Department of Health and Human Services, designed to study and evaluate the use of natural supports for persons with disabilities within the workplace and social settings. Project staff work within target schools to obtain support for a variety of peer-networking activities, such as peer tutoring and friendship clubs. Although the primary focus of this peer-network project is to ensure post-school employment in inclusive natural settings, the system also empowers students with disabilities to gain access to high school culture, relationships, and experiences like those of any other student in a large suburban public school system. In addition, because social networking and the development of friendships is an essential part of successful recreation and leisure programs, the exercises and activities described in this chapter will be very helpful to professionals planning such programs in their communities.

The peer-networking project is located in Montgomery County, Maryland, a school system that serves over 100,000 students. Students with disabilities in this system receive their education in both inclusive settings and segregated schools, but those students with disabilities who attend classes with their peers do not usually do so in their home schools. The system is, however, moving toward the neighborhood-school concept in its plans for future programs.

Ten high schools were targeted by the peer-networking project. Prior to its initiation, schools were informally assessed through group meetings held with various individuals, including school administrators, county special education staff, special education and resource-room teachers, and high school students. Project staff categorized the schools according to the frequency and level of participation of students with disabilities in general education classrooms; the categories that they used are described below.

Pre-inclusive high schools place students with disabilities in segregated classrooms and/or segregated schools (special centers). Usually, these students participate in separate activities and community work programs. The school becomes a "temporary layover" for the student prior to any community activities. Six of the ten schools targeted by the project fit into this category.

Inclusive high schools also place students with disabilities in segregated classrooms, but some of these students leave the segregated classroom to participate in inclusive classes in subjects such as computers, art, Spanish, English, physical education, chorus, and band. All students also participate in community work activities, and some participate in extracurricular activities at the school. Four of the ten schools targeted by the project fit into this category.

The goals for the peer-networking project are to: 1) increase the awareness of typically developing students concerning students with disabilities, 2) increase interactions between students with and without disabilities, 3) increase social inclusion efforts for students with disabilities, and 4) develop peer-advocacy training programs for students without disabilities. In order to meet these goals, the proj-

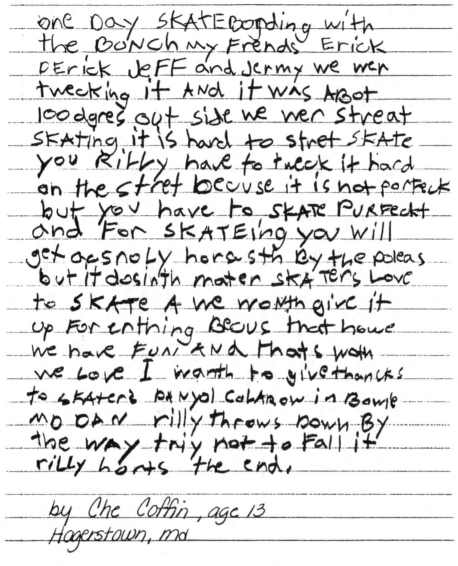

one Day skatbording with the bonch my frends Erick Derick Jeff and Jermy we wen twecking it and it was abot 100dgres out side we we streat skating it is hard to stret skate you rilly have to tweck it hard on the stret becuse it in not porfeck but you have to skate purfeckt and for skateing you will get ocsnoly horasth by the poleas but it dosinth mater skaters love to skate a we wonth give it up for enthing becus that howe we have fun and thats woth we love I wanth to give thancks to skaters Danyol Colarow in Bowie md Dan rilly throws down By the way triy not to fall it rilly horts the end.

One day, skateboarding with the bunch of my friends, Erick, Derick, Jeff and Jeremy, we went tweaking it. It was about 100 degrees outside. We were street skating. It is hard to street skate. You really have to tweak it hard on the street because it is not perfect, but you have to skate perfect. For skating, you will occasionally get harrassed by the police, but it doesn't matter. Skaters love to skate and we won't give it up for anything, because that's how we have fun. That's what we love. I want to give thanks to skater Daniel Calarow in Bowie, MD. Dan really throws down. By the way, try not to fall. It really hurts.

by Che Coffin, age 13
Hagerstown, Md.

Figure 1.   This letter demonstrates the benefits of social inclusion for a young boy with a disability.

ect concentrates on several different activities within each school. These activities, which vary according to each school's degree of inclusiveness, are briefly described below.

PEER-NETWORKING ACTIVITIES

Disability Awareness Training

These training sessions, one of which is outlined in Appendix A, are aimed at increasing typically developing students' awareness of negative attitudes, showing the adverse affects of stereotypes, eliminating myths about disabilities, and increasing students' acceptance of their peers with disabilities. The training, which is individually tailored to each school, is initiated by contacting department heads and administrators to discuss the potential benefits of this addition to the curriculum. When possible, these activities are incorporated into civil rights and contemporary issues curricula.

The training curriculum includes attitude surveys, exercises on famous people and on strengths and weaknesses, awareness points, and discussions of myths and facts about people with disabilities. Each session takes approximately 40–45 minutes. Following a pretraining attitude survey, project staff usually begin the training with a Jumbled Sentence or Jumbled Paragraph activity aimed at helping students understand what it's like to have a learning disability. Students are given 60 seconds to unscramble a sentence or paragraph and told that this exercise will count toward their grade for the day. Throughout the 60-second time period, students typically complain, look on each other's papers, give up, or refuse to complete the exercise. No teacher or staff response occurs until after the 60 seconds is up. At that point the students are asked about their impressions regarding the expectations for the exercise, and they discuss accommodations that could be made to ensure the success of a student facing similar challenges.

The famous-people exercise is used to focus on individual strengths and serves as a lead-in to an exercise in which each individual in the room, beginning with the members of the project staff, states his or her name and one positive and one negative aspect about him- or herself. As the class members introduce themselves, the staff focus on the negative facets of the students' self-descriptions, asking questions about and drawing attention to their faults. This exercise is meant to demonstrate that although *all* people have both strengths and weaknesses, most prefer to be identified by their interests and abilities, not by the things that they are unable to do.

Based on a particular teacher's curriculum, project staff may also provide information on the Americans with Disabilities Act (ADA) and the legislation that preceded it (see Chap. 5, this volume).

Throughout the training, the goal of project staff is not to force a change of attitude, but rather to encourage students to examine their assumptions, to try to understand why they feel the way they do, and to adopt more positive beliefs.

Disability Awareness Week   Each of the 10 high schools participating in this project dedicates one week of each school year to exposing students and faculty to a variety of disability issues and activities (see Table 1). Staff and students are notified of the week's activities through posters, announcements, staff meetings, and word of mouth.

Simulation Exercises   During each school's disability awareness week, simulation exercises are used to allow typical students the opportunity to experience, to

Table 1. Disability awareness week information ideas

1. Morning announcements of myths and misconceptions paired with facts
2. Displays of posters and slogans
3. Packets or flyers on disability issues
4. Simulated wheelchair exercises
5. Photography project with the general education students and the photography class
6. Movies on disability issues and acceptance
7. Guest speakers on disability issues in the classroom
8. End of the week assembly with guest speaker on disability issues
9. Students to have a disability and then report the results . . . to be published in the school newspaper or shared at the assembly program
10. Open House of the classrooms, with a videotape of the students explaining interests, likes, dislikes, etc.
11. A teacher participation survey on inclusion activities

some small extent, what it is like to have a disability. One such activity is conducted at lunch time in the cafeteria. Using a wheelchair, each student must try to negotiate an obstacle course of tables, trashcans, and lines of students. This exercise should give the typical students some idea of the obstacles faced by students with physical disabilities even in everyday activities. These types of exercise should also serve to open lines of communication between students with and without disabilities. After the wheelchair simulation, for example, an interview period with a person with a physical disability can be helpful and informative for the typical students, who may want to ask how long he or she has used a wheelchair, how he or she learned to use it, or how he or she gets to and from school and from class to class.

Other activities for disability awareness week may include displaying slogans created by students with disabilities, hanging posters of famous people with disabilities, discussing myths and misconceptions about disabilities in the morning announcements, and distributing packets or flyers or writing school newspaper articles on disability-related issues. Students in peer groups and friendship clubs can plan and orchestrate these activities, with Project staff providing support and guidance that may include: 1) acting as liaisons between the school administration, students, and teachers; 2) being available at the school during activities to assist in keeping the students on track; 3) answering any questions that students may have; and 4) proofreading pamphlets and posters for such things as person-first language and good public relations (see Figure 2). A disability awareness week generally requires several months of planning by the peer groups and friendship clubs within a school.

Inservice Training

Inservice training is provided for all school personnel who come into contact with students with disabilities. The purpose of this training is to foster a deeper understanding of students with disabilities, to introduce staff to the concept of social inclusion, and to present ideas on how it can be implemented. Inservice training sessions can range from 45–90 minutes, depending on the preferences and relevant previous experience of school personnel.

Each inservice training session was designed to convey three basic truths: 1) everyone has the potential to learn; 2) teachers and other students should focus

IT'S THE 'PERSON FIRST'
THEN THE DISABILITY

WHAT DO YOU SEE FIRST?

◆ The wheelchair?

◆ The physical problem?

◆ The person?

If you saw a person in a wheelchair unable to get up the stairs into a building, would you say "there is a handicapped person unable to find a ramp"? Or would you say "there is a person with a disability who is handicapped by an inaccessible building?"

What is the proper way to speak to or about someone who has a disability?

Consider how you would introduce someone -Jane Doe- who doesn't have a disability. You would give her name, where she lives, what she does or what she is interested in- she likes swimming, or eating Mexican food, or watching Robert Redford movies.

Why say it differently for a person with disabilities? Every person is made up of many characteristics- mental as well as physical- and few want to be identified by only their ability to play tennis or by their love for fried onions or by the mole that's on their face. Those are just parts of us.

In speaking or writing, remember that children or adults with disabilities are like everyone else- except they happen to have a disability. Therefore, here are a few tips for improving your language related to disabilities and handicaps.

1. Speak of the person first, then the disability.

2. Emphasize abilities, not limitations.

3. Do not label people as part of a disability group; don't say "the disabled"; say "people with disabilities."

4. Don't give excessive praise or attention to a person with a disability; don't patronize them.

5. Choice and independence are important; let the person do or speak for him/herself as much as possible.

6. A **disability** is a functional limitation that interferes with a person's ability to walk, hear, talk, learn, etc.; use **handicap** to describe a situation or barrier imposed by society, the environment, or oneself.

Disability Etiquette
Don't Say/Say

disabled, handicapped child
child with a disability

palsied, C.P. or spastic
person with cerebral palsy

mute or dumb
without speech, nonverbal

slow
developmental delay

crazy or insane
**emotional disability
or mental illness**

deaf and dumb
deaf or hard of hearing

confined to a wheelchair
uses a wheelchair

retarded
person with retardation

epileptic
person with epilepsy

mongoloid
Down Syndrome

is learning disabled
has a learning disability

normal, healthy
non-disabled

crippled
has a physical disability

birth defect
congenital disability

fits
seizures

midget or dwarf
of short stature

Figure 2. Guidelines for the proper phrasing to use when speaking or writing about those with disabilities. (From Pacer Center. [no date]. *Pacesetter*, Minneapolis, MN: Author; reprinted by permission.)

on the person first, not the disability; and 3) everyone has the right to develop to his or her full potential.

It is important to note that inservice training at pre-inclusive schools focuses on awareness issues and basic social inclusion activities—for example, stressing that students with disabilities, like other students, should be allowed to keep personal items in a locker, as opposed to keeping them in the classroom—while schools that are already inclusive are given presentations that deal with social inclusion—participation in extracurricular activities such as sports, cheerleading, and drama, for example. One activity used in both types of inservice training is the Concerns Survey (see Figure 3), which teachers are asked to complete prior to the beginning of their first inservice session. The teachers are told that any of their concerns not addressed during the preplanned part of the session will be covered afterward. The Concerns Survey addresses issues such as safety, demands made on teachers' time, the attitudes and reactions of students without disabilities, quality of education, accommodations, ability, how to deal with failure, communication, and self-doubt.

Inservice training sessions are concluded by presenting teachers with a tool for judging attitudes and decisions concerning persons with disabilities. The teachers are told to take anything that they say or hear about a person with a disability, remove the word disability, and replace it with a reference to race, gender, or religion. If the statement is not acceptable in this form, then neither is it acceptable when referring to people with disabilities.

Peer Tutor/Mentor/Buddy Training

Students without disabilities who volunteer to be peer tutors, mentors, or buddies are provided with a 1-day training program. Peer tutors, for the purpose of this project, are students who attend a class with a student with a disability and are willing to assist that student with assignments, group work, and homework. Mentors or buddies assist students with disabilities with the daily rigors of high school culture. This could include orienting someone to the layout of the school building, teaching a student how to use a locker or locate his or her classes, showing him or her how to use the cafeteria, or discussing peer-related problems. Students are nominated as mentors by their guidance counselors, teachers, and administrators. This is strictly a volunteer program, for which some schools award credit. The volunteers' commitment to this program can vary from 2 weeks to a semester; the relatively short time period allows many students an opportunity to be a mentor or buddy during the school year.

One week prior to mentor or buddy training, students are asked by the sponsoring teacher to write down one question that they would like answered. Project staff then develop the training based on these questions. Students discuss age-appropriateness, typical high school behaviors, and peer pressure. They are also provided with specific information on particular disabilities that students within their school may have, problem-solving strategies, and the benefits of having students with disabilities included in high school culture. Project staff have noted that the Circle of Friends activity (Snow & Forest, 1987) seems to have a notable impact on students in terms of helping them understand the importance of friendships. This activity entails an individual's cataloging the relationships in his or her life, beginning with immediate family, close friends, and acquaintances, then branching out to people from whom they receive services, such as doctors. The typical students' circles are

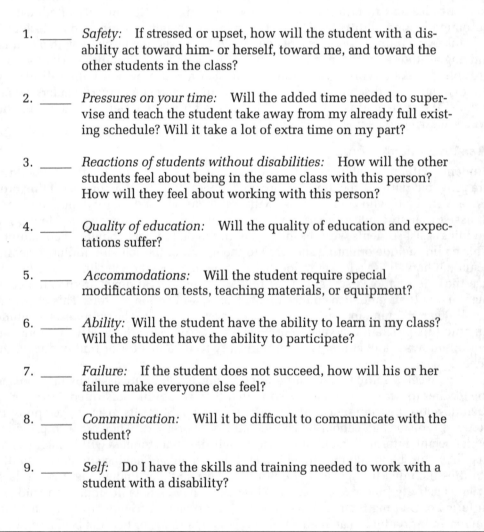

CONCERNS SURVEY

You have recently been asked to include a student with a disability in your classroom. Please review the following list of concerns and rate each one on a scale of 1–5 (with 1 meaning that you would be very concerned; 5 meaning you have no concern at all).

1. _____ *Safety:* If stressed or upset, how will the student with a disability act toward him- or herself, toward me, and toward the other students in the class?

2. _____ *Pressures on your time:* Will the added time needed to supervise and teach the student take away from my already full existing schedule? Will it take a lot of extra time on my part?

3. _____ *Reactions of students without disabilities:* How will the other students feel about being in the same class with this person? How will they feel about working with this person?

4. _____ *Quality of education:* Will the quality of education and expectations suffer?

5. _____ *Accommodations:* Will the student require special modifications on tests, teaching materials, or equipment?

6. _____ *Ability:* Will the student have the ability to learn in my class? Will the student have the ability to participate?

7. _____ *Failure:* If the student does not succeed, how will his or her failure make everyone else feel?

8. _____ *Communication:* Will it be difficult to communicate with the student?

9. _____ *Self:* Do I have the skills and training needed to work with a student with a disability?

Figure 3. The concerns survey can be a helpful tool for deciding which topics to cover during inservice training for teachers.

then compared to that of a student with a significant disability. Usually, the circle of the student with a disability is much smaller and consists mostly of family members and paid individuals. After comparisons are made, students discuss the differences and their probable causes.

Classroom Open House

An open house provides faculty and students with disabilities an opportunity to meet each other in an informal setting. The open house usually follows inservice training, to give the teachers the benefit of raised awareness. The special education classroom teacher, in conjunction with the peer tutor, mentor, and/or buddy students, produces a video in which each student with a disability describes his or her strengths and academic desires. For those students with communication difficulties, the peer tutor reads a script developed by the student. The videos are then shown throughout the day in the teachers' lounge. General education teachers are asked to fill out an informal survey on the possibility of including a student with a disability in particular classes (see Figure 4). The teachers are then invited to the special education classroom to discuss any concerns that they might have and to develop tentative inclusion plans. Project staff present these ideas to the special education teacher, who then coordinates all aspects of the open house.

Friendship Club

Friendship clubs are designed to help students with disabilities become more involved in high school social activities. They are student-operated clubs in which a sponsoring teacher is present merely for the purpose of guidance; the teacher does not make any final decisions on activities unless necessary. Essential components of the club include a supportive school administration, an interested faculty advisor, parental support, active recruitment of students with and without disabilities, mutually satisfactory meeting times and places, and social activities planned by students with and without disabilities. (Wilkinson, 1986).

Recruitment procedures for the Friendship Club are no different from those followed by any other school club. Morning announcements, advertisements in the school newspaper, and word of mouth are some of the methods used to recruit members. Project staff involvement in activities varies depending on the goals, needs, and interests of the members of a particular club.

Any professional within the school system who supports social inclusion would be able to help start a friendship club; in the peer-network project, facilitators include principals, speech therapists, special education and resource personnel, and general education teachers. It is important to remember that friendship clubs should be student centered and operated and governed by the same regulations and privileges as other clubs or extracurricular groups connected with a school.

CONCLUDING COMMENTS

PL 94-142, the Education for all Handicapped Children Act of 1975, mandates that *all* children and youth with disabilities be provided a free and appropriate public education in the least restrictive environment (LRE). In an attempt to comply with the LRE requirement, inclusion has become a priority in special education. Students were formerly considered to be mainstreamed if they spent any part of the

TEACHER SURVEY

I would like to take an informal survey of teachers who are interested in having a student with a disability in their class. Students would be included in order to learn appropriate social skills as well as to meet academic goals set by the cooperating teacher and me. One example of an academic goal might be to learn to count to 10 in a foreign language. Please understand that by participating you will be in no way responsible for grades. Please take the time to fill out the following form and return to _____ at your earliest convenience.

___ Yes, I am interested in having a student with a disability in my class.

___ I would like to discuss this possibility with you in further detail.

___ No, I am not interested at this time, because:

_____

___ Next marking period would be better.

If you have indicated above that you would like to include a student with a disability in your class or you would like to discuss this possibility further, please fill out the following:

Class: _____

Period: _____

Would you like a special education teacher or classroom assistant to accompany the student?

___ yes   ___ no   ___ yes, initially

Figure 4. An informal survey distributed to teachers during an open house in the special education classroom in order to gauge interest in inclusion.

school day with their peers without disabilities. Unfortunately, physical integration has not always resulted in social inclusion.

In response to this issue, a number of programs have been developed with the specific goal of achieving social inclusion. It is important to recognize that a broad range of activities should be used to reach this goal. Furthermore, activities to enhance social inclusion must be considered an essential component of each student's educational and life experience.

Increased comfort with diversity is of utmost importance if true inclusion is to occur for persons with disabilities, and fostering social relationships between students with and without disabilities can certainly be a catalyst for increasing comfort levels. All efforts to encourage the growth of peer networks enable students with disabilities to increase their social skills and encourage students without disabilities to become more aware of and sensitive to the needs of individuals with disabilities. It is important to recognize that today's students will be the coworkers, supervisors, and parents of persons with disabilities in the future.

When positive relationships are established and nurtured at school, there is a greater likelihood that an individual with a disability will display acceptable social skills in the workplace, in recreation and leisure settings, and in all other parts of the community. These "normalized" relationships lead to important networks of friends that can assist with job searches, provide natural supports on the job, and decrease dependency on human services providers. The peer networking exercises discussed in this chapter are examples of activities designed to facilitate the social inclusion of students with disabilities and the development of peer networks.

It is important to note that the activities discussed in this chapter should be used to *encourage* the development of peer networks and friendships. No student with or without a disability should ever be forced to support or make friends with any other student or group of students. True enduring friendships can only be based on free choice and personal preference. As advocates, teachers, parents, and leisure facilitators, we must provide opportunities for inclusion and support positive attitudes that enhance experiences for individuals with and without disabilities. Successful social inclusion will become widespread only if we are willing to push and work for change.

~ Appendix ~

Disability Awareness
Training Session

1. Attitude Survey

The attitude survey (see p. 222) should be completed by students just before they begin the activities that follow, and once again after the activities have been completed, in order to gauge the effect of the training session.

2. Jumbled Sentence or Paragraph

Display or pass out copies of a jumbled sentence or paragraph such as the one that appears below:

gnirutcurtser yb pacidnah a nessel ot syaw ynam era erehT eht tnemnorivne ro eht ksat.
(*Answer:* There are many ways to lessen a handicap by restructuring the environment or task.)

Ask students to take out a piece of paper and a pencil. Instruct those who are right handed to use their left hands to write, students who are left handed will continue to use their left hands. All students will have approximately 60 seconds to complete the task. When the time is up, ask the following questions:

*   If this had been a test, how many of you would have passed?
*   How did it make you feel to know that this exercise counted toward your grade?
*   How could we have made this exercise easier for you?

3. Famous People

Read about 10 names from the list of famous people on pages 223 and 224, but without mentioning the disabilities. Ask students to write down the first thing that comes to mind when they hear each name. After the names have been read, ask students what they think these people all have in common. Finally, point out that all of the people mentioned have a disability, but that we recognize each of them first for their individual talents and abilities.

Discuss with the students the implications of what they have learned for their feelings about inclusion and about persons with disabilities.

4. Strengths and Weaknesses

Have students introduce themselves and name one positive and one negative thing about themselves. Then have staff members focus on the negatives in the students' self-descriptions, asking questions about and drawing attention to them. Explain at the end of the exercise that people do not want to be known by negative qualities, but by their interests and abilities.

5. Basic Values

Discuss with students the fact that people with disabilities have the same personal values as anyone else, which include:

- Being seen as an individual *first*
- Having love, friendships, and relationships
- Being treated with respect and dignity
- Having opportunities to grow and learn
- Having the information and experience necessary to make educated choices and to have those choices respected
- Participating in and contributing to their local community
- Living in a quality home and working at a satisfying job

6. Myths and Misconceptions about People with Disabilities

Have students discuss the common myths on page 225, as well as any other stereotypes about people with disabilities that they may have heard.

7. Question and Answer Session

Ask students if they have any questions about people with disabilities or about a specific disability.

8. Closure

Explain to students that an appropriate and realistic attitude toward people with disabilities is based on three basic assumptions:

- Everyone has the potential to learn.
- Focus on the person first, not the disability.
- Everyone has the right to develop to their fullest potential.

REFERENCES

Americans with Disabilities Act of 1990 (ADA), PL 101-336. (July 26, 1990). Title 42, U.S.C. 12101 et seq: *U.S. Statutes at Large, 104,* 327–378.

Boone, R., Fabian, E., Sloniker-Larson, M., & Zygmunt, L. (1992). Peer advocacy and peer networks in transition from school to work: Focus on the consumer. *Rehabilitation Education, 14*(3), 225–234.

Brown, L., Long, E., Udvari-Solner, Davis, L. VanDeventer, P. Ahlgren, C., Johnson, F., Gruenewald, L., & Jorgensen, J. (1989). The home school: Why students with severe intellectual disabilities must attend the schools of their brothers, sisters, friends and neighbors. *Journal of The Association for Persons with Severe Handicaps, 14*(1), 1–7.

Education for All Handicapped Children Act of 1975, PL 94-142. (August 23, 1977). Title 20, U.S.C. 1401 et seq: *U.S. Statutes at Large, 89,* 773–796.

Chadsey-Rusch, J. (1990). Social interactions of secondary-aged students with severe handicaps: implications for facilitating the transition from school to work. *Journal of The Association for Persons with Severe Handicaps, 15*(2), 69–78.

Cole, D., Meyer, L., Vandercook, T., & McQuarter, R.J. (1986). Interactions between peers with and without severe handicaps: Dynamics of teacher intervention. *American Journal of Mental Deficiency, 91*(2), 160–169.

PRE- AND POST-TRAINING ATTITUDE SURVEY

INSTRUCTIONS: For each sentence, circle the answer that best describes how you feel, choosing between "Yes," "No," and "Maybe." Remember, there are no right or wrong answers!

1. Yes No Maybe   Students with disabilities can be as happy as those who do not have disabilities.

2. Yes No Maybe   People with disabilities can be good parents.

3. Yes No Maybe   Students who have disabilities are the same in many ways as those who do not have disabilities.

4. Yes No Maybe   I would like to plan an activity with a student who has a disability.

5. Yes No Maybe   Students who have disabilities can be just as smart as students without disabilities.

6. Yes No Maybe   Workers with disabilities can be just as successful as workers without disabilities.

7. Yes No Maybe   Students who have disabilities should go to the same schools as everyone else.

8. Yes No Maybe   I would invite someone with a disability to my house.

9. Yes No Maybe   People who have disabilities can live on their own when they grow up.

10. Yes No Maybe   Students with disabilities can have many friends.

11. Yes No Maybe   Students with disabilities are expected to do many of the same things students without disabilities do, like helping around the house and doing homework.

12. Yes No Maybe   I would like to make friends with someone who has a disability.

13. Yes No Maybe   A person who has a disability could marry a person who does not have a disability.

14. Yes No Maybe   I think people with disabilities should live and work like everybody else.

15. Yes No Maybe   I feel OK around people who have disabilities.

Adapted from National Easter Seals Society (1990).

FAMOUS PEOPLE EXERCISE

1. Abraham Lincoln

   Depression and Marfan syndrome Marfan syndrome is a growth disorder that causes you to grow very tall, very quickly. The heart has a difficult time keeping up with the growth of the rest of your body.

2. John F. Kennedy

   Physical disability Kennedy's back was injured during World War II; he used crutches to get around the White House when not in the public's eye.

3. Franklin D. Roosevelt

   Polio Roosevelt used a wheelchair because of polio. Most people did not know that he had a disability when he was elected because there was no television at the time and newspaper writers did not write about it (it was considered a taboo subject).

4. Winston Churchill

   Learning disability

5. George Patton

   Learning disability

6. Whoopi Goldberg

   Learning disability (dyslexia) Goldberg uses a reading coach to help her learn scripts.

7. Tom Cruise

   Learning disability (dyslexia) Cruise went to the LAB school in Washington, D.C., and uses a reading coach to learn scripts.

8. Cher

   Learning disability (dyslexia) Cher uses a reading coach to learn TV, movie, and commercial scripts.

9. James Earl Jones (actor)

   Communication disability (stutter) Jones did not speak in school because he was so embarrassed. He learned to speak without stuttering by reading poetry (poetry has a rhythm to it and people who stutter often can sing or read poetry).

10. Danny Glover (actor)

    Learning disability Glover was placed in a class for students with mental retardation until he was in high school and did not learn to read or write until after he had graduated from school.

11.	Chris Burke (actor)	*Mental retardation (Down syndrome)*
12.	Marlee Matlin (actress)	*Deafness*
13.	Katherine Hepburn	*Parkinson disease*
14.	Richard Pryor	*Multiple sclerosis*
15.	Sammy Davis, Jr.	*Visual impairment* (Davis had one glass eye)
16.	Walt Disney	*Learning disability* Disney did not learn how to read until he was 9. He drew pictures to help him remember what he was learning.
17.	Muhammed Ali	*Brain injury*
18.	Magic Johnson	*HIV*
19.	Jim Abbott (baseball pitcher)	*Physical disability* (has one hand) He pitched a no hitter in 1993.
20.	Kenny Walker (football player)	*Deafness*
21.	O.J. Simpson	*Learning disability*
22.	Greg Luganous (Olympic diver)	*Learning disability*
23.	Beethoven	*Deafness*
24.	Ray Charles	*Blindness*
25.	Stevie Wonder	*Blindness*
26.	Freddie Mercury (rock singer)	*AIDS*
27.	Vincent Van Gogh	*Depression*
28.	Edgar Allen Poe	*Alcoholism and mental illness*
29.	Helen Keller	*Deafness and blindness*
30.	Albert Einstein	*Learning disability* Einstein was kicked out of school for behavior problems. His teachers thought he could not learn. He did not learn to read until he was 9.
31.	Howard Hughes	*Hearing impairment and depression*

MYTHS AND FACTS

Myths about people with disabilities often lead others to treat them inconsiderately. Below are a few misunderstandings about people with disabilities, along with the facts.

Myth: People with disabilities are courageous.

Fact: Adjusting to a disability actually requires adapting to a new lifestyle, not bravery and courage.

Myth: All people who use wheelchairs have chronic illnesses.

Fact: The association between wheelchair use and illness probably evolved because hospitals use wheelchairs to transport sick people. A person may use a wheelchair for any one of a great number of reasons, many of which have nothing to do with a lingering illness.

Myth: People who are blind develop a "sixth sense" for directing themselves.

Fact: While it is true that most people who are blind develop their remaining senses more fully, they do not develop a "sixth sense."

Myth: People with disabilities are more comfortable "with their own kind."

Fact: Years of grouping people with disabilities together in separate schools and institutions has reinforced this misconception. Today, more and more people are taking advantage of opportunities to join their peers in the community.

Myth: People without disabilities are obligated to take care of people with disabilities.

Fact: Individuals may offer assistance to anyone they choose, but most people with disabilities prefer to be responsible for themselves.

Adapted from Gordon (1991, April).

Lewis, R.B., & Doorlag, D.H. (1987). Chapter 1: Mainstreaming for success. *Teaching Special Students in the Mainstream.* 4. Columbus, OH: Charles E. Merrill.

Pacer Center. (no date). It's the 'person first,' then the disability. *Pacesetter.* Minneapolis, MN: Author.

Peck, C., Donaldson, J., & Pezzoli, M. (1990). Some benefits non-handicapped adolescents perceive for themselves from their social relationships with peers who have severe handicaps. *Journal of The Association for Persons with Severe Handicaps, 15,* 241–249.

Remmes, H. (1986). My life as a Ph.D.: Physically handicapped disaster. *The Exceptional Parent, 16*(3), 36–38.

Schwartz, S.E. (1991). Chapter 1: Exceptional people. *Exceptional People: A Guide for Understanding.* 6–11. McGraw-Hill Publishers.

Snow, J., & Forest, M. (1987). Circles. In M. Forest (Ed.), *More education integration* (pp. 169–176). Downsview, Ontario, Canada: G. Allen Roeher Institute.

Stainback. W., & Stainback, S. (1987). Facilitating friendships. *Education and Training in Mental Retardation, 22,* 18–25.

Stainback, W., Stainback, S., & Wilkinson, A. (1992). Encouraging peer supports and friendships. *Teaching Exceptional Children, 24*(2), 6–11.

Strully, J., & Strully, C. (1985). Friendship and our children. *Journal of The Association for Persons with Severe Handicaps, 10*(4), 224–227.

Truesdell, L.A., & Abramson, T. (1992). Academic behavior and grades of mainstreamed students with mild disabilities. *Exceptional Children, 58*(5), 392–398.

Villa, R.A., & Thousand, J.S. (1992). Student Collaboration: An essential for curriculum delivery in the 21st century. In S. Stainback & W. Stainback (Eds.), *Curriculum considerations in inclusive classrooms: Facilitating learning for all students* (pp. 117–142). Baltimore: Paul H. Brookes Publishing Co.

Wilkinson, P. (1986). *Developing a school social club: A guide to the development of an extra-curricular club which facilitates integration of students with handicaps with their same school, non-handicapped peers.* Montgomery County Public Schools.

Index